THE EL MOZOTE MASSACRE

HEGEMONY AND EXPERIENCE:
CRITICAL STUDIES IN ANTHROPOLOGY AND HISTORY

SERIES EDITORS
HERMANN REBEL AND WILLIAM ROSEBERRY

The
EL MOZOTE
Massacre

ANTHROPOLOGY AND HUMAN RIGHTS

LEIGH BINFORD

THE UNIVERSITY OF ARIZONA PRESS   TUCSON

The University of Arizona Press
© 1996
Arizona Board of Regents
All rights reserved
♾ This book is printed on acid-free, archival-quality paper.
Manufactured in the United States of America
01   00   99   6   5   4   3   2
Library of Congress Cataloging-in-Publication Data
Binford, Leigh, 1948–
The El Mozote massacre : anthropology and human rights / Leigh
Binford.
p.   cm. — (Hegemony and experience)
Includes bibliographical references (p.) and index.
ISBN 0-8165-1661-8 (cloth : acid-free paper). —
ISBN 0-8165-1662-6 (pbk. : acid-free paper)
1. El Salvador—History—1979–1992.   2. El Mozote (El Salvador)—
History.   3. Massacres—El Salvador—El Mozote—History.   4. Human
rights—El Salvador.   5. Ethnology—El Salvador.   I. Title.
II. Series.
F1488.3.B55   1996
972.8405'3—dc20   96-10097
CIP

British Library Cataloguing-in-Publication Data
A catalogue record for this book is available from the British Library.

Publication of this book is made possible in part by the proceeds of
a permanent endowment created with the assistance of a Challenge
Grant from the National Endowment for the Humanities, a federal
agency.

TO DOÑA LOLA: midwife, coffee grower, human rights activist, and confidante of a thousand *compas*

CONTENTS

ILLUSTRATIONS

MAPS

FIGURES

TABLES

ACKNOWLEDGMENTS

Every intellectual work is a social product in the broadest sense, and this one is no exception. I owe special debts to Phyllis Robinson and Shelli McMillen, who assisted me in carrying out the primary fieldwork on which this book is based. Phyllis conducted the initial interviews with former inhabitants of El Mozote in the fall and winter of 1992; she also made a site survey of *el Llano* (the Plain) and gathered information on many prominent El Mozote families. Shelli McMillen worked intensively in El Mozote in June and July 1993 and interviewed most of the repopulating families. Shelli helped me enlarge the overall site map from about 25 to more than 150 structures and collected a great deal of genealogical information. She proved an astute interviewer, very sensitive to the special circumstances and histories of her informants, and I like to think that she sowed considerable goodwill among those repopulating El Mozote and other former residents (though I'm sure they would exchange our goodwill for housing and electricity). I also owe a debt of appreciation to Roxanna Duntley, currently a graduate student at the University of Michigan, who worked on the larger project of which this book is one part and gathered information that contributed to my understanding of the historical context within which the El Mozote massacre transpired.

However, it would be a political and ethical mistake to overstate the contributions of the foreign researchers, myself included, when the real credit should go to the many people who shared with us their pride for the prewar accomplishments of their community and their tragic stories of its wanton destruction. Men and women throughout the northern Morazán region took time out of their busy days to explain El Mozote's founding, its growth, the religious and political dispositions of its inhabitants, their repression, and their relations with the army and the FMLN. One *campesino* (peasant) who had lost four children and sixteen grandchildren guided us around this very dispersed community for four days and shared his intimate knowledge of its social geography. This book is my effort to compose a story from those told by José, Magdalena, Raquel, Carlota, Rufina, Ricardo, Ovelia, Davíd, Florentín, Francisco, Juan Evangelista, Andrea, Felipe, Pedro, and many other people. Obviously, the story will be both more and less than the stories told by particular informants, shaped as it is by a social scientist who came along ten years after the fact and was spared the suffering of those about whom he is reporting.

I know words cannot do justice to the experiences, not only of those who lived in El Mozote, but of hundreds of thousands of other Salvadorans, nor can words capture the difficulty of reconstruction and the pain of national reconciliation.

I also want to thank "Nolvo" and "Benito," ERP activists who worked in La Guacamaya and El Mozote in the late 1970s; "Felipe," a catechist from La Guacamaya who preached in the El Mozote chapel in the late 1970s; "Bracamonte," who shared with me his memories of the operation; "Franco" and "Matias," former members of an FMLN health brigade who were sent to El Mozote soon after the massacre to bury the dead; and Jacinto Márquez, who worked as my field assistant from November 1994 to August 1995. "Clelia" and "Salvador" of the Museo de la Revolución Salvadoreña, Heroes y Mártires, in Perquín, as well as Oscar Chicas, executive director of the Community Development Council of Morazán and San Miguel, allowed me to copy maps in their possession. My thanks as well to "Chele Cesar" for his friendship and inspiration, and to "Roberto," "Licho," and "Santiago" (as well as to many other compas and campesinos) for having taught me about the history of northern Morazán.

My understanding of the events surrounding the investigation of the massacre was shaped by conversations with Father Esteban Velásquez and with Gloria Romero and Mercedes Castro of the Human Rights Commission of Segundo Montes. Documentation of human rights violations in northern Morazán was made available by the Human Rights Committee of El Salvador, Nongovernmental (CDHES-NG), Tutela Legal, and the Human Rights Commission of Segundo Montes. Documentary research was also carried out in the newspaper archives and other files available at the Documentation Center of the University of Central America. Licensiado Franzi Miguel Hasbún, then Director of the Office of Project Promotion of the University of Central America and now in charge of External Relations, has been a consistent supporter of social investigation in northern Morazán and elsewhere in El Salvador.

The personnel at the National Security Archive provided an important service by filing thousands of Freedom of Information Act requests and making the resulting documents available to libraries in the form of beautifully indexed microfiche files, and someone on the staff of the library at the University of Connecticut had the foresight to purchase them. I employed materials generated by the National Security Archive extensively in chapter 4. I also benefited from the editorial work of Mark Danner, who published several important documents released in November 1993 in the appendix of his 1994 book on the El Mozote massacre.

Nancy Churchill, Jerry Phillips, and Mary Gallucci bore up extremely well under an incessant barrage of household commentary on El Mozote, and they helped me work through more than a couple of trouble spots. William Roseberry and Hermann Rebel read early drafts of the manuscript and made several critical suggestions. The manuscript also benefited from suggestions made by Margaret Low, Shelli McMillen, Nancy Churchill, Jerry Phillips, Edward Herman, and two anonymous reviewers. Whatever merit the photographs that accompany the text may have should be credited to my good friend Frank Noelker, who patiently answered numerous questions and provided sound laboratory advice to this novice photographer and printer. Mark Hoffman kindly contributed the photograph in the epilogue. I would like to thank Chris Franson for the very fine job he did on the maps and figures. Claudia Santelices and Elise Springer transcribed hundreds of pages of interviews with impressive precision; to my chagrin and embarrassment I now have an accurate written record of my Spanish-language errors. Joanne O'Hare was a sympathetic editor at the University of Arizona Press. I owe a special debt of gratitude to Gloria Thomas Beckfield, who copyedited the manuscript with a discerning eye for both the misplaced comma and the contradictory thought. Finally, I must thank Ben Magubane, Scott Cook, and James Faris (the troika) for the years of assistance that they have rendered me first as teachers and since 1985 as colleagues. To various degrees this work reflects the influence of each, although I despair of ever being able to synthesize three such disparate approaches—each meritorious in its own way—to social analysis.

The University of Connecticut Research Foundation helped fund the research for this book with three grants, for which I am most appreciative. Information obtained during a 1994–95 Fulbright-Hays Fellowship contributed to the materials in the epilogue. I should mention that in order to protect them from potential repercussions, I changed the names of many informants. Because many former FMLN combatants continue to be known by and feel more comfortable with their wartime pseudonyms, I have included such pseudonyms in quotation marks when referring to them. All translations from Spanish are my own.

ABBREVIATIONS

ABECAFE   Asociación Salvadoreña de Beneficiadores y Exportadores de Café (Salvadoran Association of Coffee Processors and Exporters)

ACOPAVEM   Asociación Cooperativa de Producción Agropecuaria "23 de Mayo" (Cooperative Association of Agricultural Production "23 May")

ANSESAL   Agencia Nacional de Servicios Especiales de El Salvador (Salvadoran National Security Agency)

ARENA   Alianza Republicana Nacionalista (Nationalist Republican Alliance)

ASCAFE   Asociación Salvadoreña de Café (Salvadoran Coffee Association)

BIRI   batallón infantaría de reacción inmediata (immediate reaction infantry battalion)

CARE   Cooperación Americana de Remesas del Exterior (Cooperation for Assistance and Relief Everywhere [note that the same acronym is employed in the United States and in El Salvador but with somewhat different meanings])

CDHES-NG   Comité de Derechos Humanos de El Salvador, No Gobernamental (Human Rights Committee of El Salvador, Nongovernmental)

CEBES   Comunidades Eclesiales de Base de El Salvador (Christian Base Communities of El Salvador)

CISPES   Committee in Solidarity with the People of El Salvador

COMADRES   Comité de Madres y Familiares de Presos Políticos, Desaparecidos y Asesinados de El Salvador "Monseñor Romero" (Committee of Mothers and Relatives of Political Prisoners, Disappeared, and Assassinated of El Salvador "Monseñor Romero")

CONADES   Comisión Nacional de Asistencia a la Población Desplazada (National Commission for Assistance to the Displaced Population)

COPPES   Comité de Presos Políticos de El Salvador (Committee of Political Prisoners of El Salvador)

DIDECO   Dirección General de Desarrollo Comunal (General Direction of Communal Development)

END   Ejército Nacional de Democracia (National Army for Democracy)

EPICA   Ecumenical Program on Central America and the Caribbean

ERP   Ejército Revolucionario del Pueblo (People's Revolutionary Army, one of five political-military groups composing the FMLN)

FALANGE   Fuerzas Anti-Comunista de Liberación (Anti-Communist Liberation Armed Forces)

FARN   Fuerzas Armadas de Resistencia Nacional (Armed Forces of National Resistance, one of five political-military groups composing the FMLN)

FDR   Frente Democrático Revolucionario (Democratic Revolutionary Front)

FECCAS   Federación Cristiana de Campesinos Salvadoreños (Christian Federation of Salvadoran Peasants)

FENASTRAS   Federación Nacional de los Trabajadores Salvadoreños (National Federation of Salvadoran Workers)

FMLN   Frente Farabundo Martí para la Liberación Nacional (Farabundo Martí National Liberation Front)

FOIA   Freedom of Information Act (United States)

FPL   Fuerzas Populares de Liberación (Popular Forces of Liberation, one of five political-military groups composing the FMLN)

IDEA   Iniciativa para el Desarrollo Alternativo (Initiative for Alternative Development)

IDESES   Instituto de Desarrollo Económico Social de El Salvador (Social Economic Development Institute of El Salvador)

IDHUCA   Instituto de Derechos Humanos de la Universidad Centroamericana (Human Rights Institute of the University of Central America)

LP-28   Ligas Populares "28 de Febrero" (Popular Leagues "28 February")

MAC   Movimiento Auténtico Cristiano (Authentic Christian Movement)

MCM   Movimiento Comunal de las Mujeres (Communal Women's Movement)

NACLA   North American Congress on Latin America

ONUSAL   Misión de Observadores de las Naciones Unidas (United Nations Observers Mission)

ORDEN   Organización Democrática Nacionalista (Nationalist Democratic Organization)

PADECOMSM   Patronato de Desarrollo de las Comunidades de Morazán y San Miguel (Community Development Council of Morazán and San Miguel)

PAR   Partido de Acción Revolucionaria (Revolutionary Action Party)

PCN   Partido de Conciliación Nacional (National Conciliation Party)

PCS   Partido Comunista Salvadoreño (Salvadoran Communist Party)

PRTC   Partido Revolucionario de los Trabajadores Centroamericanos (Central American Workers Revolutionary Party)

PRUD   Partido Revolucionario de Unificación Democrática (Revolutionary Party of Democratic Unification)

SRN   Secretaría de Reconstrucción Nacional (Secretariat of National Reconstruction)

UCA   Universidad Centro Americana, José Simeón Cañas (University of Central America, José Simeón Cañas)

UES   Universidad de El Salvador (University of El Salvador)

USAID   United States Agency for International Development

UTC   Unión de Trabajadores del Campo (Rural Workers Union)

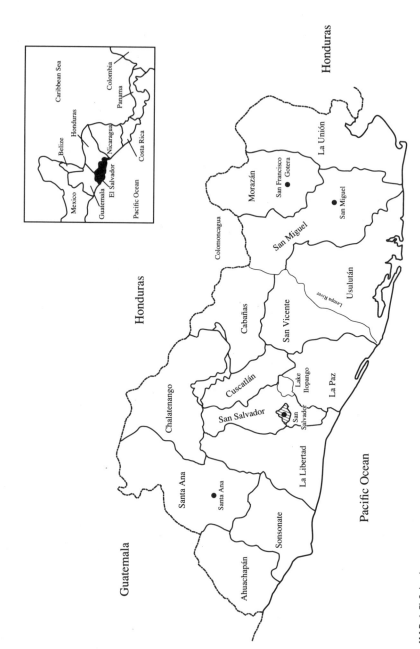

MAP 1 El Salvador

THE EL MOZOTE MASSACRE

REDUCING CULTURAL DISTANCE

IN HUMAN RIGHTS REPORTING

Between 11 and 13 December 1981, the Atlacatl Battalion, the first immediate-reaction infantry battalion in the Salvadoran army to be trained and equipped by the United States, massacred more than a thousand people in six hamlets located in the municipalities of Meanguera and Joateca, northern Morazán, El Salvador. As many as half of the victims were murdered in El Mozote on 11 December. Because the largest number of people died in that hamlet, or perhaps because El Mozote produced the principal eyewitness—a woman who miraculously escaped from the soldiers moments before she was to be machine-gunned to death—the whole three-day massacre has come to be designated as the massacre at El Mozote.

Raymond Bonner of the *New York Times* and Alma Guillermoprieto of the *Washington Post* investigated the massacre and brought it to public attention, and Ambassador Deane Hinton and Assistant Secretary of State for Inter-American Affairs Thomas Enders denied it. For a few weeks in early 1982, "El Mozote" was discussed in the press and debated in Congress, but after March the international press lost interest in the issue, which assumed the status of just one more (among many) "alleged" army massacres in "violence-torn" El Salvador. Major daily newspapers printed thirty-two articles in 1982, but only two of these articles appeared between April and December, following Thomas Enders's testimony before the House Subcommittee on Western Hemisphere Affairs. No additional investigative work followed on the Bonner and Guillermoprieto efforts. From January 1983 through December 1989, "El Mozote" was cited in a mere fifteen articles published in major U.S. and Canadian newspapers. (During this same period the U.S. government provided the Salvadoran military with more than $500 million in direct military assistance.) Eight of the fifteen citations appeared in 1984, mostly in connection with the death of Domingo Monterrosa Barrios, the lieutenant colonel "alleged" at the time to have ordered the massacre. As the end of the war approached following the FMLN final offensive of November 1989, the number of citations rose to eighteen for the period 1990–91. El Mozote was resurrected as a newsworthy issue in 1992 following the Peace Accords and forensic work carried out at the site (eighty-eight citations), and it became a mandatory subject of moral outrage for every liberal daily in 1993 (a whopping one hundred fourteen citations), when the United Nations Truth Commission accused the U.S. government of covering up the massacre.[1]

The coverage of El Mozote shows us that for journalists, no less than for most people in the West, the daily lives of billions of people in the rest of the world do not exist outside the parameters of crisis or scandal: hurricanes, earthquakes, volcanic eruptions, droughts, crop failures, and civil wars (for another example, see Kaplan 1994). Latino, African, and Asian peoples are as invisible to the vast majority of European Americans as are the ubiquitous dust particles that permeate the air. They become visible to European Americans only in the light of some spectacular event, often one that involves massive loss of life.[2] And even then, the attention they command is only transitory and is quickly superseded by the next crisis in some other part of the world. Such victims are treated as inherently "unworthy," at least as far as the mainstream media are concerned. The only worthy victims are those abused in enemy states (Ortega's Nicaragua, Castro's Cuba, Allende's Chile) (Herman and Chomsky 1988:37).

Human rights organizations challenge this configuration, but their challenge is limited by the fact that their interest in non-European peoples begins at the point that a person becomes a victim: one who, in human rights discourse, has been arbitrarily and without just cause deprived of freedom, security, or life, or has been threatened with such, according to international accords such as the Geneva Convention (e.g., Americas Watch Committee 1984b). Human rights organizations document violations, picking up the stories when or shortly before the violations occurred; they attribute blame; and they work to bring political, economic, and moral pressure upon those deemed responsible in order that the violations be punished and that actions be undertaken to ensure that they not reoccur. However, unless the victim is well known as a union president, manager of a cooperative, or member of the press, or occupies some other equally noteworthy status, identifying markers tend to be limited to basic information such as name, age, sex, and occupation.

Human rights organizations pay little attention to victims' "histories" or the histories of their communities, i.e., their lives *before* the interruptions wrought by capture, torture, or murder. Personal biography and collective history assume significance primarily when they are thought to lend insight into the oppressors' motives, as when violations of the human rights of known labor leaders or politicians are attributed to their organizational or political activities, or to their beliefs. Nothing in the personal histories of nonpolitical victims of scorched-earth policies or random bombings explains why *they* are repressed—nothing, that is, beyond the fact that they are peasants, students, or members of the Catholic Church.

Consider, for instance, the very important *Report on Human Rights in El Salvador* compiled by the Americas Watch Committee and the American Civil Liberties Union and released on 26 January 1982, one day before news stories about El Mozote appeared in the *New York Times* and the *Washington Post*. The report provided comprehensive documentation of the violation of fundamental human rights in El Salvador: the right to life, humane treatment, personal liberty, due process and a fair trial, freedom of thought and expression, etc. The authors described the background to the tragedy, the human rights situation, and the U.S. role in El Salvador, and demonstrated through a mass of testimony, statistics, and analysis that the Salvadoran government had failed to comply with both domestic and international law, and that the U.S. government was in violation of legal codes restricting its involvement abroad, particularly those laws that link foreign assistance to human rights performance.

This report presents Salvadorans as either perpetrators of human rights violations, victims, or witnesses testifying to the violations. The victims of persecution are portrayed as passive; they are acted upon. And they are discussed in categories, as *campesinos* (peasants), clergy and religious workers, political leaders, children and youth, teachers and academics, and journalists and human rights monitors, or divided into more detailed categories, as are the murder victims enumerated in Appendix 5 of the report. Of course, most Salvadorans would have no trouble identifying with the victims discussed in the *Report on Human Rights in El Salvador,* since behind each Venicio Humberto Bazzaglia, student, twenty-four years old, killed by the National Guard on 3 October 1980 (1982:50), Salvadoran readers could envision a cousin, a brother-in-law, a godfather, or a son and at least imagine the victim as a living person with a past and a personal trajectory for the future, terminated by the National Guard. But for the U.S. citizen taxpayer whose image of El Salvador approximates a dystopia of military strongmen, corrupt bureaucrats, and illiterate peasants, the report holds few surprises. For them, Venicio Humberto Bazzaglia and the thousands like him remain stick figures.

This categorizing approach to human rights is a realistic one considering the constraints—institutional, time, political, financial—under which such organizations operate. And with the constraints under which their informants operate, how could it be otherwise? Who would dare to speak openly and truthfully about victims in the midst of open civil war or where the state has undertaken a campaign of systematic repression? The fact that human rights organizations key their analyses to international laws that provide substantial protection to civilians who live in the midst of civil war makes little difference, because the laws are not obeyed. Adherence to these laws on the part of government and armed opposition would certainly alleviate an enormous amount of suffering in El Salvador and elsewhere.

But I want to suggest that, pragmatic or not, the practices that dominate human rights reporting reproduce the effects of an ideological vision that is dominant in the West of a world divided in two: a homogenous mass of poor, Third World humanity, cut more or less from the same cloth, on the one hand, and an aggregation of struggling Western individuals, each unique, each working to fulfill her or his potential, on the other. For those whose view of the world is framed by it, this discourse, I believe, depreciates the lives of Salvadorans, Sri Lankans, Senegalese, and others, and consequently depreciates the meaning of their suffering. Once depreciated, that suffering becomes a lot easier to accept, as do the explanations given for it by the governments, businesses, and others responsible. I believe that until this very bipolar and Western-centered view of the world changes, the massacre of a thousand peasants by a U.S.-trained and U.S.-equipped battalion like the Atlacatl will not be regarded in the West as being as significant, as important, or as newsworthy as the tragic shooting, drowning, electrocution, or collective suicide, etc., of ten struggling Anglos seeking to mold their individual destinies.

Let me be clear. I do not impugn the beliefs or question the motives of human rights advocates, who perform admirable work under difficult, often dangerous, circumstances. They make available to both researchers and the general public detailed knowledge of human rights violations, and they provide an important counterweight to those who claim that the situation gives no cause for concern. They do so from the perspective of an abstract humanism that, at least in theory, values all lives equally, regardless of race, ethnicity, gender, or social class. But the various factors that constrain their investigations, combined with a juridical model of reportage (Americas Watch documents often read like court briefs), place severe limits on their ability to challenge the complacent ethnocentrism of Westerners who rationalize their right to intervene in other nations' affairs by saying that "They" (the Others) cannot "keep their house in order." The universal valuation of human life and other humanitarian ideals that underpin progressive human rights reporting are not necessarily shared by the target audience. It is important, in order to improve the chances of reaching that audience, to develop new discursive strategies for presenting human rights problems.

If Americas Watch was constrained by the exigencies of the situation following the massacre, the same cannot be said of Mark Danner, who researched the case and published his results twelve years later. Danner's extensive ("book-length," as one commentator put it) article "The Truth of El Mozote" was published in the 6 December 1993 issue of the *New Yorker*.[3] "Once in a rare while," opined *New York Times* columnist Anthony Lewis (1993) in reference to the Danner piece, "a writer re-examines a debated episode of recent history with such thoroughness and integrity that the truth can no longer be in doubt." Lewis continued: "Over the years politicians and journalists have differed bitterly about what happened there—who did the killing, indeed whether there was a massacre at all. The argument is over now."

Indeed! Given that two experienced journalists visited the site and interviewed eyewitnesses less than a month after the event, the surprising thing is that the fact of the massacre and the identities of the perpetrators were ever questioned—that, in other words, an argument over "what happened there" occurred in the first place. Despite several months of research (but only a single short trip, in November 1992, to El Salvador)

FIGURE 1 Unknown persons placed these wooden crosses at the foot of an eroded adobe wall, part of the remnants of the home of El Mozote resident Israel Márquez. According to El Mozote massacre survivor Rufina Amaya, the remains of dozens of women murdered by the Atlacatl Battalion lie underneath the dirt and rubble of the interior of the ruin.

and interviews with former soldiers, Farabundo Martí National Liberation Front (FMLN) commanders, and El Mozote survivors (both the two persons who escaped after being captured by the army and others who left town before the troops arrived), Danner says very little about El Mozote as a social location, i.e., a community with a complex and interesting history and a rich tapestry of prewar social relationships. He represents the massacre victims en masse as poor, illiterate peasants—apolitical innocents butchered by a military bent on teaching the guerrilla and its *masas* (supporters—among whom the residents of this mountain community were counted by the government) a lesson. Apart from a few passing observations, Danner's prose allows El Mozote and its former inhabitants to be absorbed within a generic vision of a Salvadoran countryside populated by "people without history" (Wolf 1982). Excise a few geographical specificities and Danner could have been speaking of Cabañas, La Unión, San Vicente, or any other department in El Salvador, or some rural area of Mexico, Guatemala, Colombia, or Peru. Even Rufina Amaya, who has become the symbol par excellence of the survivors of government repression in El Salvador, as has Rigoberta Menchú in Guatemala, is dehistoricized (unlike Menchú, who, after all, was enabled to tell her story). In Danner's account, Amaya's history becomes of interest at the moment that Marcos Díaz informed El Mozote residents of the impending government military invasion; for him, her suffering begins at that point as well. He ignores the fact that for several decades prior to the massacre, Amaya endured a daily struggle against the effects of the grinding rural poverty that afflicted most El Mozote inhabitants.

Of course, it could be argued that local history was not something that Danner was aiming at. But to assert such a position would be, rather than a reasonable justification, a manifestation of the larger problem. After all, Danner wrote a lot about the Salvadoran military, the figure of Lt. Col. Domingo Monterrosa, and the thoughts and actions of U.S. Embassy personnel—powerful figures and institutions all. Would it have been too much for him to give equal time to the victims and survivors, whose beliefs and relationships were at least as varied and complex as those of the people who killed them and of those who financed and then covered up the killing?[4] I will discuss Danner's portrayal of El Mozote and suggest an alternative to it at various points in this book, especially in chapters 5 and 6.

What form, then, might a plausible alternative writing of human rights assume? The testimonial is one possibility. Testimonials are produced by witnesses who have been and continue to be the subjects of exploitation and oppression by groups in a dominant social, economic, and political position. In other words, they are by and about victims of human rights violations. Since testimonials involve witnessing—the speaker testifies to events experienced—the perspective is that of the first-person "I" rather than that of the third-person "he," "she," or "they." As a result, testimonies eschew the passive contemplation of a life to manifest a sense of urgency and involvement. Since the witness wishes to draw attention to events that have not been publicized or to disseminate them to a wider public, testimonial literature is partisan rather than neutral. The writer seeks to convince the reader of the justice of the struggle and to solicit sympathy and support for it.

Through the narrator/speaker's testimony, the reader learns about the condition of a larger oppressed sector of society: indigenous people, women, workers, peasants, or some combination of these. In this sense, the narrator is both an individual and a representative of a social stratum, any member of which could have given roughly similar testimony.

The voice of the witness fills the space of the text. The details of birth, childhood, marriage, daily life, work, suffering, and so on are the means through which social and cultural distance is reduced between narrator and reader. The text depicts the narrator as a human being with aspirations, capabilities, and morals who is embedded within a social situation that narrows the opportunities for realizing these ideals. Finally, testimonials usually project a future ideal that represents an improvement on the present and that serves as a goal toward which people struggle and against which they measure the present's shortcomings. The reader is invited to participate through her or his action in the construction of this future (Stephen 1994a; Gugelberger and Kearney 1991).

Isabel Allende said that "[p]robably the strongest literature being written nowadays is by those who stand unsheltered by the system: blacks, Indians, homosexuals, exiles and, especially, women—the crazy people of the world, who dare to believe in their own force" (1989:55).[5] El Salvador's struggle has produced important testimonials by members of opposition forces (Dalton 1987; Díaz 1992; Martínez 1992), by members of the popular movement (Stephen 1994b), and even by committed foreign participants from the North who have identified with the struggles of the poor and have elected to leave the shelters of privilege to accompany them in their struggles for social and economic justice (Clements 1984; Metzi 1988).[6]

I believe that every member of an oppressed group has a story to tell, though many people are unable to recall the details of the story or tell it well enough to maintain the interest of a culturally and geographically remote audience. Most (if not all) societies produce oral historians—guardians of collective history and truth. But unlike the collective histories transmitted by the Saramakan elders discussed by Richard Price (1981), testimonies are essentially individual accounts, even when they embody collective experience. For this reason they are constrained by the knowledge, experience, and personal orientation of the witness.[7]

Despite these limits, I find testimonies particularly useful and have incorporated segments of them in this book. In fact, during my ethnographic work in northern Morazán, what began as interviews often reverted to testimonials as the informants-cum-witnesses narrated in great detail the violence wreaked upon them by the Salvadoran military and security forces. However, this book primarily explores another approach to writing that is different from testimonials but shares with them the object of inserting individual and collective history into the investigation of human rights abuses. Without denigrating or stereotyping the individuals who lived in El Mozote—the histories-cum-testimonies told by the survivors form the basis for the following account—I attempt to locate El Mozote as a material, social, and symbolic place, the meaning of which has come to transcend the massacre that occurred there. If testimonials elucidate collective history through the eyes of one individual, I wish to situate the individuals (the oppressed and the oppressors) making that history by approaching it from a multiplicity of perspectives that will converge upon a single episode in the Salvadoran civil war: the massacre at El Mozote. Thus I will discuss El Mozote as a unique community and will locate it within a regional context (chapters 5 and 6), but I will also place the massacre within the *longe dure* of events that gave rise to the current Salvadoran state (chapter 3). Further, and in contrast to others, I will treat the massacre as a living event rather than one that is dead and can be buried (chapters 7 and 9). Throughout this book I will argue that, in a very real way, the success or failure of the Salvadoran people, and particularly of their government, to "come to terms" with El Mozote—the single largest massacre of the civil war—says a great deal about the potential for peaceful reconciliation in post–civil war El Salvador.

To those ends this work is organized as follows. Chapter 2 briefly describes the massacre at El Mozote. Chapter 3, "The Eye of the Oligarchy," traces the roots of the massacre into the social and economic transformation of the past century that gave rise, through a gradual though violent process, to a small, immensely wealthy oligarchy intent on protecting its ill-gotten gains from the workers and peasants who produced them. The chapter also documents the post–World War II U.S. role in the creation and installation of a security apparatus that reached into the heart of most rural communities. The U.S. government may not have injected the virus of cold war ideology into El Salvador, but it certainly nourished it. Chapter 4 summarizes the cover-up of the massacre. Here I acknowledge my debt both to Mark Danner's investigative work and to the National Security Archive for having made available to researchers a plethora of documents acquired through Freedom of Information Act requests.

Chapters 5 and 6 are in many ways the core chapters of the book because they present a portrait of El Mozote at odds in almost every way with previous depictions. Chapter 5 outlines El Mozote's short history as a congregate community and analyzes prewar social and economic relationships there. I hope that after perusing this chapter the reader comes to the same conclusion that I did when writing it: that El Mozote was a relatively successful example of liberal rural development theory put into practice, the kind of community about which USAID bureaucrats rhapsodize. This makes it all the more ironic that it was targeted for eradication by the Salvadoran military. In chapter 6, "The Politics of Repression and Survival in Northern Morazán," I discuss experiences within the community during the two-year period leading up to the massacre; there I attempt to rebut three broadly held misconceptions about El Mozote: that the population's political neutrality could be attributed to its embrace of evangelical Christianity; that the inhabitants had previously escaped repression at the hands of military and security forces; and that the entire population of the community (with notable exceptions) was wiped out, meaning that few survived to pass on El Mozote's collective history. I should mention that eight months of fieldwork in northern Morazán (June–July 1991, July–December 1992) carried out prior to taking up the El Mozote case provided me the broad background knowledge of northern Morazanian history and society that proved critical in understanding both El Mozote's "typicality" and its "exceptionalism."[8]

Chapter 7, "Investigation and Judgment," turns toward the present to describe efforts to pursue justice in the case. In that chapter I discuss the critical role played by the northern Morazanians who initiated the case and pressed it forward; by contrast, public credit for this tended to go to Tutela Legal and the Truth Commission. Chapter 8, "A Reformed Military?" counters claims that the Salvadoran military reformed following the period of massacres and death-squad killings of the early 1980s. Though much of that chapter focuses on the period of the Duarte presidency, I extend the analysis to the present in order to argue that the greatest obstacle to reconciliation remains the military institution. Chapter 9, "History and Memory," discusses a memorial mass and museum exhibits about the massacre and argues that El Mozote will remain a "live" issue for generations to come. I also show that through its repopulation (155 households with more than 750 people as of October 1994), El Mozote has acquired a concrete, as well as symbolic, existence after over ten years of total abandonment. In the concluding chapter I return to some of the themes raised here, mark the limits of this text, and suggest an alternative practice of anthropology.

THE MASSACRE

In 1974 Rafael Arce Zablah, a founder of the People's Revolutionary Army (ERP), reconnoitered northern Morazán and discovered it to be one of the few areas in highly populated El Salvador appropriate for the establishment of a guerrilla rear guard.[1] The region's 225 square miles of terrain located north of the Torola River is topographically rugged, endowed with a reliable year-round water supply, and home to a peasantry integrated into capitalist production relations principally through seasonal migration (Henríquez 1992:25; see map 2). Juan Ramón Medrano (Comandante "Balta")[2] recalled that

> In contrast to the peasants of Usulután, who were undisciplined, worked the cotton harvest and related more with the city, were more affected by alcohol and were violent among themselves, the Morazanian peasants were better organized and structured in Christian communities, [and] were middle and poor peasants many of whom had resolved their subsistence needs, although others were quite impoverished. But all were very united and displayed profound Christian values. (Medrano and Raudales 1994:69)

The ERP organized in the region on the back of the progressive Catholicism that was sweeping Latin America in the 1960s and 1970s (Lernoux 1980) and that played an instrumental role in the revolutions in El Salvador (Pearce 1986; Montgomery 1982; Hassett and Lacey 1991),

Nicaragua (Lancaster 1988), and Guatemala (Menchú 1984). In northern Morazán the main proponent and practitioner of this "theology of liberation," through which the Church identified with the poor and demanded "that Christians be a force actively working to liberate the vast majority of the people from poverty and oppression" (Montgomery 1982: 100), was Father Miguel Ventura, who was sent to the region in 1973 to direct the newly formed parish centered in Torola (see chapter 6). Through the Bible-reading and discussion groups organized by a network of peasant catechists working with Ventura, many peasants developed a growing awareness of the relationship between their poverty and the tremendous wealth that accrued to the oligarchy; lamented the state's unwillingness to address the most fundamental needs for infrastructure, health care, and education; discussed the failure of liberal efforts to democratize the country (especially the fraudulent elections of 1972 and 1977); and recounted the daily injustices that they suffered at the hands of the National Guard and the Treasury Police,[3] which occupied posts in the municipal townships and worked hand in glove with large landowners and wealthy merchants.[4] By the time Rafael Arce Zablah called the first meetings with the "natural leaders" of the communities west of the *calle negra*—the asphalt road that divides northern Morazán—many peasants understood the web of interests and contradictions that produced their poverty and oppression, and opted to join clandestine military committees in order to prepare for the conflict that Arce told them was on the horizon. Others less disposed to take up arms participated in the aboveground political protests of the Popular Leagues "28 February" (LP-28), the ERP's mass organization formed in 1977 and called Popular Leagues "28 February" in commemoration of the 28 February 1977 government massacre in the Plaza Libertad in San Salvador of up to 200 demonstrators protesting the fraudulent election that brought Gen. Humberto Romero to power (Whitfield 1995:101–102). Developments in northern Morazán followed a course similar to that in Chalatenango and elsewhere, except for the absence in northern Morazán of organizations such as the Rural Workers Union (UTC) and the Christian Federation of Salvadoran Peasants (FECCAS) that provided an intermediate ground between progressive Catholicism and armed insurgency (see Pearce 1986).

For several years the ERP worked quietly and clandestinely to expand its support base in northern Morazán. Meanwhile, its urban cadres carried out a series of brazen bank robberies and spectacular kidnappings of wealthy landowners in order to build up the war chest (see Martínez

1992). Following the fraudulent election in 1977 of Gen. Humberto Romero, who added his name to the long list of military presidents that had ruled El Salvador since Maximiliano Hernández Martínez seized power in 1932, tensions in the country approached the breaking point. The rapid growth of mass organizations in the cities was countered by a tidal wave of state-sponsored repression.

In northern Morazán the National Guard and the Treasury Police met rumors of guerrilla activity with increasing surveillance, harassment, and captures of suspected civilians. The ERP responded by progressing from clandestine military training (often carried out at night on soccer fields by the light of the moon) to weapons recuperation and propaganda operations. At the end of the 1970s, the peasant guerrillas repaid security-force massacres and death-squad operations by assaulting National Guard and Treasury Police patrols. By late 1980, National Guard and Treasury Police forces, along with local Civil Defense forces, patrolled areas around the town centers while surrendering large areas of the countryside to the day-to-day control of the ERP and its civilian collaborators.[5]

The die of the future was cast in October 1980, when the ERP joined with four other leftist political-military groups to form the Farabundo Martí National Liberation Front (FMLN).[6] The groups maintained their prewar names and identities and tended to operate in different areas of the country where each had developed its historic following. However, they also developed an impressive capacity for collective planning and action. That same month northern Morazán became the target of the largest military operation since El Salvador fought Honduras in the Hundred Hours War of 1969. Contingents of National Guard soldiers and Treasury Police officers joined troops from Military Detachment No. 4 in San Francisco Gotera and commandos from the Third Brigade base in San Miguel to entrap ERP units in a hammer-and-anvil operation west of the calle negra. Grossly outnumbered and possessing only a few high-powered rifles, the novice guerrillas used thousands of homemade contact bombs to hold off more than two thousand troops. For over two weeks they shifted their defensive lines gradually southward. Finally, the ammunition ran out and the rebels were forced to retreat to safety across the Torola River, leaving behind in Villa El Rosario hundreds of civilians whom they had been protecting. In the largest massacre in northern Morazán to that date, army and security forces killed over thirty unarmed men, women, and children who had taken refuge in the Villa El Rosario church. More civilians would have been killed but for the efforts of Capt. Francisco Emilio Mena Sandoval, a member of the progressive Military Youth Movement, who called off a planned bombardment (see accounts in Mena Sandoval 1991 and López Vigil 1991). The October 1980 invasion established northern Morazán as a region of great strategic concern to the Salvadoran military and FMLN guerrillas alike. Peace would not come to the area for more than eleven years, and at a cost of more than five thousand residents dead between civilians and combatants— over 10 percent of the 1980 population.

During the next thirteen months additional army operations and security-force and death-squad murders combined to terrorize the civilian population. Human rights documents from the Human Rights Commission of Segundo Montes contain denunciations of massacres of ten or more people in December 1980 in Torola, January 1981 and July 1981 in Villa El Rosario, and March 1981 in Cacaopera. Survivors also testified to sixty assassinations in northern Morazán during the eleven-month period prior to the El Mozote massacre (see chapter 6, tables 1 and 2). Were an accurate accounting possible, the numbers would surely be much higher.

But the massacre at El Mozote differed greatly from preceding repressive acts. The El Mozote massacre did not involve a spur-of-the-moment decision to eliminate guerrilla sympathizers following three weeks of intense battle and numerous losses, as may have occurred in October 1980; instead, it was a meticulously planned operation carefully calculated to drain the civilian "water" from the sea and thereby strand the guerrilla "fish." Operation Rescue, as the 7–17 December operation was ironically designated by the Salvadoran military, was an operation of *tierra arrasada* (scorched earth). And to carry out the plan, what better instrument of destruction than the Atlacatl Battalion, the first immediate-reaction infantry battalion armed and trained by the United States and named, ironically, after a heroic Pipil chieftain who died resisting the Spanish during the conquest?

The facts of the El Mozote massacre are contained in a detailed document composed by Tutela Legal (Legal Protection), the human rights organization of the Catholic archdiocese of San Salvador, from the testimony of more than a dozen witnesses (Tutela Legal 1991). This information was later supplemented by the investigative work of Mark Danner in his book *The Massacre at El Mozote* (1993, 1994). According to both Tutela Legal and Danner, the Atlacatl Battalion disembarked from helicopters in Perquín, Morazán, on 8 December 1981. Battalion officers forcefully

MAP 2 Northern Morazán

recruited ten local men to act as guides during the operation, and for the next seventy-two hours the battalion's five companies, a total of about twelve hundred men, marched south toward El Mozote and other areas located east of the *calle negra*. Whereas the October 1980 invasion had been focused west of the asphalt road, in Torola, Jocoaitique, San Fernando, and Villa El Rosario, municipalities in which the ERP developed its early nuclei, the December 1981 assault was aimed primarily at La Guacamaya (located in the municipality of Meanguera), site of the ERP command post and the clandestine Radio Venceremos, although the largest number of people were killed at El Mozote (also in Meanguera).

The rural hamlet of El Mozote is located less than an hour's walk north from La Guacamaya.[7]

The operation's planners designated the Atlacatl Battalion as the "strike force" that would confront guerrillas fleeing from units of regular-army and security-force troops penetrating the area from the Torola River to the south and Joateca to the east. During their march southward from Perquín, Atlacatl companies cleaved off at different points to pursue objectives that lay along roughly parallel routes running from the northwest to the southeast. The battle plan laid out for the First Company took it through Arambala and on to El Mozote, Los Toriles, and La Guacamaya (see the map in Danner 1993:68, 1994:54).[8] As Danner notes in his text and on the map that accompanies it, other companies left the calle negra at Los Quebrachos and assaulted La Joya, La Ranchería, and Cerro Pando.

The bloodletting began on Wednesday, 9 December, in Arambala, where soldiers killed between three and twenty men—witnesses testified to six deaths for the Truth Commission—whose names were on a list of suspects carried by one of the officers. The following day the First Company proceeded toward El Mozote. After a confrontation with a guerrilla unit somewhere around El Portillón (Danner 1993:68, 1994:55), the troops arrived outside El Mozote on 10 December and encamped while planes and helicopters strafed and bombed surrounding hillsides to "soften up" the area.

In the late afternoon of 10 December, forty-three years to the day after the United Nations adopted the Universal Declaration of Human Rights (Dundes Renteln 1990:27–28), soldiers entered El Mozote, rousted the inhabitants from their houses, and assembled them in the central plaza area, or the Plain, where they forced them to lie down in the street. At the time, El Mozote was swollen with refugees from the surrounding countryside who had been warned by a respected local store owner named Marcos Díaz, acting on the advice of an army officer in San Francisco Gotera, that the military was going to invade the area and that anyone caught outside town would be killed, while the lives of those congregated in El Mozote would be respected (Tutela Legal 1991:6). Many people had already left the area out of fear, while others had gone to seek dry-season jobs elsewhere in northern Morazán or in more distant places (see chapter 6).

But the soldiers' behavior was not reassuring. They kicked and threatened people, robbed them of their jewelry and other valuables, accused

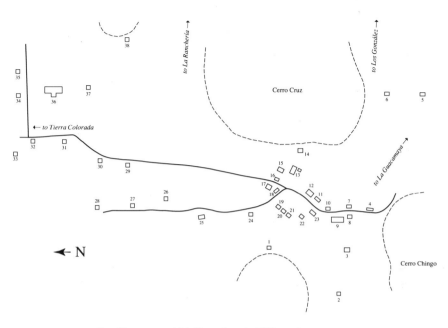

List of Structures and Inhabitants from the El Mozote Survey

1.	Ponciano Argueta	lived	14.	Sofía Márquez	?	27.	José María Márquez Argueta	massacred
	Dominga Argueta	lived	15.	Rosendo Vigil	lived		Hilda Hortensia Márquez	massacred
2.	Teofilo Márquez Alvarenga	lived	16.	Casa Comunal		28.	Narciso Márquez	lived
	Saltación Argueta	lived	17.	José María Claro Guevara	?	29.	Graciliano Argueta	massacred
3.	Israel Márquez	massacred	18.	Benita Díaz	?		Sofía Márquez	?
4.	Efraín Márquez	massacred		Cervando Guevara	?	30.	Sofía Argueta	lived
	Lucía Chicas	massacred	19.	Ignacio Chicas	lived		Leoncio Díaz	massacred
5.	Santos Márquez	massacred	20.	Daniel Romero	massacred	31.	Fernando Hernández	?
	Augustina García	massacred		José Carmen Romero	lived		Andrea ?	died before
6.	José María Márquez	massacred		María Romero	massacred	32.	Leonardo Márquez	lived
	Donatila Periera	massacred		Raquel Romero	lived		María Diana Claros	lived
7.	Ambrosia Claros	massacred	21.	Francisca Díaz	died before	33.	Leocario Argueta	lived
	José Nilo Claros	massacred	22.	Claros Guevara	?		Carmen Argueta	lived
8.	Eloy Márquez	lived	23.	Alfredo Márquez	lived	34.	Santana Díaz	lived
9.	Marcos Díaz	massacred		Martina Claros	lived	35.	Martina Díaz	massacred
10.	Angel Ramos	lived	24.	Eufraio Márquez	lived	36.	School	
	Valentina Chicas	lived		Anastacia Vigil	massacred	37.	Tranquilino Argueta	lived
11.	Pedro Rodríguez	lived	25.	Perfecto Díaz	massacred		Ovelia Márquez	lived
	Andrea Chicas	lived		Andrea Claros	massacred	38.	Israel Márquez	lived
12.	Maximiliano Rodríguez	lived	26.	Santos Argueta	lived		Petronila Vigil	lived
13.	Church and Sacristy			Victoriana Díaz Márquez	massacred			

FIGURE 2 El Mozote

them of being guerrillas, and demanded to know where they had hidden their arms. After about an hour, the soldiers ordered their captives back into the houses for the night and warned them not to show "even so much as their noses" outside (Danner 1993:72, 1994:64). The houses were crowded, hot, and stuffy, and the peasants remained awake during the night, hungry and apprehensive about what the dawn might bring.

Meanwhile, the Atlacatl troops celebrated the town's capture with laughter, singing, and gunfire.

At five o'clock on the morning of 11 December 1981, soldiers pounded on the doors, forced the people again from the houses, and concentrated everyone in the Plain in front of the small, whitewashed-adobe Church of the Three Kings. After compelling the people to stand for several hours, the guards divided them into two groups: the men and older boys were driven into the church, while the women, girls, and young children of both sexes were interned in the vacant home of Alfredo Márquez, a local merchant who had left town. Together the groups numbered between four hundred and six hundred people. Many of the men were blindfolded, tied up, and forced to lie *boca abajo* (face down) on the dirt floor of the church. Soldiers carried out perfunctory and superficial interrogations with the prisoners in both places, prodding them with bayonets, beating them, and demanding to know where their arms were located and whether or not they collaborated with the guerrillas (Danner 1993: 78–79, 1994:68–69). But gathering information does not seem to have been a high priority, because soon the killing began:

> About eight o'clock on the fourth day of the operation, in the interior of the church, there began a series of massive assassinations by members of the armed forces that participated in the operation against the civilian population. From eight o'clock various of the men concentrated in the church were lifted up from the soil by military troops and decapitated with machetes. The decapitations did not take place simultaneously but one after the other, after which the soldiers dragged the bodies and the heads toward the sacristy [a room attached to the church, where the priest was lodged during his occasional visits] where they piled up the remains. Some men tried to escape when the assassinations started but were machine gunned in their flight by military troops who subsequently decapitated some of the cadavers. . . . The approximate number of persons concentrated in the church was two hundred. (Tutela Legal 1991:8)[9]

But as Danner observed, "Decapitation is tiring work, and slow, and more than a hundred men were crammed into that small building" (1993: 79, 1994:70). Thus the majority of the men were assassinated outside the town center proper. They were bound, blindfolded, marched in small groups into the surrounding hills or to the brick-walled and tile-roofed elementary school, and forced to lie face down on the ground, after which, according to a witness quoted in the Tutela Legal report (1991:8), "they received a burst of gunfire in the head." Between eight o'clock in the morning and four o'clock in the afternoon, several hundred people were killed in this manner.

About midday Atlacatl troops arrived at the Alfredo Márquez house, selected out older girls and young women, and forced them to walk up the wooded hillsides of Cerro Cruz and Cerro Chingo, where they repeatedly raped them over the course of the next twelve to eighteen hours and then murdered them. Some were shot; others may have been stabbed or strangled. Late in the afternoon the soldiers began to remove the remainder of the adult women in groups of about twenty, followed by the older women, and lastly the children. Not a living soul was to be allowed to escape, although at least one person did. While the armed escort sought to control one of the last groups of twenty elderly, pleading, crying, and praying campesinas—some of whom had earlier seen men cut down and then marched off to be shot—Rufina Amaya, wife of Domingo Claros and mother of six, slipped off the path and hid herself behind a tree. The guards accompanying the group did not notice her, and she eventually fled the area. But not before the children, four of hers included, were murdered within earshot on that dark December night (Danner 1993:81– 84, 1994:73–76).[10]

The church, the sacristy, and the homes of Israel Márquez, Isidro Claros, and José María Márquez—wherever the bodies of the victims had been dumped—were set on fire, and the flickering flames must have effected a macabre counterpoint to the cries of the dying children. From her hiding place behind a crabapple tree next to the house of Israel Márquez, Rufina Amaya heard the following conversation among a group of resting Atlacatl soldiers: "Well, we've killed all the old men and women. . . . But there's still a lot of kids down there. You know, a lot of those kids are really good-looking, really cute. I wouldn't want to kill all of them. Maybe we can keep some of them, you know—take them home with us." His confederate objected: "We have to finish everyone, you know that. That's the colonel's order. This is an operativo de tierra arrasada here and we have to kill the kids as well, or we'll get it ourselves" (cited in Danner 1993:84, 1994:74–75).

And so the order was given and the order was completed. Based on the testimony of Rufina Amaya and according to Tutela Legal (1991:10), the soldiers of the Atlacatl proceeded to assassinate the small children, who numbered several hundred, concentrated in the house of Alfredo Márquez. During said assassinations, the children's shouts for help could be heard. . . . "Mama, they are killing us," "they are strangling us," "Mama, they are sticking us with knives." After assassinating the minors, the soldiers set fire to the house of Alfredo Márquez in whose interior were found the bodies of the children. While the home blazed in flames the cry of a minor who called for his mother could be heard, after which an unidentified soldier gave the following order: "go and kill this bastard *[cabrón]* that you haven't killed well." Subsequently several shots were heard, soon after which the cries of the minor were no longer heard.

In a story that has been told many times in many places and has assumed mythic dimensions in northern Morazán, Amaya crawled across the road and under a barbed-wire fence in the blackness of the night and hid herself in a patch of maguey. There she carved a little hole in the ground and stuck her face into it so that she could silently mourn for her murdered family (Tutela Legal 1991:12–13).

The Tutela Legal (1991:14–27) report listed 393 known victims at El Mozote by name (where known), age (often estimated), and family association; the total number of victims listed from Operation Rescue for all hamlets was 794. In 1994 Mark Danner reviewed the Tutela list on the basis of more recent information and reduced the count slightly, to 370 victims in El Mozote.[11] But there can be little doubt that numerous other victims went unrecorded, their names lost to posterity because ten years after the fact the witnesses had forgotten them, or because they were among those from surrounding rural areas who had come into El Mozote on the advice of Marcos Díaz and were not known to residents of the community. I shall attempt to demonstrate in chapter 6 that about one-third of the pre-war population died in the massacre.

Having wiped out the population in El Mozote, the First Company continued on to Los Toriles the following day, and thence to La Guacamaya, which had long been abandoned by the guerrillas. During the same period (11–13 December), other companies were besieging other hamlets. The modus operandi varied slightly from one site to another, but the results were everywhere the same: the extermination of every human being and every animal that could be located, and the destruction of homes, beehives, sugar mills, and other personal and productive property. Drawing on the testimony of those who by good fortune or by foresight escaped the Atlacatl's deathtrap, the Tutela Legal report narrates how the Atlacatl arrived at this or that rural hamlet; slaughtered men, women, and children; killed or carted off the domestic animals; and set fire to the homes. It plods along, systematically describing the horror, hamlet by hamlet, with the account of each locale followed by a list of the identifiable dead: in La Joya the number of dead was estimated at 138; 54 were murdered in La Ranchería, 63 in Los Toriles, 17 in Jocote Amarillo, and 113 in Cerro Pando. Another 15 people who sought refuge from the operation in a cave near Ortiz Hill were killed when patrolling soldiers lobbed a grenade into the cave mouth, their attention attracted by the sound of a crying child (Tutela Legal 1991:27–62).

In the midst of the operation, the colonels in charge held an early morning meeting. Col. Jaime Ernesto Flores Grijalba, who led the Third Brigade in San Miguel; the colonel in charge of the Fourth Military Detachment in San Francisco Gotera; and Lt. Col. Domingo Monterrosa Barrios, the Atlacatl Battalion commander, met with the Atlacatl's executive officer, Maj. Jesús de Natividad Cáceres Cabrera, and with the captains who commanded its five companies. They killed and butchered a steer to eat, and Monterrosa "expressed his satisfaction regarding the results of the operation: 'Mission completed,' he told the commanders. Some soldiers carried a green cloth with white letters that said, 'If the guerrilla returns to Morazán, the Atlacatl will return to Morazán'" (Tutela Legal 1991:62).

THE DISCOVERY

Though many people in the area of El Mozote heeded the advice of Marcos Díaz, others were skeptical and fled before the approaching soldiers, either alone or with the assistance of guides provided by the FMLN (see chapter 6). From refuges in heavily wooded ravines, caves, or on the other side of the Sapo River, outside the noose laid by the military, these survivors could observe the movement of the Atlacatl troops and the coming and going of helicopters that ferried the commanding officers to and from the killing fields. They knew that something bad had occurred when they saw smoke rising from the burning homes, since during earlier periods of the civil war the army had set fire only to uninhab-

FIGURE 3 The home of Marcos Díaz, El Mozote's wealthiest inhabitant, was destroyed in the massacre. This photograph was taken in late 1992, prior to reoccupation of the house by a surviving sister. Cerro Chingo can be seen in the background.

ited houses. When the vultures appeared, circling in the sky and then descending in corkscrew spirals to feast on the human and animal remains, the reality of what had occurred began to sink in.

As the Atlacatl exited northern Morazán on 17 December, the guerrillas filtered back in. The Salvadoran military had left a company of regular-army troops to guard La Guacamaya, and on 29 December the ERP mounted a "tremendous attack" and retook the area (Henríquez 1992: 106). But even before the area had been secured, ERP commanders were counting the bodies and sending in health teams *[brigadistas]* to bury the human corpses and dispose of the animal corpses in order to guard against an epidemic. "Franco" participated in one such group and discussed his experiences with me. Entering from the direction of Cerro Cruz, his team encountered the bodies of four young women about fifteen years old who had been shot and stabbed to death on top of the hill. They walked down the slope to the church in El Mozote, where they found many bodies in advanced states of decomposition; these they buried in mass graves of twenty to twenty-five bodies each. The strong, sickening smell of decaying flesh—now more than two weeks in the tropical sun—was practically intolerable, and after digging mass graves all day, the brigade members had to camp outside the area to sleep.

The guerrillas "more or less cleaned up" the central Plain area, but they missed numerous bodies scattered throughout the surrounding countryside. Passing east through La Ranchería, they came upon a macabre sight: "There was a tall man about two meters in height. He was with other people, seated as though he was alive, and a pig was biting his left foot. And the pig couldn't move it [the body] because it was obstructed by a stone next to the abdomen. . . . [The body was] seated leaning against a stone fence. . . . Then the compañeros said, 'This pig cannot be eaten because it has consumed human flesh.'"

After burying as many of the dead as they could, the members of the brigade returned to camp and burned their clothing to rid themselves of the odor of death. Even so, "Franco" stated, the smell of decay clung to their skin for days afterward.

"Santiago" (Carlos Henríquez Consalvi), the Venezuelan international who had become "the voice of Venceremos," reentered northern Morazán on 24 December, ordered back by the FMLN from Jucuarán, a town on the Pacific Coast to which the radio team had been sent two weeks earlier to wait out the invasion (Henríquez 1992:97–106). That same day he broadcast the first news of the massacre to the world. On 30 December, a day after the zone was secured, Santiago entered El Mozote with a mobile team to interview survivors and describe the scene firsthand. I quote from his memoirs:

> To the degree that we approach El Mozote, hallucinatory signs envelop the senses, a mortal silence where before there were murmurs of children playing and old people weaving rope. Servando, the combatant who accompanied me, covers his nose:
> "The turkey vultures are eating the dead," he tells me.
> The plaza is deserted, on all sides there is a disorder of broken plates, scapularies, straw hats, papers, and pieces of bloody clothing. I remove the camera from the backpack and photograph a solitary infant tricycle in the middle of the street that symbolized all the intensity of the tragedy. We enter the church. Microphone in hand I describe the scene: desolation, destroyed benches, virgins [shot] full of holes, a headless saint, the walls riddled by the machine guns. Scattered over the floor: shoes, ID cards, dolls, prayer pamphlets, a daguerreotype, ornamental combs, bibs, bras, and torn shoes.

In the confessional booth a skull outlined with chalk, together with an inscription:

Batallón Atlacatl, Los angelitos del infierno.

[Atlacatl Battalion, The little angels from hell.] (Henríquez 1992: 107)

Santiago left the church and approached the small sacristy next to it: "The sacristy had been destroyed. Cadavers are entombed beneath its ruins. I shudder when I discover among the rubble a raised arm whose hand is extended toward the sky, as if in agony he had cried out for help without finding it" (Henríquez 1992:107). He then took testimony from survivors:

In a house with a collapsed roof a peasant studies the rubble that entombs little infant bodies.

"I am searching for my four children. I've been looking for them for two days. By God, look what they have done! This is an ingratitude. . . . what were these people guilty of?"

With his cry the man tries to revive his dead. We continue from house to house. In every one there are scenes filled with sadism. (Henríquez 1992:107–108)

The mobile crew took direct testimony from Doroteo, Anastacio Chicas, sixty-one-year-old Sebastián, and the witness Rufina Amaya. Sebastián pointed out the body of Israel Márquez, the town patriarch, who was "well liked, a real worker." They saw hundreds of spent 5.56 mm cartridges used in the M-16 littered about.

In the caseríos of Rancherías, Los Toriles, La Joya, Poza Honda, El Rincón, El Potrero, Yancolo, Flor de Muerto, Cerro Pando, the scene is repeated everywhere: in the patios of the houses mountains of massacred peasants, the infants embracing their mothers. The skin appears like parchment. The turkey vultures are having a banquet, the sun raises the unbearable smell of death. On a plank, written in charcoal there is an inscription:

The Atlacatl was here.

The father of the subversives. Second Company.

Here we shit on the sons of whores

and if you are missing your balls

ask for them by mail from the Atlacatl Battalion.

We the little angels from hell will return.

We want to finish you off. (Henríquez 1992:109)

THE EYE OF THE OLIGARCHY

We have no record of the deliberations that entered into the design of Operation Rescue, but it is inconceivable that they took place without the mention of "communism," equated in El Salvador with "terrorism," and the role that Operation Rescue would play in a grand design to defeat what the oligarchy and the military defined as "the communist threat." What the "communists" threatened in El Salvador was to undo the economic monopoly of the oligarchy and the monopoly on formal state power of the Salvadoran military men who had ruled in the oligarchy's service since 1932. Playing different but complementary roles, the military and the oligarchy collaborated to sustain a capitalist economy with semifeudal characteristics and an authoritarian state apparatus that secured by violence and paternalism the minimal political conditions necessary for the system's maintenance and reproduction.

The fact that the military played a "service" role for the oligarchy suggests to us that we should begin by examining the oligarchy and its ideology and then attempt to demonstrate some of the mechanisms through which that ideology has been imparted across sectors.[1] There is no better vehicle for this task than the Nationalist Republican Alliance, or ARENA Party, founded on 30 September 1981 by ex–National Guard Major Roberto D'Aubuisson to contest the March 1982 Constituent Assembly elections against the Christian Democratic Party, the National Conciliation Party, and other political parties. Although ARENA now attempts to dress in the clothing of moderation and reform (see NACLA 1986), at its founding in 1981 it crystallized the ideology of the most conservative sector of the oligarchy and through the efforts of D'Aubuisson gained a large following within the officers' corps (Schwarz 1991). His charisma aside, it is clear that D'Aubuisson's views appealed to sentiments that were widely shared but that were given coherence only when the oligarchy found it necessary to enter active political competition following Christian Democratic Party participation in the military-civilian junta formed in October 1979 (Gaspar Tapia 1989:3).

ARENA's ideology, according to Ignasio Martín-Baró (1991a), has its basis in a belief in the sanctity of individual effort and by extension the protection of the individual's right to acquire, retain, and use property. As a result, private enterprise becomes "an essential part of the individual," and "the liberty demanded for private enterprise is a logical extension of the liberty demanded for the individual." A 1988 handbook for ARENA activists states clearly, "The individual is recognized as the fundamental base of the nation, and the family as the fundamental nucleus of society" (ARENA 1988:2). ARENA's ideology is anchored by three basic values related to this belief in individual effort—nationalism, anticommunism, and capitalism—related by Martín-Baró (1991a:296–297) in the following manner:

> Any measure that threatens the right to private property or the freedom of private enterprise is an assault on the basic principles of the capitalist economic system, which is the foundation of national unity, and is therefore a threat to national security. Thus in practice the nationalism ARENA upholds is a nationalism defined by its anticommunism and by its profession of capitalist faith and which utilizes the principles and mechanisms of national security in order to preserve the system of production for profit and individual development which has prevailed in El Salvador for decades.

ARENA does not articulate a clear concept of "communism" comparable to its articulation of the concepts of "private property" or "capitalism." It defines "communism" neither as a political philosophy nor as an economic doctrine. Nor is it, as used by ARENA, the opposite of "capitalism" and "private property," since well-known defenders of both have been tarred by ARENA with the communist brush. But, then, how can "communism" be defined when it takes in so much: all that cannot be encompassed within the narrow frame that underwrites the oligarchy's right to endless accumulation? For Martín-Baró (1991a:296), ARENA's militant anticommunism

> is an anti-value since it is interested primarily in what is to be rejected, and only negatively in what is to be sought for the future. What ARENA means by communism is never defined except on a very generic level. . . . Communism is any system, movement, or ideology that is not fully identified with the prevailing system in El Salvador or that calls for some kind of social change. Communism is thus the denial of the nationalism that ARENA upholds. Therefore, in the discourse of the Salvadoran far right, Fidel Castro and Jimmy Carter, the Communist Party and the Jesuits, the FMLN and the United States Senate can all be equally communist.

"[C]an all be equally communist." *Can* is a modal verb of affirmation, and its use in this context conveys possibility rather than certainty, meaning that it is equally possible that at least in some cases they—whoever "they" are—might also not be communist. This makes of "communism" a moving target, a signifier with a shifting field of referents defined less in the realm of ideas than in the realm of action. Regardless of what a person may declare, he/she is branded a communist when and if undertaking (or espousing) an action that is adjudged threatening to the system of oligarchical domination. For ARENA, communism is not about "those others" at all but about "themselves" and anything that threatens them. A logic of the concrete that turns around the current interests of a few hundred families of the super rich, it masquerades as a logic of the abstract. It serves as a dumping ground for the "refuse" of uncomfortable propositions, whatever their source, and in the early eighties it empowered the activities that memorialized el Playón (the Big Beach) and la Puerta del Diablo (the Devil's Doorway) as macabre dumps that death squads filled up with the tortured bodies of those people regarded as dangers to the status quo.

Tina Rosenberg, a journalist who attempted to grasp violence in Latin America by studying "those who make cruelty possible" (1991:9), explains the attitudes of El Salvador's rich this way:

> I began to understand El Salvador's violence only after listening to repeated admonishments from the wealthy to tell the truth. They meant not the truth as I saw it but the truth as they saw it, the basis of which is the belief that the members of the private sector, the produc-

tive people who create wealth for El Salvador, are under attack from the twin evils of terrorism and socialist policies. This is the central Truth....

But the details of the Truth do not matter. What matters is that the oligarchy believes in it passionately. Finding the Truth is a question not of metaphysics but of real estate. It was born behind concrete walls, barbed wire, and bulletproof glass that delineate the world of the upper class like the lines in a coloring book. The Truth is a version of reality distilled and sharpened each day as the rich talk only to one another, as government ministers whisper the names of the rich softly and lovingly, as the army acts as their personal guards and the newspapers as their personal press agents. (Rosenberg 1991:223)

The Salvadoran rich have been speaking only to one another for a long time. Many of the families trace their arrival in El Salvador back to the colonial period (1525–1821), when planters grew indigo on both plantations and scattered peasant plots and then processed and exported it to the mills of Manchester, England, as hard blocks of dark blue, colorfast dye. In the second half of the nineteenth century, indigo gradually gave way to coffee cultivation, and the accompanying expansion of what had up to that point been a stillborn economy attracted a modest number of immigrants from Europe, Latin America, and the Middle East. "There were," as Lindo-Fuentes (1990:181) notes, "no large national groups moving en masse to El Salvador; immigrants were individuals (often male and single) with a specific expertise." Beginning in commerce and industry, they moved into land ownership and eventually intermarried into the mestizo elite. Within a few generations only the surnames remained to suggest their origins: Hill and Wright (England); Álvarez (Colombia); de Sola (Curaçao); Llach (Germany); Hasbún and Zablah (Palestine).

For a time El Salvador must have been a heady place for people with marketable skills and capital. Erected on economically "weak foundations" (the term is that of Lindo-Fuentes [1990]), the coffee economy stimulated saving and investment, a centralized bureaucracy, and the construction of a transport system. Most important, the prospect of producing this *grano de oro* (golden grain) led the elite to use state power to privatize communal and ejidal lands in what Rosenberg (1991:240) referred to as "a land reform in reverse" (cf. Browning 1971). Once most of the potential coffee land located on the upper slopes of the volcanic chain in the central cordillera had been occupied, the golden age of upward mobility into the elite pretty much came to an end: "The right time to start a big fortune, it seems, were the last twenty years of the nineteenth century and the first twenty years of the twentieth. . . . After that the door was virtually closed" (Lindo-Fuentes 1990:184). By 1928 coffee made up 92 percent of El Salvador's exports (Browning 1971).

The consolidation of the coffee economy fixed the contours of the modern oligarchy, which accommodated very few newcomers in the ensuing sixty years. In 1977 Eduardo Colindres pointed out in his book on the economic foundations of the Salvadoran bourgeoisie that only four of the sixty-three richest families in the country had made their fortunes after the 1950s. Thus the local beneficiaries of the postwar cotton boom of the 1960s, the expansion of insurance and banking services, or the industrial growth connected to the import substitution policies and the Central American Common Market were, principally, the same interconnected families that formed the coffee oligarchy. (Of course, the *principal* beneficiaries were the foreign—mainly U.S.—banks, merchants, and companies that financed, supplied, and purchased the products of postwar economic expansion [see Williams 1986].) As Baloyra (1982) notes, " '[D]iversification' in El Salvador did not increase the social heterogeneity of the dominant group. The older families, represented in the first group (planters), simply moved outside the coffee sector into other areas of the agricultural sector and into other areas of production" (23). If the "planters" did not move into retail trade, neither did the "merchants" move into agriculture.

More recently Paige (1993) distinguished a more "progressive" agro-industrial faction of the coffee elite (who favored a negotiated solution to the civil war and limited democracy) from a politically retrograde agro-financial faction.[2] The ideological differences between the two groups are overshadowed by their ideological similarities: members of both groups believe that private control over coffee production, processing, and marketing is the *only* plausible route to economic development; both oppose structural changes that would lead to the redistribution of wealth and political power; and both attribute the civil war to "a tiny group of terrorists of foreign inspiration if not foreign origin" (Paige 1993:25). Writing shortly before the end of the war, which lasted from 1980 to 1992, Paige (1993:38) concluded, "Despite the current acceptance of democracy and negotiations, elite ideology has changed remarkably little since the liberal revolutions that ushered in the coffee era a century and a half ago."

Observers frequently attribute the elite's narcissistic view of the world to the relatively closed circle of wealth and influence in which it resides. For instance, Lindo-Fuentes (1990:190) wonders "if the absolute power of the planters has something to do with their political inflexibility and narrow-mindedness." Since "[t]hey were beyond credible challenges, they did not have to learn the art of compromise, [and] they could insulate themselves from the rest of the population." Rosenberg's statement about conversations taking place behind "concrete walls" and "bulletproof glass" and endorsed by a coterie of yes-men (journalists, politicians, military officers) has the same import.

The fact is that we know little about what takes place behind those walls, in the foreign luxury automobiles, and in the beach houses where the oligarchs and other elites reside, "work," and congregate to relax. What does social isolation—an isolation maybe only a few degrees more severe than that of many American suburbs—contribute to social myopia and personal megalomania?[3] How does social positioning react upon social ideology? Should we assume with Louis Althusser (1971) and to a lesser degree Paul Willis (1979) that language learning, ideology, and desire are inseparable components of a single process of class-based socialization? If so then there would be little surprise that except for the occasional renegade "almost every Salvadoran seems to get through school in the United States without acquiring any beliefs that contradict those of his parents" (Rosenberg 1991:238).

But this is in the theater of ideological transmission, which is less critical for thinking about El Mozote than representation. It is enough for the moment to point out that a relatively small and interrelated group of wealthy capitalists live as though under a state of siege; they believe that the barbarians are at the gates and any measures are legitimate to save civilization. With notable exceptions (such as the martyred Enrique Álvarez) the oligarchy is an ideological black hole. So convinced is it of a few densely packed maxims that light cannot escape its strong gravitational field.[4] Yet, is it inconceivable that in the midst of this self-indulgence, a large eye looks out upon the world—a world that the oligarchy refuses either to acknowledge or to accommodate—and blinks?

THE 1932 INSURRECTION

The Salvadoran oligarchy has reason to blink, because it must know, or suspect, that it is both envied and hated. It has already weathered the feared storm once. In the crux of world depression and a massive decline in coffee prices in 1930, indigenous peasants organized by the Communist Party under the leadership of Augustín Farabundo Martí rebelled and seized several towns in the coffee-producing departments of Sonsonate and Ahuachapán. In the 1880s the peasants had been thrust into wage labor after being dispossessed of their communal lands by decree, and in 1930 they were threatened with starvation when the coffee planters responded to a depression-induced collapse of the world coffee market by reducing workers' wages. Though plans of the rebellion reached the army and Martí was arrested, the uprising proceeded. Gangs of angry, machete-wielding indigenous peasants seized Izalco, Nonualco, and other towns and killed some twenty or thirty wealthy planters, government officials, and security-force personnel before the army arrived from the capital and elsewhere to arrest the insurrection. The restoration of peace—for the bourgeoisie, though not for workers and peasants—was followed by the systematic slaughter of between 10,000 and 30,000 people ordered by Gen. Maximiliano Hernández Martínez, who had seized power from civilian president Arturo Araujo a few months earlier. Thomas Anderson, who has produced the most careful examination of the *matanza*, as the 1932 peasant massacre came to be called, wrote, "As most of the rebels, except the leaders, were difficult to identify, arbitrary classifications were set up. All those who were found carrying machetes were guilty. All those of a strongly Indian cast of features, or who dressed in a scruffy, *campesino* costume, were considered guilty" (1971:131).

Government authorities tricked the residents of Izalco, Juayúa, and other towns by inviting people who had not taken part in the insurrection to present themselves in order to acquire safe-conduct passes. The authorities examined those who arrived, and they took out and shot those who matched the broad criteria used to identify insurgents. Had the people living in and around El Mozote known more about the deceptions employed in the 1932 massacre, which took place far to the west of Morazán, they might have reacted differently when Marcos Díaz allegedly informed area peasants that those who congregated in the community center would have their lives respected by the invading military force.

However, the government maintained silence about the 1932 events and destroyed files, books, and newspapers dealing with the revolt (Anderson 1971:144). The silence contributed to a plethora of rumors that have become accepted as fact by many people. One common belief is that the peasants killed hundreds of members of the bourgeoisie; Anderson arrived at a maximum of one hundred after a meticulous accounting, which "means that the government exacted reprisals at the rate of about one hundred to one" (136). Ever since the massacre, the oligarchs and their allies have taken measures to impede the independent organization of rural peasants and wage workers.

Farabundo Martí was shot on 1 February 1932, along with two of his confederates, but the oligarchs' fear of communists and campesinos did not die with him. Although rural organization was stifled by oppressive labor laws and rural security forces (Treasury Police, National Guard), it is clear that among Lázaro Cárdenas, Fidel Castro, Jacobo Arbenz, Rafael Trujillo, and others, there were enough real and imagined communist threats nearby to keep the Salvadoran bourgeoisie on alert. When that threat did finally consolidate again in 1980, it is not surprising that the revolutionaries named their organization after Augustín Farabundo Martí (the FMLN) or that the extreme Right organized a death squad named after General Martínez: the Maximiliano Hernández Martínez Brigade.

It is my contention that elite ideology was firmly established by the first quarter of the current century and that the "weak foundations" of the Salvadoran economy set the stage for the elite's inflated sense of its self-importance. Members of bourgeoisies everywhere believe that they and not workers are the real producers, as though risking capital—which under capitalism is nothing more than a congealed form of other people's labor—is morally superior to risking one's life eking out a meager living as a peasant or wage laborer. But the Salvadoran bourgeoisie takes the position to its extreme, speaking as though they are not just the *real* producers but the *only* producers. They work; others merely pretend to. We have here something very close to a frontier mentality, in which economic gain is the reward for those who successfully carry out a risky conquest of nature. Yet in El Salvador the "conquest" of coffee lands on the slopes of the central cordillera involved the dispossession and displacement of the resident indigenous and mestizo peasantries, which were impelled into the ranks of the *minifundistas* (small landholders), share-croppers, *colonos* (plantation residents who worked in exchange for a small parcel of land), and wage laborers. (The process was repeated following World War II, when insecticides opened up the south coast to cotton production [Williams 1986:13–73, 155–158; McClintock 1985:152–153; Browning 1971].) As large-scale growers replaced peasants with coffee trees and opportunities to get in on the bonanza declined, the winners in the land rush became less willing to share the wealth and more willing to label those who would insist upon it in diabolical terms, among which *communist* came to occupy the front ranks. Even when capital diversified, the domination of agrarian over industrial capital and the interpenetration of the two prevented industrialists from promoting the land reforms needed to broaden the internal market for their goods (Williams 1986:173; see note 8).

In what manner, we must now ask, did these views succeed in insinuating themselves into the army and the security forces, which were led not by members of the upper classes but by the sons of small-scale merchants and petty tradesmen? To begin, it is relevant to note that the army, National Guard, National Police, and Treasury Police were created at different times and under somewhat different conditions at the behest of the Salvadoran bourgeoisie and were assigned the task of maintaining internal security. *Security* is synonymous with *protection, safety, shelter, certainty.* To say that security was to be maintained rather than created presumed that it already existed and that the mandate of these "security" forces was to preserve in a "secure" state a system that showed signs of deviating from it, or, alternatively, to remove those signs of deviation before they affected the system. In this usage, *security* was a gloss for "order," and maintaining it meant preserving the system of private property and elite dominance against efforts of the poor to defend their lands or to secure better wages and working conditions. Hence *security forces* (composed of the National Guard, Treasury Police, and National Police) was a disingenuous choice of terminology that internalized a class bias: the (hyper)security of the few that such armed bodies sought to maintain necessarily involved the *insecurity* of the majority. From a subaltern perspective, the so-called "security forces" were "insecurity forces," virtual threats to shelter, safety, and so on since they enforced a system of insecurity: of poverty, want, pain, and suffering. Similar deconstructions could be undertaken of the names given to the National Police and the National Guard, where *national* glosses the territorial range of the police or guard but not the mandate. Clearly, those who "police" or "guard" a class-differentiated system promote the national interest only if that interest is assumed to be identical with the interest of the dominant class.

The forces of "insecurity" became elite bodies between their founding in the 1910s and the early 1940s. They were better armed, better trained, and much better paid than the army, which was composed largely of peasant—often indigenous peasant—conscripts and perhaps for that reason was a less trustworthy force. This changed when the army was professionalized after World War II. The 1932 rebellion was snuffed out mainly with contingents of National Guard members from the capital, although hastily organized groups of civilian militias (the *cívicos*), drawn mainly from among the elites, joyfully helped to mop up the "communist insurgents." The authorities believed that the army was thoroughly infiltrated by the rebels, and in many areas it was (Dalton 1987:241–242). Where the troops were not accused of being communist collaborators or sympathizers and shot, as occurred with an entire company of the First Cavalry Regiment posted in San Salvador, they were disarmed and confined to barracks for the duration of the uprising (McClintock 1985: 119–120).

Following the rebellion, the Legislative Assembly passed laws that required people to register in their home municipalities and to carry identity cards with photographs and a record of sex, occupation, date and place of birth, and other information. They also reinvigorated the defunct cantonal patrols, composed largely of army reservists, to police the rural population. These regulatory measures were designed to prevent a repeat of the 1932 debacle, though more generally to secure control over the rural workforce to the benefit of large landowners. The Agrarian Code, the key piece of legislation, had been passed years before, in 1907, though it was revised in 1941. "The Agrarian Code," according to McClintock (1985), "relates the security system to a specific economic and social framework, and freezes the peasant into his subservient social niche by spelling out the relationship of rich and poor to the land and instructing the National Guard and other security forces to preserve this relationship" (125). The code depicted "an 'us' and 'them' society composed of rich and poor" in which *jornaleros* (day laborers) were portrayed as *reos* (criminals) to be kept under careful surveillance through the identity cards and records on their work performance compiled by the landowners (125). Propertyless people unable to present proof of employment could be forced to work on private farms or in public works.

Too much could be made of these regulations, which were enforced unevenly—with more rigor in major zones of export agriculture and less in "refuge" zones of small-scale corn production and petty stock raising, such as Morazán and Chalatenango. The key point is the way in which the regulations divided the population into two groups, one of which— composed of those people without significant access to property—was viewed as both necessary for economic prosperity (hence the concern with controlling their labor) *and* a potential threat to public order. Nowhere is the class bias in these regulations better illustrated than in the fact that anyone who donated one hundred *colones* (exceeding a farm worker's monthly income) to a "Patriotic Subscription of National Cooperation" was exempted from having to carry an identity card (122). In conclusion, McClintock notes that the Agrarian Code

> provided the framework within which the security services operated, with little modification, through to the 1980s. It prohibited the peasantry from forming labour organizations and confirmed the powers of the landowners to set conditions for the labourers on their property at their own discretion. The organization of security forces was designed deliberately to keep the peasantry under tight control, at the service of the large estate owners, in a special, virtually criminal class without rights or protection under the law. The Agrarian Code, and the Martínez security apparatus, were the foundation of the tacit agreement by which the agrarian aristocracy yielded the reins of government to the military, confident that their position of privilege was ensured. (1985:126)

The 1932 rebellion proved to the oligarchs that rural workers and peasants composed a useful but dangerous class of people who had to be tabulated, classified, watched, and regulated; this job was handed over to what I have called the "forces of insecurity," including the "National" Guard and the "National" Police. If the matanza proved the weakness of the domestic communist movement and the strength of the repressive forces, it also alerted authorities to the importance of maintaining a high degree of vigilance lest the "international conspiracy" gain ground again in the future. They would not be caught off guard a second time.

TOWARD THE NATIONAL SECURITY STATE

It is not enough, in order to comprehend the El Mozote massacre, to study the era of the matanza, when the oligarchy's fears of communism were confirmed by the insurrection led by Farabundo Martí. We must also look to the post–World War II period, when a much more malignant communist threat was imagined into existence and a sophisticated repressive apparatus was put in place to seek out that threat and eradicate it. These changes owed much to activities of the United States government.

John F. Kennedy, remembered in liberal circles as the architect of the Alliance for Progress, was much more concerned with protecting U.S. client states from Soviet-Cuban contamination following Fidel Castro's 1959 overthrow of Batista than he was with their socioeconomic development. Under Kennedy's tutelage, the theory and practice of "counterinsurgency" diffused downward from the White House to the Department of Defense and outward to U.S. neocolonies such as El Salvador and Guatemala that were deemed "weak" and vulnerable to subversion because of high levels of poverty, massive income inequality, and authoritarian political structures. Later administrations followed JFK's lead (McClintock 1985:13; Schöultz 1981:211–266).

McClintock notes that counterinsurgency doctrine identified "Communism as the threat and the enemy as its agents" (1985:30). The "enemy" was interpreted in the broadest possible terms:

> The US Joint Chiefs of Staff in 1962 defined insurgency as a condition of "illegal opposition to an existing government" that could range from passive resistance, illegal strike action or demonstrations, to large scale guerrilla operations, but fell short of civil war. Next to overt guerrilla warfare, the principal instances of insurgency were "urban political demonstrations, riots and strikes," and responsibility for insurgency was placed squarely on independent political opposition groups, student demonstrators, university communities, and labour organizations. (30)

In El Salvador (and most other Latin American countries) such ideas reinforced existing political concerns. More innovative perhaps—from the Salvadoran point of view—was the U.S. military's promotion of "counterterror" as a legitimate governmental response to insurgent threats. According to the doctrine, communist insurgents would use any and all methods, including those that violate international standards of warfare; they could only be combated by employing their own methods against them. Hence the presumed legitimacy of, or at least the rationalization for using, counterterror, including torture, assassination, and kidnapping. But to rationalize the use of counterterror, military theorists drew questionable parallels between domestic resistance movements defending their territory against a foreign occupying government (e.g., the French Resistance struggling against the Nazis) and a "Third World" government "defending" its right to rule against a domestic insurgency. Counterinsurgency doctrine asserted that communist insurgents were equivalent to foreign invaders and that the government was entitled to employ *any measure* to "recover" the national territory from "occupation" by them (30, 210).[5] In El Salvador these theories were materialized through the development of a centralized intelligence apparatus to provide early warning signals of communist infiltration and a nationwide system of paramilitary irregulars as the first line of defense (see below). However, the massacre of hundreds of unarmed civilians in guerrilla-occupied territory can also be rationalized from within the counterterror paradigm.

McClintock noted that "[t]raining foreign military forces, both inside and outside the United States, was the principal vehicle by which the counter-insurgency orientation was instilled in Latin America. . . . The message was taken home by trainees, and propagated by doctrinal materials from US military publications (notably the *Military Review*) regularly reproduced in publications of Latin American armies" (31). Between 1950 and 1979 the United States trained 1,971 Salvadoran officers, "including at least seventeen in Urban Counter-insurgency, fourteen in Military Intelligence, one hundred eight in Basic Combat and Counter-insurgency, and one hundred twenty-four in Basic Officer Preparation" (Americas Watch Committee and the American Civil Liberties Union 1982:179). Also, the United States trained 448 Salvadoran police between 1957 and 1974, when police training terminated. U.S. assistance for grants, credits, and training totaled an "extremely modest" (178) $16.7 million between 1950 and 1979 (including $7.4 million for the military assistance program and $2.1 million for police training), though the real cost was much higher because many programs were paid for by the Defense Department rather than through foreign assistance allocations (McClintock 1985:326; Schöultz 1981:215). The programs in Argentina (over $250 million) and Brazil ($598 million) dwarfed the one in El Salvador, but then, those are much larger countries. The effect was regional, as Fagen (1992:43) noted: "Thanks to U.S. military and police assistance, an entire generation of Latin American military officers and police were armed, trained, and 'professionalized.'" During the 1970s, when military assistance and training programs came under attack, congressional supporters argued that regardless of human rights records it was important to continue the funding in order to be able to influence an important group of social actors. But what sort of influence would this be? Lars Schöultz (1981:247) answered the question, "To provide military aid to a government that bases its existence upon the repression of its citizens' human rights is to support the repression of human rights, since any government sustained primarily by threats of physical force is obviously strengthened by the acquisition of greater amounts of force or, in the case of military training, by the acquisition of the skills necessary to employ coercion."

Capt. Francisco Emilio Mena Sandoval, whose 1991 memoir provides the only available insider's view of the Captain General Gerardo Barrios Military School, stated that in the late 1960s fourth-year cadets customarily received several months of counterinsurgency training at the U.S. School of the Americas in the Panama Canal Zone prior to their return to El Salvador and commissioning as second lieutenants (1991:49–52). Unfortunately, Mena does not discuss the political and ideological content of the courses there and thus does not confirm McClintock's assertion that "[t]he basic message of indoctrination was negative: the enemy is the Communist, insidious and omnipresent, unyielding and pernicious, powerful and perverted" (1985:31). If Manlio Argueta's (1983) fictional portrayal of "the authorities" in his influential novel *One Day of Life* is correct, the military school leaders exhibited a contradictory blend of military pride, self-hatred, denigration of civilians, anticommunism, and belief in the imminence of the apocalypse:

> Get this, the gringo says that the soul of the people has been poisoned. They're brainwashed. This is something scientific, but in these parts, because we're backward countries, we don't understand. It's not that we're stupid but that we're a country of illiterates, lugs, as they say; well, because we were born lazy. We had the bad luck of being conquered by the Spanish, who were nothing but drunkards, while up there in the north arrived the English, who are all great workers. What's more, the English killed off the Indians but the Spaniards didn't. That was the big mistake. . . . we Indians are all fucked up; we want everything to fall from heaven into our laps. . . .
>
> . . . What happens is that you were born to be a beast of burden, brother. . . .
>
> The thing is, all civilians are shit, brother; you're no exception. They envy our uniforms, the fact that we've gotten ahead in life. (1983: 93–94, 98)

Such devaluation and dehumanization of the victims was undoubtedly a prerequisite for officers to order, and to a lesser degree for the troops to carry out, the El Mozote massacre and other massacres. Ignasio Martín-Baró—Jesuit priest, teacher, psychologist, and himself a murder victim of the Atlacatl Battalion in 1989—put it clearly: "Obviously, it is easier to shoot at a 'terrorist' than at a young *campesino,* easier to torture a 'communist beast' than a political dissident, easier to bomb a group of subversives than a group of families" (1991c:338).

Still, many atrocities are ordered and carried out by people well aware that what they are doing is morally (and legally) wrong, but who participate because the exercise of raw power leaves them no alternative, or because they develop a more complex series of rationalizations to justify the brutality. Even hardened Atlacatl troops sought to avoid murdering young children at El Mozote but did so because they believed that they would have been killed had they refused the order (see chapter 2; Danner 1993:84, 87–88, 1994:74–75, 79), or because sparing the children would have strengthened the guerrillas in the future.

Officers who could order such a massacre would certainly have been capable of including recalcitrant troops among the victims, if such had been required to maintain discipline. Some of the soldiers argued about the ethics of what they had been ordered to do, but when their officers found out, they curtailed the objections with displays of brutality that must have shocked even many of the troops (Danner 1993:87–88, 1994: 79). Finally, we may never know whether any of the soldiers passively resisted by deliberately shooting past prospective victims, as did various individuals during World War II in the Polish Reserve Police Battalion 101, which killed an estimated 38,000 Jews between July 1942 and November 1943 (Browning 1992). I do believe the El Mozote operation (and other lesser massacres perpetrated by the Atlacatl, not to speak of other units in the Salvadoran military) produced hundreds of psychologically disabled soldiers who are haunted by the pleading of the unarmed men, women, and children whom they wantonly dispatched.[6]

For the sake of social (rather than individual) analysis, however, I believe that we must assume with Michael Taussig that "[a]ll societies live by fictions taken as real" (1987:121), and then investigate the circumstances under which such fictions seize the social imagination and acquire the status of frames that give meaning to experience. In a sketchy way, I began that process in earlier sections of this chapter when I suggested that the social and spatial segregation of the Salvadoran elites nourished both fear and hatred of the workers and especially the peasants, whose unremunerated labor was (and is) the basis of elite wealth. Here I wish to discuss the existence of similar attitudes on the part of the Salvadoran military officers who control the state's repressive forces. The dynamics of ideological formation among them differ from those among the oligarchy and bourgeoisie, for the military officers for the most part have a different class origin. True, some officers have recently joined the economic elite by exploiting unprecedented opportunities for profit making that accompanied the massive inflows of U.S. economic and military assistance during the civil war (Millman 1989). But through the 1970s and into the 1980s the army was a service institution granted political power by the class that maintained it but lacking the economic independence required to move Salvadoran society in new directions. As Baloyra (1982:17) observed, "[T]he military controlled but did not dominate the society."[7] The limits of military power came to the fore especially during those rare periods when military politicians attempted to introduce reforms that threatened powerful sectors of the elite.[8]

Military school creates military officers, but the "raw materials," i.e., the youths who enter, come not from the oligarchy and bourgeoisie but from among the petit bourgeoisie of tradespeople and shopkeepers, social strata with only limited potential for upward mobility but possessed of adequate resources to provide their children with a basic secondary education. The four years of training for future officers in the Captain General Gerardo Barrios Military School entails both selection from among the array of ideological beliefs and social practices of the raw recruit and inculcation of new beliefs and practices. For instance, male strength and valor are highly valued in Salvadoran culture, and the military trainers need merely emphasize them. Other aspects of the recruits' upbringing must be weeded out. Joel Millman, who spent a year studying the Salvadoran military, explained the total immersion process (my term) designed by school administrators to wean young cadets (fifteen to eighteen years old at entry) away from whatever identification they may have maintained with the popular classes:

> It is a tough school. Many more cadets are accepted than can ever rise to positions of power, so attrition begins the first day. There are forced marches, beatings, all-night calisthenics, ordeals designed to reduce each class to a hardened core of officers. The soft boys from the good families go first, followed by the scholars—those most equipped for success outside the military. The survivors are cloistered in the academy, isolated from a civilian world they are taught to view as decadent, amoral and corrupt. (1989:95)

Mena Sandoval concurred:

The well-to-do families have in the military their most sincere ser-
vants and defenders. In exchange for this, they give them power, a
power that converts the military into a privileged caste, accustomed to
shout at and command its subordinates but to obey its patrons. That
is the military officer that is forged in the school—a man ambitious
for power, full of arrogance. It is significant that by tradition, the
fourth year cadets are called "The Gods of Olympus." . . . In the military school they teach one the art of war and the concept of fatherland, but without relating it with the interests of the people and the
defense of democracy and sovereignty, but they do identify it with the
anti-communist struggle. (1991:41, 344)

Millman and Mena describe a rigid hierarchy within which each cadet
is encouraged, indeed compelled, to learn his place, that of total superiority to the classes below his and complete deference to those above. The
hierarchy is internalized through its inscription in ritual humiliations of
subordinate classes by the dominant ones (Mena 1991:43–45). Surviving
these humiliations, as well as the long hours of study, physical trials, and
stress, requires cadets to discipline themselves and to work together,
assisting others within their class. I view the hierarchical relations of
the military school as homologues of the social and economic class relations that (partially) structure the larger society; as each class of military
school cadets must learn its place, so must the social groups that compete
in public space. There, as the military sees it, the military institution is
the most important stratum, as indicated by the motto "The Army shall
live as long as the Republic shall live" (Dickey 1984:36). The military sees
itself as the linchpin in society; it is the guarantor of order without which
(for the military) society cannot survive. Thereby, the military is the
guarantor of society itself.

That minority of cadets, 10 percent according to one account (Millett
1984:33), who surmount the difficulties of military school to graduate
four years later as second lieutenants have many opportunities to pad
their military salaries (Millman 1989; Dickey 1984; Mena Sandoval 1991).
A few of the lucky ones even have the good fortune of being incorporated into wealthy families by marrying women "with sonorous last
names and juicy bank accounts" (Mena Sandoval 1991:46). As the officers
rise in rank through the system, together with their *tanda*—the reduced
group of classmates that, through mutual support, survived the rigors of
military school and forged itself into an indivisible unit—the opportuni-

ties for enrichment grow. Gifts, kickbacks, the contracting out of soldiers and security agents as private security guards, offers to invest with members of the bourgeoisie, and even (during the war) the sale of arms and munitions to the FMLN are but a few of the schemes that allow the sons of artisans and petty shopkeepers to retire as "fat cats" thirty years to the day after they enter military service (Christian 1986:96; Millman 1989; Mena Sandoval 1991: 115–121, 136–138, 146, 151; Schwarz 1991:19–21).

Let me note that this process of "socialization" or "indoctrination" is not without a degree of slippage. Since 1945 military officers have occasionally joined popular forces to oppose the oligarchy and bourgeoisie.[9] Shirley Christian even spoke of "El Salvador's divided military" (1986: 90), which she considered to be "at war as much with itself as with the guerrillas" in the late 1970s and early 1980s. Writing in 1983 she stated that the military "has reached a degree of consensus about the need to change the country's social and political attitudes, and to make the military put a high value on human life. But there are sectors in the armed forces not in agreement, men who believe that it is still possible to use the threat of a Communist takeover to justify oppression" (103).

But in her haste to align her views with those of the Reagan administration, Christian grossly overstated the case. Real military reformers, men with an alternative vision and the will and courage to pursue it against entrenched institutional resistance, have always been a small minority within the Salvadoran officers' corps. When large numbers of officers have committed to a course of social change, they have done so invariably out of a sense that change was necessary for the preservation of the military institution itself. More often than not, military "activists" have been younger, poorer (relatively speaking), and more idealistic officers with fewer compromising economic entanglements with wealthy elites. Even well-intentioned reformers have proven vulnerable to appeals to institutional unity cast by older, higher-ranking, and more politically astute conservatives. The slippage, in other words, has always been managed.

But if the Salvadoran military is not on the road to democracy, as Christian claims, neither is it the semifeudal holdover portrayed by Christopher Dickey (1984).[10] Rather, it displays an institutional structure and ideology appropriate to its mission of maintaining conditions for capital accumulation (domestic and foreign) in a U.S. neocolony marked by one of the Western Hemisphere's highest levels of income inequality. Most military officers have been relatively untouched by the suffering of masses of destitute workers and peasants, and they have echoed the U.S. military doctrine that lumped together "any and all opposition to the status quo as either incipient or actual insurgency" (McClintock 1985:30). Thus counterinsurgency doctrine reinforced preexisting beliefs and accorded to them the stamp of approval of the hemisphere's preeminent defender of "democracy." The doctrine also rationalized military efforts to block reforms—attributed to "communists"—and sustain the status quo, practically guaranteeing that opposition groups would eventually be compelled, for lack of alternatives, to seek the overthrow of the state through violent means.

Under the twin banners of counterinsurgency and counterterror, U.S. advisers helped the Salvadoran military and security forces set up a security network to provide intelligence, assessment, and operational units to defeat the "communist threat." These programs were initiated in the early sixties, when no significant organized leftist opposition to the government existed. In August 1960 Herbert O. Hardin, chief of the Latin American branch of the Public Safety Division of the International Co-operation Administration (ICA, the predecessor to USAID), wrote that El Salvador faced a "growing threat to internal security as a result of infiltration of the country's borders by subversive persons." The security situation was not yet out of control, Hardin said, but he warned that "now is the time to lend attention, before the point of acute danger is reached" (cited in McClintock 1985:197). Washington responded to Hardin's plea for "an urgent programme of security assistance" (198) and set off on a twenty-year campaign to build a centralized intelligence apparatus based on a nationwide network of paramilitary informers who would provide early warning signals of communist activity and interdict such activity.

Army Colonel José Alberto ("Chele") Medrano, with the assistance of the CIA, constructed the intelligence apparatus "practically from scratch." Housed in the presidential palace, Servicios de Seguridad (Security Services), as the agency was called, became a clearinghouse for intelligence information generated by the intelligence units of the National Police, the National Guard, and the Immigration Service. Medrano set up a grassroots paramilitary organization called the Nationalist Democratic Organization with the acronym ORDEN, which is Spanish for "Order," to gather intelligence in towns and villages scattered over the densely populated countryside.

ORDEN members were drawn from among army reservists who in lieu of active duty spent a year in cantonal patrols under the authority of noncommissioned officers (usually sergeants) stationed in municipal centers. McClintock (1985:205, 207–208, 220) suggested that an invitation to join ORDEN followed careful observation of the potential recruit and assessment of his patriotism and loyalty. In northern Morazán this was not always the case, as in the late 1970s guerrilla sympathizers often acquired ORDEN credentials, which they used to smooth relations with the authorities. But in general ORDEN channeled information to local National Guard and Treasury Police commanders and carried out repressive activities when so ordered (Pearce 1986:147–148, 150–152). These security functions (or "insecurity functions," from the point of view of the victims) were hidden behind ORDEN's public face: "Its stated political mission was to promote an ill-defined patriotism and a message of anticommunism. Its previous security functions underlay an overt political role as support group for the military government's Party of National Conciliation" (McClintock 1985:206).

The creation of ORDEN was a breakthrough for U.S. counterinsurgency doctrine in El Salvador. Historically the army had distrusted civilian irregulars (though they were used to help crush the 1932 uprising) and had left control of the "communists" to the political police, a special branch separate from the security forces (209). But the Salvadorans were convinced to take counterinsurgency seriously by the stream of Public Safety Program advisers, the U.S. Military Mission, and the Army Mobile Training Teams from the United States—examples of what Petras (1988: 317) calls "the special training missions of the imperial terror state." They hammered home the message that communism was sponsored from without (Cuba, Moscow), that communists were invaders, and that a paramilitary civilian "resistance" was instrumental if the nation was to be saved. Any and all tactics were deemed legitimate. The communist "terror" had to be met with "counter-terror" (McClintock 1985:210). That, as McClintock relates, is exactly what occurred:

The government move against the guerrillas gradually brought into full operation the paramilitary and intelligence apparatus built up since the early 1960s. The traditional style of repression—prolonged imprisonment and exile—was gradually transformed, until, by 1977 [one year after the aborted Molina land reform (see note 8)], "disappearance" and extra-judicial executions became the accepted way of dealing with the opposition. This gradual transformation was punctuated by dramatic incidents of government violence and innovations both in the style of execution and the choice of victims, drawn from ever widening sectors of society. (172)

TERROR, THERE AND HERE

The Salvadoran officers who ordered and led the El Mozote massacre viewed mass terror as a legitimate tactic of counterinsurgency warfare; in so doing they demonstrated that they had mastered, perhaps too well, the lessons imparted by their instructors in courses attended in Panama, the United States, and elsewhere. The "communist" was the labor organizer, the student, the social activist, the priest and nun, the peasant catechist—virtually anyone making demands on the system or seeking to change it from below. Obviously, the main responsibility for the massacre must lie with those officers and soldiers who participated in its planning and execution. But it would be a mistake, when parceling out responsibility, to overlook postwar U.S. governments, as do Mark Danner (1993, 1994), the Truth Commission (United Nations 1993), and other writers. The United States not only armed the Atlacatl troops with the most effective (most murderous) weapons available and trained the unit, but for over thirty years it disseminated a paranoid anticommunist ideology that reinforced preexisting fears and justified the use of any and all methods to defeat the presumed enemy. In "Barbarism: A User's Guide," Eric Hobsbawm recently noted that "after about a hundred and fifty years of secular decline, barbarism has been on the increase for most of the twentieth century, and there is no sign that this increase is at an end" (1994:45). Is it not curious that "the classic era of Western torturing" between the mid-1950s and the late 1970s (52) coincided with the rapid expansion of postwar capitalism?

Nine of the eleven Salvadoran officers cited by the United Nations as participants in the El Mozote massacre were trained at the U.S. Army School of the Americas at Fort Gulick in the Panama Canal Zone (United Nations 1993:124–125; SOA Watch n.d.; Bourgeois 1994:15).[11] Lt. Col. Domingo Monterrosa Barrios, the Atlacatl commander from February 1981 to November 1983 (when he was promoted to commander of the Third Infantry Brigade in San Miguel), attended a parachute ranger course at the Fort Gulick school from March to May 1966. Monterrosa went on to receive helicopter flight training in France (1973) and took a political warfare course in Peitou, Taiwan, from September to December 1978 (Defense Intelligence Agency 1984; Danner 1993:125, 1994:143). He was widely viewed as the best and most capable officer in the Salvadoran army, "the gringo's man," because he was one of the few officers who pursued the FMLN relentlessly rather than fighting a nine-to-five war. Monterrosa believed that "[t]he guerrilla always carries his *masas* [supporters] into battle with him," which Danner understood to mean that "in this bloody war, in the red zones, there was really no such thing as a civilian" (1993:62, 1994:41).

Finally, let us note one additional manifestation of terror: the daily public discourses about terror in the capitals of the United States and Europe that enable the terror technocrats and the terror agents there and elsewhere to pursue their work unmolested. For most European Americans, terror always happens somewhere else and is someone else's problem—a dinnertime or coffee break topic of conversation for them and an unavoidable daily reality for the Rest. But "[i]n talking terror's talk," Michael Taussig asks, "are we ourselves not tempted to absorb and conceal the violence in our own immediate life-worlds, in our universities, workplaces, streets, shopping malls, and even families, where, like business, it's terror as usual?" And do those daily, wearing mini-terrors here not enable the horrific, attention-grabbing ones there? Writing in a slightly different context, Joel Kovel states that

> The racist sentiment which pervades the life of virtually all white Americans is, though real and potent, not the only obstacle to the achievement of racial justice. Equally important as a general psychological factor is the general apathy and remoteness, the nonspecific coldness that prevails in our time. By and large we do not care for one another; we can be momentarily aroused to compassion, fear, or even rage, but as a rule we soon slip back into the comfortable torpor that typifies our life. (1984:34)[12]

The Salvadoran civil war was a dirty war from the very beginning, and support for it in the United States was never particularly strong. But neither was resistance generalized—despite the proliferation of antiwar and pro-refugee groups (a veritable underground railway). Too many people, numbed by boredom and the alienation of daily life, stood by and cynically mocked the government's feeble defense of the Salvadoran military and its equally feeble rationalizations for its spiraling involvement without actively working themselves to terminate that involvement. This, too, was a product of terror.

THE U.S. COVER-UP

"Hear nothing, see nothing, say nothing, and you will live to be a hundred
years old."   Sicilian proverb

News of nine hundred civilian deaths in Morazán reached Eugene Stock-
well at the National Security Council in late December or early January
1982, and he requested information from Deane Hinton, the U.S. ambassador to El Salvador. Hinton replied, "I certainly cannot confirm such reports nor do I have any reason to believe that they are true." He claimed
that none of the embassy's "tested sources" had given any indication of
large-scale civilian casualties inflicted by the government military, and
asserted, "given [the] savage measures of civil war here, that had anything
like this number of civilian casualties been inflicted by government military, the guerrillas would not have taken prisoners as they did during
their counter-attack in El Mosotes [sic] sector." He stated that he believed
the FMLN's clandestine Radio Venceremos was "not a credible source"
(Hinton 1982c).

Journalists from the *New York Times* and the *Washington Post* filed
stories in late January on the El Mozote case based on personal inspection of the site and interviews with survivors such as Rufina Amaya
(Bonner 1982a; Guillermoprieto 1982). Raymond Bonner of the *New York
Times* was accompanied by Susan Meiselas, a well-known photojour-
nalist, who documented their observations (Meiselas 1993). Bonner and
Meiselas crossed the Honduran border into El Salvador on 3 January 1982
and reached the El Mozote area three days later; Alma Guillermoprieto of
the *Washington Post* followed the same route into the zone over a week

later (Danner 1994:96–102). By the time Bonner and Meiselas arrived in the region in early January, most of the bodies from the massacre had been buried either by FMLN health teams, which feared the outbreak of an epidemic, or by survivors who had avoided the soldiers by hiding among the brush and steep ravines that dot the area (see chapter 2).

Bonner's reconnaissance of El Mozote preceded that of Guillermoprieto by several days, but both newspapers published front-page articles on 27 January (Bonner 1982a; Guillermoprieto 1982). The resulting public furor, which was intense but short lived, led the State Department to request that the embassy "seek any additional available evidence that might give further details about the incident or substantiate MOD [Minister of Defense] García's denials that it took place" (Stoessel 1982b). The report resulting from the investigation by Todd Greentree, an embassy officer, and Maj. John McKay, the assistant defense attaché, formed the basis for the U.S. government's response to news media and congressional queries about El Mozote. This report was based on four sources of information acquired during a tour of the area on 30 January: briefings by Salvadoran army officers in San Miguel and in San Francisco Gotera; a short helicopter flyover of the area around El Mozote; interviews in refugee camps in San Francisco Gotera with people who had fled from El Mozote and nearby hamlets; and visits and discussions with peasants in Jocoaitique, Perquín, and other towns accessible from the blacktop highway (Danner 1994:104–109).

Although the report was cabled out over Hinton's name, Greentree drafted the text, which was circulated among and edited by other embassy personnel before release.[1] His report concluded that "no evidence could be found to systematically confirm the massacre of civilians in the operation zone, nor that the number of civilians killed even remotely approached [the] number being cited in reports circulating internationally." El Mozote was characterized as lying "in the heart of guerrilla territory," and its inhabitants were said to have spent "most of the last three years willingly or unwillingly cooperating with the insurgents" (Hinton 1982a).[2]

The embassy document employed a variety of arguments to undermine or debunk press reports based on direct inspection. First, it claimed that the FMLN had known since 15 November that the army was planning an invasion but that it did nothing to remove civilians from the path of battle. Soldiers participating in Operation Rescue encountered stiff resistance from trench lines south of the village, the document claimed, and more fighting occurred as they broke through into the settlement, with the consequence that "the town was partially destroyed" and "[c]ivilians remaining in any part of the canton could have been subject to injury as a result of the combat" (Hinton 1982a). In this account, then, the dead civilians were innocent victims of war, but the FMLN bore the blame since it knew that the battle was coming but failed to forewarn civilians and remove them from the area.

A more insidious interpretation is codified in the claim that civilians in El Mozote had for three years been "willingly or unwillingly cooperating with the insurgents," a charge that appears to have come from a priest, almost certainly Father Andrés Argueta, who "travels freely along the main road."³ The report stated that prior to the operation "the guerrillas . . . had mobilized their forces, *including civilian supporters* [my emphasis] to harass government forces while withdrawing large numbers from the operation zone." The logical (though unstated) conclusion is that the "collaborating" civilians were also combatants and may well have been firing back when the army "moved forward into the settlement where they again came under fire and took casualties" (Hinton 1982a).

The cable posed two scenarios without deciding the case in favor of either: the civilians were either unfortunate victims, caught in a cross fire because callous guerrillas failed to remove them from the line of fire, or legitimate military targets "mobilized" and perhaps armed by the FMLN guerrillas to shoot back at the invading army. In either case, blame for any civilian casualties that might have occurred was laid at the feet of the FMLN. Uncertain as to what had actually transpired at El Mozote, the embassy stacked the deck from both sides.

Other sections of the document contradict these claims, or at least insinuate the possibility of an army massacre. For instance, embassy investigators interviewed an aged couple from El Mozote in Jocoaitique, where they had taken refuge after the massacre. They said that "[g]uerrillas had told them to leave in early December because they were so old, but they did not want to because they had spent their whole lives there and had never been outside the community." Here, against earlier assertions to the contrary, is evidence that people were warned of military operations but refused to heed the advice. And in a portentous statement that hangs over one long paragraph like a large, dark cloud, Jocoaitique's mayor deferred discussion of the comportment of government soldiers, saying, "This is something one should talk about in another time, in another country" (Hinton 1982a).⁴

Greentree also discussed the FMLN's successful takeover of Jocoaitique on 12 January 1982, an event unrelated to El Mozote but one that he used to drive a wedge between FMLN accusations of army human rights violations and the FMLN's own human rights practices. Greentree asserted that in its attack the FMLN killed four National Guard members and twenty-seven other inhabitants, "primarily members of the Civil Defense and their family members. *Some of the latter did not die during the assault on the town but were shot after being captured*" (my emphasis). In contrast to the fog enveloping the "alleged" massacre at El Mozote, the FMLN murder of civilians in Jocoaitique was reported as *fact*, even though it was based on after-the-fact testimony and none of the three journalists present in the town verified this story in print. One of those journalists was Bonner, who was a Vietnam veteran knowledgeable about military affairs. Bonner followed behind guerrillas during the attack on Jocoaitique and entered the town with them (Bonner 1984:121–128, 1982b). He wrote that twenty-six members of the rural defense force surrendered, and that, if for no other than political reasons, "[t]he rebel commanders . . . insisted that prisoners be treated well" (1984:127).

The embassy also told the State Department that the FMLN carried away typewriters and town hall registries listing the names of all inhabitants of the surrounding *cantones* (rural zones) before they vacated the town when the army arrived to retake it on 18 January 1982. Greentree estimated that there were no more than 300 people in El Mozote prior to December 1981 and speculated that the names of victims circulating in the U.S. press and in Europe, presumably the 217 identified by name on Radio Venceremos and later in print by the FMLN (FDR/FMLN 1982:13) and the list given to Bonner during his visit, "may well have been extracts in whole or part" from the stolen civil registries (Hinton 1982a).[5] This was pure speculation. "I don't recall thinking it was what happened," Greentree told Danner more than ten years after the fact, "but I thought it was a possibility." However, the FMLN showed Bonner a list of victims before its January attack on Jocoaitique; the embassy never spoke to Bonner, whom embassy personnel suspected of having a leftist bias, in order to confirm Greentree's suppositions (Danner 1993:111, 1994:118).

The claim that El Mozote contained no more than 300 people was used to debunk FMLN assertions that the massacre involved a thousand or more victims. Yet from the beginning the FMLN listed El Mozote as one of twelve massacre sites and the site that accounted for the largest single number of victims (FDR/FMLN 1982:16).

The ostensibly objective embassy report is actually a highly ideological document aimed at debunking guerrilla claims of massive human rights violations perpetrated by the Salvadoran military. The ideological content is manifest in a variety of ways: the selective weighting of information according to source; the discrediting of press reports; and the suggestions that civilians collaborating with the guerrillas were in some sense guilty and deserved their fate but also that most of the civilians were really guerrillas. In fact, the discourse serves to conflate combatants and civilians, when the Geneva Convention and other international treaties draw clear distinctions between the two, distinctions that the embassy could have used (see chapter 8).

Based on the material in this, the only field investigation of the El Mozote case carried out by the embassy, the State Department drew up a briefing and distributed it to the press on 1 February 1982 (United States Department of State 1982). It is reproduced below. Reading it, we see how the State Department attempted to convince the press corp that it had made a "determined effort" to look into the El Mozote situation through visits to neighboring communities and interviews with "a wide variety of sources, including refugees from El Mozote." The briefing does not state that none of these refugees were present in El Mozote during the Atlacatl invasion and occupation of the town, nor does it mention that embassy investigators were accompanied on interviews by Salvadoran military personnel and what effect that might have had on what they did learn about the case (see below). In stating conclusions without always providing the details on which they were based, the report leaves little room for disagreement. Most notable by its absence is the "dark cloud" cast forth by the Jocoaitique mayor's statement, rife with foreboding, that "[t]his is something one should talk about in another time, in another country" (Hinton 1982a).

El Salvador: Alleged Atrocities at Mozote

Our embassy in San Salvador has made a determined effort to look into the press accounts that there was a massacre of civilians at the small northeast town of El Mozote in December 1981. While Embassy personnel have not been able to visit El Mozote, because it is now once again in guerrilla hands, they have visited neighboring communities and interviewed a wide variety of sources, including refugees from El Mozote. The Embassy is continuing its investigation but as of now this is what we know.

— El Mozote is a rural community located in the heart of a guerrilla infested area in the war-ravaged northeast department of Morazan. Many inhabitants of the area have fled the violence for the relative safety of the larger cities.

— El Mozote's remaining inhabitants have spent most of the past three years willingly or unwillingly cooperating with the guerrillas. Government forces have not been posted in the town since August 1981.

— From December 6–17, the military conducted a sweep through central Morazan to clear the area of guerrillas. The guerrillas had known about this operation since at least November 15, and had mobilized their forces, including civilian supporters, to harass government troops while withdrawing large numbers from the operation zone.

— Both guerrillas and civilians were present when government forces approached El Mozote from the south. The guerrillas resisted from a trenchline south of the settlement. Fighting there lasted about four hours. Soldiers then moved forward into the settlement, where they again came under fire and took casualties. Fighting continued and the town was partially destroyed.

— Civilians remaining in any part of the town could have been subject to injury or death as a result of the combat. It is not possible to prove or disprove that excesses of violence against the civilian population occurred. There is little doubt that some civilians were killed, but no evidence could be found to confirm that government forces systematically massacred civilians in the operation zone. It is clear, however, that the guerrilla forces who established defensive positions in El Mozote did nothing to remove civilians from the path of the battle which they were aware was coming and had prepared for.

— Radio Venceremos issued its first report of the alleged incident on December 27, two weeks after the sweep occurred, claiming that 192 non-combatants had died at El Mozote. On January 2, it increased that figure to 472. On January 27, press reports in the U.S. raised the figure to 700 killed "in and around" El Mozote. Since our interviews in the area indicate that there were no more than 300 inhabitants in the entire canton in which El Mozote is located, these figures would appear to be highly exaggerated.

— Subsequently, the guerrillas have circulated lists of "victims" of the alleged massacre. These names may well be extracted from the civil

registries for the area stolen from the nearby town of Jocoaitique
when guerrillas occupied it, killing in the process four national guards-
men and 27 others, including the family members of civil defense
personnel.
— We have not yet identified the army unit involved in this action but
expect to do so in the near future.

With one addition and one alteration, this press release was used as
the standard State Department response to queries from other embassies
and congresspeople about the El Mozote case. Whereas the Greentree cable stated (albeit erroneously) that "the population of El Mozote . . . was
estimated at no more than 300" at the time of the operation (Hinton
1982a), the press briefing asserted that "there were no more than 300 inhabitants *in the entire canton* in which El Mozote is located" (my emphasis; see above). It follows from the latter statement that El Mozote, as one
among many hamlets in the cantón, would have had far fewer than 300
residents in December 1981. In this way the press briefing further reduced
El Mozote's population and cast additional doubt on the veracity of the
Radio Venceremos broadcast. One statement, present neither in the original report nor in the press release, was added in later responses at the beginning of the third to last paragraph ("Radio Venceremos issued . . ."), to
the effect that "it is also clear that the guerrillas have grossly inflated the
number of civilian deaths for propaganda purposes" (see Stoessel 1982a;
Moore 1982a, 1982b). This addition is more significant than it might appear. Its placement at the beginning of the paragraph discussing civilian
casualties gives it the status of a thesis statement, which it is the purpose
of the subsequent description of Radio Venceremos to substantiate. It
leads the reader down one interpretative path rather than leaving the
reader to draw his/her own conclusions about the credibility of FMLN reporting based on the evidence cited.

THE EMBASSY INVESTIGATION

Journalist Mark Danner has carried out a thorough review of the embassy investigation. His work benefited from the November 1993 declas-
sification of additional documents pertaining to the case, as well as a
willingness of the principals (with the marked exceptions of Deane Hinton and Col. Moody Hayes, the Military Group commander) to discuss the
case. Thanks to Danner's meticulous work, it is now possible to recon-

struct the "investigation," denote its limits, and understand better the process through which extremely ambiguous observations and conversations in the field were organized into a narrative consistent with U.S. government policy in El Salvador. We will find that the Greentree cable's ambiguities and contradictions were confined to the margins of the text and assigned the status of parenthetical remarks. This cleared the field for the principal conclusion, really a nonconclusion: that there was no convincing evidence that a massacre had actually been committed.

I noted above that Greentree and McKay never really reached El Mozote, that their evidential base was confined to a brief helicopter overflight, debriefings from the Salvadoran military, and discussions with refugees. The aerial observations revealed nothing beyond evidence of a military sweep (trench lines, collapsed roofs, destroyed buildings). When the chopper circled and dropped down for a closer look, it came under fire from the ground, forcing McKay and Greentree to cut short their reconnaissance and return to San Francisco Gotera. Accompanied by Deputy Chief-of-Mission Kenneth Bleakley, they drove to a nearby refugee camp that had recently received an influx of refugees from northern Morazán, some rumored to have come from El Mozote and surrounding hamlets. Then, leaving Bleakley in the camp, they took a trip up the asphalt road north of the Torola River to Jocoaitique and Perquín, which were alleged to harbor others who had fled El Mozote. Throughout, McKay and Greentree were escorted by Salvadoran soldiers whose mere presence forged a conspiracy of silence among the refugees (Danner 1994: 105–109). Who could be expected to speak freely about an army massacre in the presence of the possible perpetrators? The irony of the situation was not lost on McKay: "You had a bunch of very intimidated, scared people, and now the Army presence further intimidated them. . . . I mean, the Atlacatl had supposedly done something horrible, and now these gringos show up under the pretense of investigating it, but in the presence of these soldiers. It was probably the worst thing you could do. I mean, you didn't have to be a rocket scientist to know what the Army people were there for" (cited in Danner 1993:104, 1994:107).

In the camp outside San Francisco, McKay jawed with the soldiers in order to give his partner an opportunity to talk to some of the refugees, and though Greentree conversed with "more than a dozen," and though "each person I talked to confirmed the impression that something bad had happened . . . nobody was willing to go ahead and give the exact story" about what had gone on in the El Mozote area (cited in Danner 1993:105, 1994:108). Nonetheless, both investigators came away with the impression, based on the high levels of fear and trauma that they "observed" among the population, that something quite serious had occurred during Operation Rescue. Greentree recounted to Danner that he became convinced "that there probably had been a massacre, that they [the army] had lined up people and shot them," while McKay drew upon his experiences in Vietnam to make a similar point: "I was in Vietnam, and I recognized the ambiance. The fear was overriding and we sensed it and we could tell that fear was not instilled by the guerrillas" (cited in Danner 1993:104, 1994:108).

But feelings—even though the feelings were reinforced by conversations in Jocoaitique and other towns north of the Torola River— "couldn't," as Bleakley warned McKay, "answer the fundamental question—you know, the difference between subduing a town and pulling out the civilians, My Lai style, and massacring them" (Danner 1993:105, 1994:108). Given the circumstances, truth was destined to be an elusive target. Bleakley seemed to be recommending to McKay that he approach it by means of a loose version of the sociological null hypothesis: in the absence of a credible amount of information to the contrary, assume that the independent variable (Salvadoran military) had no effect (massacre) upon the dependent variable (El Mozote's civilian population). However, as we have seen, the investigation unfolded in a controlled context that mitigated against the acquisition of enough information to reject definitively the null, i.e., no massacre, hypothesis. Greentree recalled, "We reported what we saw, and the main requirement was to distinguish between what you saw and what other people said—you know, what was information and what you thought—and, even more than the standards of journalism, to keep your 'slant' out of what you were reporting. What this leads to, though, is great frustration, and that was my feeling. I mean, I was frustrated because it wasn't a satisfactory account" (cited in Danner 1993:108, 110, 1994:115).

A cursory reading of the cable is sufficient to demonstrate that it was not the product of an "even-handed" assessment of the evidence. The embassy systematically applied different standards to information supplied by different groups: the military and the government were given the benefit of the doubt, while the Left, Left sympathizers, human rights organizations, solidarity groups, and many people within the Catholic

Church, etc.—that is, practically anyone opposed to the government from any position other than that of the extreme Right—were assumed to be biased and untrustworthy sources.

Government-sponsored violence wiped out the political center in El Salvador in the late 1970s and early 1980s: government critics were killed off, forced to flee the country, intimidated into silence, or impelled into the ranks of the FMLN. Those who remained in the early 1980s, most of whom were connected to the Catholic Church or human rights organizations, were suspect from the embassy's point of view. The remaining political center (large portions of the Christian Democratic Party, Social Democrats, and others) was forced into opposition, and its credibility plummeted. The U.S. government employed this epistemological catch-22 to erect a Maginot Line around the embattled Salvadoran government, one consequence being that government critics in El Salvador and the United States were forced to expend an excess of energy arguing about methodologies and asserting objectivity rather than focusing on the issues (cf. Americas Watch Committee 1984b; Danner 1994). Raymond Bonner was one of the victims of a right-wing propaganda campaign led by Accuracy in Media and the *Wall Street Journal*.[6] His recall from El Salvador and transfer to the Metro desk at the *New York Times* in August 1982 served as an object lesson for other reporters who might have thought to buck the Reagan administration line (Massing 1983:45–46).[7]

Apropos these observations, Greentree failed to report much of what he and McKay did intuit: the fear, anxiety, and "controlled hysteria" of many refugees, which gave pause when the possibility of a massacre was entertained. But as he recalled to Danner, "It was just an impression. There was no direct corroborating evidence" (1993:110, 1994:115). Of equal importance, much of what did go into the report was *not* seen or experienced, but was culled from Salvadoran military briefings and was *assumed to be credible* in ways that Radio Venceremos, the eyewitness testimony of Rufina Amaya and other witnesses Bonner and Guillermoprieto interviewed, and the circumlocutory testimony of various refugees was not. Danner finds it curious that the investigators,

> instead of building on their observations, inferences, and conclusions to present the best version possible of what *probably* happened . . . emphasize the gap between what could be *definitively* proved to have happened—which, of course, wasn't much, given the reticence of the people and the constraints on the investigators' movements—and

what the newspapers and the guerrillas were claiming had happened. It is a peculiar way of reasoning, built, as it is, on the assumption that in the absence of definitive proof nothing at all can really be said to be known. In effect, officials made active use of the obstacles to finding out the truth. (1993:107–108, 1994:113)

True enough. But what Danner misses is that much of "what could be *definitively* proved to have happened" (at least what was accepted as definitive) was based on military testimony, which Greentree and others privileged over the testimony of other parties. Consider the full text of Greentree's description in his cable of the government attack on El Mozote, much of which was incorporated verbatim into the State Department press release:

> Both guerrillas and civilians were present there when government forces approached El Mozote from the south during mid-operation on about December 11. Attacking troops encountered stiff guerrilla resistance from a trench line south of the settlement. Fighting there lasted about four hours until troops were able to penetrate the line with 90 mm recoilless rifle fire. Soldiers then moved forward into the settlement where they again came under fire and took casualties. Fighting continued and the town was partially destroyed. Civilians remaining in any part of the canton could have been subject to injury as a result of the combat. (Hinton 1982a)

The cable that Greentree penned for Hinton stated as *fact* that Salvadoran troops came under fire and took casualties *in El Mozote* and that the partial destruction of the town was one outcome of the battle. Based on the progression of events built up, he tendered the conclusion that some erstwhile civilian guerrilla supporters trapped in this battle zone "could have been" part of the combat's collateral damage. Had Greentree assumed a different starting point, privileged other sources of information, listened to the subaltern voices of the traumatized refugees in San Francisco Gotera, Jocoaitique, and elsewhere seeking to communicate with him through a wall of military interference, he might have come to different conclusions. He did not do so. For all of his unease over his experiences in Morazán, and his personal belief that "something had gone on, and that it was bad" (Danner 1993:100, 1994:95), the cable employed the army's description of the El Mozote situation as a baseline of fact from which to concoct a case against the rebels, American journalists, and human rights workers who argued that a massacre had occurred there. Of course, Greentree was "assisted" in this task by Kenneth Bleakley, Deane Hinton, and others more attuned to the larger dimensions of the policy that the embassy was mandated to defend (Danner 1993:110, 1994:116). We may never see Greentree's initial draft, but we know that by the time Hinton signed off on the cable, it had passed a "clearing process" (Danner 1993:108, 1994:114) that confined Greentree's apprehensions to the text's margins and prevented them from leaking into the center.[8]

His apprehensions were completely eliminated when the cable was transformed into a State Department press release in Washington. The cable itself was, after all, confidential and was released (with eight lines excised) only after Raymond Bonner filed an FOIA request in 1983. It was of no consequence for the public and congressional debate about El Mozote except insofar as it provided ammunition to sustain the official administration position that claims about a massacre were probably fabricated by the FMLN. As the press release was no watertight document, particularly as regards the ambiguous characterization of El Mozote's civilian population, State Department officers patched up several of the more prominent leaks in the process of "translating" the confidential cable authored by Greentree into a public document.

The U.S. government's unquestioned support for the Salvadoran military as the only bulwark against a communist takeover in El Salvador formed the ideological ground upon which the El Mozote massacre investigation proceeded. The U.S. government needed the colonels to orchestrate the slaughter of poor Salvadorans by other poor Salvadorans in order to preserve U.S. regional political and economic hegemony that the Sandinista victory in Nicaragua, the revolution in Guatemala, and the FMLN uprising jeopardized. The colonels were aware of their role and felt that they could count on gringo largess as long as they could "plausibly deny" that they were behind the slaughter (cf. Danner 1993:114–115, 1994: 123–124). Thus the Carter, Reagan, and Bush administrations combined in various degrees Orwellian language, allegations of a continent-wide catastrophe if a leftist triumph were to occur, lies and deceit, logic strained to the breaking point, and medieval numerology to back up these denials. The task was facilitated by the fact that no congressperson, Republican or Democrat, wanted to stand accused of having "lost" El Salvador, as if this nation of 5.5 million people were theirs (or ours) to lose.[9]

The embassy never mounted a frontal challenge to the Salvadoran military over the El Mozote case, despite the tremendous unease that the investigation and a series of other reports generated among some staff members. By 1 February, two days after Greentree's investigation, even Ambassador Hinton had arrived at the position that "it is quite possible Salvadoran military did commit excesses," although he continued to reject the Radio Venceremos account as leftist propaganda (Hinton, cable to secretary of state, 1982, cited in Danner 1994:207). Of course, this sentiment was not made public at the time. Twice Hinton prodded Defense Minister Jose Guillermo García to explain what had occurred at El Mozote (Hinton, cable to secretary of state, 1982, cited in Danner 1994:225–228), and on 1 February Major McKay was sent to the Atlacatl base to "put the question about El Mozote directly to Lieutenant Colonel Domingo Monterrosa and his officers" (U.S. Defense Attaché's Office, cable to Defense Intelligence Agency, cited in Danner 1994:203–206). These efforts yielded tidbits of information (that the Atlacatl Battalion was, indeed, present at El Mozote) and vague references, parables really, about guerrillas fighting from within houses containing civilians, but they clarified nothing. Led by Defense Minister García, the Salvadoran military closed ranks and stonewalled on the issue, leaving the gringos to carry the ball before Congress.

Ironically, embassy staff never followed up the best opportunity to learn what happened. Shortly after the massacre, emissaries from the Left contacted Todd Greentree and offered him an FMLN safe-conduct pass to visit Morazán and document what had occurred at El Mozote. Greentree told Danner that he knew at the time that the FMLN would never have made such an offer unless there was substance to the claims. He volunteered to go, but Hinton refused to allow him to do so because of the presumed danger (Danner 1993:100–101, 1994:95–96). History has proven Hinton correct. While it *could* have been dangerous for Greentree, who would actually have been well cared for by the FMLN, the Reagan administration *would* have run the greater danger for the revelations that might have come with a visit to the site. "[T]he fact that we didn't get to the site turned out to be very detrimental to our reporting," McKay explained to Danner. "The Salvadorans, you know, were never very good about cleaning up their shell casings" (1994:124).

The embassy's initial investigation of El Mozote turned out to be its final investigation. The purpose was damage control, to prevent a leakage of negative information that might jeopardize military aid or place in question the utility of holding elections for a Constituent Assembly in March 1982 to replace the discredited civilian-military junta. The FDR/

FMLN (1982) did seek to link El Mozote with the certification process. The entire second half of its pamphlet entitled *A Massacre in El Salvador's Morazan Province* was called *On President Reagan's Certification for Aid to El Salvador* and provided evidence that the junta had failed to meet any of the five requirements for certification. The Atlacatl's slaughter of civilians in El Mozote, if accepted as the truth, would have meant violations of two of the five requirements for certification: compliance with internationally recognized human rights and establishment of control over the military to bring an end to indiscriminate torture and murder of Salvadoran citizens. However, the FDR/FMLN version of events was published by Solidarity Publications, San Francisco, California, a small leftist press with a distribution network heavily weighted toward alternative booksellers, so it was not widely read. The embassy and State Department account of the El Mozote "nonevent" held, and, swimming in the wake of an enormous amount of evidence to the contrary, President Reagan signed the presidential certification (see Americas Watch Committee 1991:120–122), the first of four certifications before November 1983, when he eliminated the bill requiring certification through a pocket veto, interpreted in some quarters as "a *de facto* acknowledgment that the humans rights situation in El Salvador [was] so bad that he would have had difficulty in certifying" (Americas Watch Committee 1984a:1–2). Following the certification the United States increased military aid to El Salvador from $35.5 million in 1981 to $82.0 million in 1982; economic aid rose from $113.6 to $182.2 million (Americas Watch Committee 1991:141).

In the last unclassified record about El Mozote, on 6 May 1982, the U.S. Embassy in El Salvador compared the Central Elections Council voter lists with lists of "alleged" victims from three leftist sources (Radio Venceremos, the FDR/FMLN, and Socorro Jurídico, which is the Legal Aid Society of the Archdiocese of San Salvador). Only 50 of 432 available victims' names matched up. The embassy concluded, "The correspondence of names does not prove that these individuals died during the operation, merely that their names also appeared on the list of alleged victims" (Hinton 1982b). Deane Hinton's final word was as follows:

> The embassy is unable to reach a definite conclusion regarding civilian deaths in El Mozote during the December 1981 operation. Neither the rudimentary comparison, nor eyewitness accounts provided by Radio Venceremos, nor versions of journalists who traveled to the area in January 1982 concretely indicate that anywhere near 1,009 civil-

ians were massacred there. The January 1982 embassy investigation concluded that civilians who were either willing or unwilling guerrilla collaborators did die in and around El Mozote as a result of military operations, but not as a result of systematic massacre, and not in the numbers widely reported in the international press. Leftist propaganda to the effect is almost certainly exaggerated. (Hinton 1982b)

El Mozote remained an important symbol in El Salvador, but by March 1982 the case had been "outrun" by other events, particularly the March Constituent Assembly "demonstration elections," which the North American press, parroting the State Department line, heralded as a major defeat for the FMLN and the harbinger of democracy in El Salvador (see Herman and Brodhead 1984). For U.S. citizens, El Mozote simply slipped off the map, the reporting of Bonner and Guillermoprieto notwithstanding. This point can be easily verified through examination of the number, never mind the context or the quality, of articles mentioning "El Mozote" in the U.S. and Canadian press (see chapter 1).[10] With a solemn bow to the U.S. government, the media buried the story, depriving the Atlacatl's victims of a hearing before the court of world opinion. Not a single journalist thought to track down the El Mozote residents who had fled to Colomoncagua, Honduras, and could have, at the very least, refuted many of the egregious claims made by Ambassador Hinton and Assistant Secretary of State for Inter-American Affairs Thomas Enders (e.g., about the size of the population, its political orientation, the invading unit, FMLN influence in the area, etc.).

COVER-UP REDUX: THE CHRISTOPHER COMMISSION

The circumstances underlying the embassy investigation of the El Mozote massacre were finally made public in 1993. For this we thank, not the State Department, but the United Nations Truth Commission and the report it issued in March 1993 (discussed in chapter 7). The Truth Commission report, based on the testimony of over two thousand individuals testifying to twenty-two thousand human rights violations, concluded that 85 percent of the violations—the El Mozote massacre among them—were committed by government forces, 10 percent by death squads, and the remaining 5 percent by the FMLN. On what basis, then, had the Reagan and Bush administrations consistently maintained that respect for human rights in El Salvador was improving; denied that the army

systematically massacred innocent people in the early 1980s; and parceled out responsibility for repression to shadowy forces of the Right and
the Left, while proclaiming the innocence of the state's military and security forces?

More out of a need for damage control than a desire to get to the bottom of the matter, Secretary of State Warren Christopher responded to
the Truth Commission report on 24 March 1993 by appointing George S.
Vest, a former director general of the Foreign Service, and Richard Mur-
phy, a former assistant secretary of state for Near Eastern and South
Asian affairs, to head a panel that would "investigate charges that State
Department officials misled Congress about atrocities by the Salvadoran
military throughout the 1980's" (Krauss 1993a). This panel has come to
be known as "the Christopher Commission."

"Respect for human rights is a cornerstone of U.S. foreign policy,"
Christopher stated, "and when questions arise that challenge our commitments, we have an obligation to seek answers." In a sense, the degree
of such respect—which has been sorely tested and one might even say
shown (once again) to be a mere ideological sham in the wake of U.S. invasions of Panama, Iraq, and Somalia, and the rough treatment accorded
Jean-Bertrand Aristide—would be measured by just how candid and
critical a report the commission produced. Given that the report was
sponsored by a Democratic administration investigating Republican
ones, President Bill Clinton *seemed* to have much to gain and little to lose
by a thorough airing of the matter.

The commission released its report about four months later, on 15 July
1993, and the results were, to say the least, disappointing. On reviewing
the evidence available to the embassy and the conclusions that Hinton
and others drew from it, the commission explained that "[t]he El Mozote
issue then appears to have been lost in the flood of ongoing embassy
business. The election and its aftermath dominated the Salvadoran political scene. People the Panel interviewed underlined that it had dropped
off the scope of the Embassy's and the Department's concerns" (cited in
Danner 1994:278). The panel concluded that, with the exception of a few
"glitches," as it referred to Enders's vehement denial before Congress that
any evidence existed to support allegations of a massacre at El Mozote,
Roberto D'Aubuisson's role in the assassination of Archbishop Oscar Arnulfo Romero on 24 March 1980, and the tendency of U.S. Ambassador
Edwin Corr to conceal "bad news" from Washington, "the Department
and Foreign Service personnel performed creditably—and on occasion

with personal bravery—in advancing human rights in El Salvador" (cited in McManus 1993).

Where criticism was expected, called for, indeed necessary, the State Department and Foreign Service received praise. As Rep. Robert G. Torricelli (Democrat, New Jersey) noted: "[T]he State Department's report indicates more about the inability of the Foreign Service to investigate the Foreign Service . . . than it provides details about deliberate attempts to mislead the American Congress and the American people. It is almost unbelievable" (cited in Krauss 1993b). But, then, how could it have been otherwise when the investigation unfolded "from within the parameters of U.S. policy" and was headed by retired Foreign Service careerists well trained in the gross hypocrisy that goes with the terrain? As Vest said in an interview following the release of the report,

> "I knew no one was going to like it," sighed Vest. . . . "We were pretty tolerant of the way political appointees presented information to Congress during that period. We know it's a fact of life. . . . Information is going to be presented in a way that tries to sell the policy.
>
> "But the embassy (in San Salvador) generally did a fair, objective and persistent job, regardless of what they said in Washington." (cited in McManus 1993)

It is interesting, and instructive, to contrast the work of the United Nations Truth Commission in El Salvador with that of the Christopher Commission in the United States. The Truth Commission was an independent body composed of internationally respected figures from the United States, Colombia, and Venezuela who were granted a broad mandate to define the scope of the investigation of human rights violations during the civil war and the methodology most appropriate to that investigation. The Truth Commission was also empowered to draw upon the results of its labor to make recommendations for sanctions that would be considered binding on the FMLN and the Salvadoran government. By contrast, the Christopher Commission was headed by retired Foreign Service personnel who "accepted the premises of United States policy in El Salvador, which was primarily to defeat a Marxist guerrilla insurgency"; they interpreted this to mean that "Embassy personnel had no real option but to work with Salvadoran counterparts to reform the military, the police, and other organizations" (Krauss 1993b).

Furthermore, the "panel was not intended to gather evidence that would lead to disciplinary action" (Krauss 1993a). "[T]his is not a witch hunt," an unnamed State Department official told Clifford Krauss of the *New York Times.* "We don't want to refight the battles of the 80's. We're not a housecleaning Administration," said another (Krauss 1993a). The composition of the commission, the limited mandate, and the commission's interpretation of that mandate guaranteed that the resulting report would be, at best, banal.

STRATEGIES OF CONTAINMENT

When people contemplate a cover-up, they almost invariably think in terms of a conspiracy of silence to prevent the release of information that would be detrimental to the interests of the conspirators. There can be no doubt that in the case of El Salvador such conspiracies by Salvadoran officials and U.S. government officials were everyday facts of life. We cannot say with certainty that the cover-up of the El Mozote massacre was not another example. The embassy and the State Department had knowledge, in many cases quite detailed, concerning the membership and activities of death squads, and they kept that knowledge from the United States public as a matter of "national security."

But cover-ups, if we can use the term, also take more subtle forms, as the El Mozote case indicates. Apart from the deliberate conspiracy, there exists also the cover-up that results from the subtle play of power upon ideology as well as the exercise of power through it. Embassy personnel "naturally" privileged military accounts over those given by journalists or victims, and they ignored contradictions or inconsistencies. They silenced or marginalized the voices of refugees and others close to the site unless they proved of value in debunking claims that a massacre had occurred. And higher-ranking members of the foreign-policy bureaucracy exercised their right to "clean" the accounts of lower-ranking members, who were perhaps more sensitive to the human consequences of U.S. policy and less fully socialized to the need for *realpolitik.* Capacity for cynicism, I would suggest, varies directly with rank within a hierarchy of power; those least likely to be touched by suffering are also those most insulated (by social and economic distance) from it. In sum, a series of "strategies of containment"—the term is borrowed from Jameson (1981)—operated to organize the available facts into a narrative about Operation Rescue compatible with U.S. policy in El Salvador and capable of limiting the damage resulting from unsavory revelations about the U.S. client military.[11] Embassy and State Department officials did their best not to see, not to hear, and therefore not to know that "something had gone wrong."

Now let us suppose for a moment that instead of Salvadoran peasants, the victims at El Mozote had been European Americans, a settler colony of farmers, say, who had moved to El Salvador from the Midwest after being run out of business by big corporate farms and foreclosed by the banks. And suppose that instead of Rufina Amaya the sole survivor had been named Patricia Waddell: churchgoer, mother of three, and member of the El Mozote PTA. Taking the public response to the 1980 murder of the U.S. nuns and lay worker as a benchmark, I believe that reports of El Mozote in this case would have raised a massive outcry for a thorough investigation, that the faint protests sounded in the presence of the soldiers by refugees in San Francisco Gotera and Jocoaitique would have been tended to much more seriously, that overnight "Patricia Waddell" would have become a household name in the United States, and that the belligerent refusal by the Salvadoran High Command to provide details of Operation Rescue or to allow interrogation of the officers and troops of the units involved would have been taken by most U.S. citizens as a clear sign of guilt.[12]

That the actual outcry subsided so quickly, and that embassy and State Department officials expended most of their energies attacking the credibility of the reports of a massacre and those who offered them, is a measure of the different values that most European Americans (and the government that rules on their behalf) place on the lives of people who look and act like them as opposed to those who do not. It also suggests that, even more than El Salvador, the United States needs, as Rep. Joseph Moakley suggested, its own truth commission.[13] To be truly effective, this truth commission would have to be completely independent of the government and staffed by workers and peasants from the neocolonies and by the poor, dispossessed, homeless, and ethnic and racial minorities of the core (the "Third World" within the "First World"). Also, such a commission would have to have access to the resources, including all classified documentation, necessary to carry out a thorough study of state-sponsored terrorism. And it would have to have the power to fine, dismiss, and incarcerate people in and out of government found guilty of human rights violations of any kind, as well as the mandate to recommend the changes necessary to minimize the likelihood of their future reoccurrence.

THE NASCENT COMMUNITY

OF EL MOZOTE

What were the social contours of El Mozote before it was thrust onto the world stage for its few minutes of infamy by the reports of Bonner and Guillermoprieto and the carefully wrought but so poorly argued U.S. government denials: "The embassy is unable to reach a definite conclusion" and "The January 1982 investigation concluded . . . "? Like Ethiopia in the mid-1980s, Rwanda in the summer of 1994, rural Peru following the rise of Shining Path, and other neocolonial social spaces, El Mozote attracted the attention of the Western news media because something "dramatic" happened there. And as usual the drama involved massive loss of life, in this case large numbers of Salvadorans dying at the hands of other Salvadorans, although as I argued in chapter 4, the hand of the United States, though often invisible, was everywhere: in the counterinsurgency training of the Atlacatl Battalion, in the arms they employed, in the rations they consumed, and even in the ideology that framed the army's view of the northern Morazanian peasantry as infected cells threatening the social body.

A striking feature of the writings about the massacre at El Mozote is how little is apparently known about the history and social relationships of the people who were killed there, and how little curiosity the authors express about the victims. Furthermore, as I will show in the next chapter, much of what is believed to be true about them is incorrect. El Mozote entered the annals of history as the site of a crime, and it is the crime rather than the victims that dominates accounts. Some accounts of the massacre—the Tutela Legal report provides the best example—read like court briefs, orderly and precise, with a language that gradually builds a case against the Atlacatl Battalion (Tutela Legal 1991; United Nations 1993; CDHES-NG n.d.). Other reports mimic the form of the detective novel, in which the narrative begins with the criminal stalking the naive victim and then winds its way through the crime, its cover-up, the investigation, and the inevitable arrest (e.g., Danner 1993, 1994). In the El Mozote story, however, the arrest never comes.

Who died at El Mozote? How did they live? What did they believe? Was the community a new one, or could its roots be traced into the distant precolonial past, when much of northern Morazán was covered by tropical forest, and Lenca Indians hunted and sowed corn in scattered plots? The failure to ask such questions can be read in at least two ways. For human rights advocates, who view all lives as equally valuable, the features that distinguish one life or group of lives from others *must* recede in importance before the facts of false imprisonment, torture, and murder. Human rights advocates *assume* that establishing the innocence of the victim is enough to engender an identification in the audience and to move them to take action: to make a financial contribution, send a telegram or protest letter, or pressure public officials to act on behalf of victims of political persecution. But far from referencing a shared humanity endowed with fundamental rights, most people operating from within the dominant ideology *essentialize* others as so many examples of categories (the "African native," "Latin American peasant," "Japanese businessman") endowed with attributes that mark those assigned to them as inferior to those making the assignment. Racial and ethnic prejudice, operating at levels from the overt to the subliminal, determine that whatever may be the abstract humanitarian principles of their bearers, the response to concrete situations of human rights violations will be muted in comparison to what they would have been had such violations occurred among people like themselves. Writing the history of human rights violations requires, therefore, that we also challenge the dominant beliefs about others that underpin, justify, or rationalize their victimization. To do so requires that we go beyond discussion of human rights "crimes" to provide information about the communities that suffer them; if we do not provide this information, we leave a space for readers to project, unchallenged, their prejudices about others that diminish the meaning of the victims' lives, the seriousness of the abuses, and the possibility (or necessity) of doing anything about them.

In the following pages I present an ethnographic sketch of El Mozote's social and economic development constructed from conversations with about forty former residents. The massacre deprived these people of the friendship, companionship, and love of numerous relatives, friends, and neighbors. It also deprived them of homes, domestic animals, agricultural tools, social space, and lifelong patterns of interaction. In short, a whole way of life, the product of several decades of struggle, was eradicated when about one-third of El Mozote's prewar population was massacred on 11 December 1981.

EL MOZOTE: SOCIAL PARAMETERS

El Mozote (which means "the thistle") is a *caserío* (hamlet) located three kilometers southeast of Arambala, a small municipal center with approximately two hundred residents in 1980.[1] However, El Mozote is in the municipality of Meanguera, the head town of which (also called Meanguera) is several times larger than Arambala and lies nine kilometers to the southwest of El Mozote. Most of El Mozote's buildings lie on "el Llano" (the Plain), a long, narrow saddle bounded by a low ridge of hills, Cerro Cruz, and Cerro Chingo (see chapter 2, fig. 2). The Catholic church, the school, stores, and community center, as well as the homes of the economically better-off sector of the population, were located in or near the plaza, El Mozote's central space, the focal point for the community's activities: meetings of the Cooperative Association of Agricultural Production "23 May," the local council, and the Caballeros de Cristo Rey (a male solidarity association linked to the Catholic Church). Children attended school there; shoppers patronized the stores, especially the well-stocked one of Marcos Díaz; and on Sundays, people streamed into El Mozote from other hamlets to visit the chapel, where José Carmen Romero, the local catechist, celebrated the word of God.

The Plain was the area to which the army tricked (probably) the population into congregating from outlying regions, and was thereby the site of the worst killing. These days tourists and others who visit El Mozote seldom venture beyond the Plain and the roofless concrete-block buildings, a recently constructed monument to the victims of the massacre, and the weed-ridden foundation of the church that are the silent reminders of the vigorous social life that characterized El Mozote before the civil war. But the Plain was the nerve center of a much larger social body spread out in dispersed homesteads along the flanks and in the valleys between the finger-like ridges that snake downward to the Sapo River to the south or drop off precipitously into steep canyons to the west, beyond which lies the valley of the Las Marias River. People in each direction regarded themselves as inhabitants of caserío El Mozote, though they also identified with some other, more narrowly bounded place: La Polleta, La Chumpa, Los González, El Jícaro, El Cántaro, or La Ranchería, among others. Of course, these other hamlets were distinct from El Mozote, which exercised no administrative authority over them, but as El Mozote grew in economic importance, it developed into an embryonic village to which residents of surrounding hamlets ideologically adhered. They began to identify themselves as living in El Mozote, an identification that has carried over into the postwar period.

The land rises from 1,600 feet in the lower-lying areas to approximately 2,600 feet on top of Cerro Cruz, a few hundred feet above the floor of the Plain. As in many areas of the tropics, altitude corresponds with various rainfall amounts and temperature highs and lows. El Mozote falls in a transitional climatic zone between the hot, henequen-producing lands near the Torola River and the cooler, coffee-growing and timbering areas in the rugged mountainous regions to the northeast. El Mozote is too low and too hot to produce much coffee or timber, but before the war, the broad geographical range of conditions did support the cultivation of henequen, sugarcane, corn, sorghum *(maicillo)*, beans, a wide variety of perennial fruits (bananas, lemons, mangoes, etc.), and other crops, as well as the grassland necessary for small-scale cattle raising.

Throughout northern Morazán the agricultural year divides neatly into wet and dry seasons. The rainy season begins in April or May and lasts until October (November or December slightly north, around Perquín, and there are always clouds and humidity in the high mountains bordering Honduras). The rainy season is normally interrupted in July by the *canícula,* a two- to three-week drought, which is dangerous because it often coincides with the maturation of the corn crop. Heavy rains in August and September gradually tail off in October and cease by November or December. During the rainy season every El Mozote farmer who owned or rented land tended corn and other crops: his own or, in the case of land-deficient households, those of other people. Following the corn harvest in October and November, El Mozote agriculturists turned their attention to processing activities, often using machinery that was rudimentary but had gradually improved over time. The owners of small sugarcane fields hired laborers from December to February to cut and carry cane to *trapiches,* small, ox-driven mills where sugarcane juice was extracted, boiled, and poured into molds to make *panela,* a hard, crude, semiprocessed sugar found in rural markets in many parts of the world (see Binford 1991). Panela substituted for sugar locally and was also sold to merchants in Jocoaitique and other regional towns.

Only a minority of El Mozote farmers accessed through ownership or rental the humid bottomlands on which sugarcane could survive the dry season. Many more El Mozote farmers raised henequen (also called maguey) than sugarcane. The henequen (or agave) plant is a dark green, almost bluish cactus whose narrow, spiny leaves sprout from a large pineapple-shaped base. Henequen prospers on the steepest slopes, requires little capital investment, can survive the worst droughts, and is highly resistant to insect pests. For these reasons it was regarded as a poor person's cash crop. El Mozote farmers neither fertilized henequen nor applied insecticide to it. Peasants often interplanted corn between rows of newly planted henequen to gain some return during the two and one-half to three years before the first harvest. Once mature, the henequen plant provided two or three crops of leaves yearly for ten to twelve years or more. Old henequen plants even produce new shoots, obviating the need to expend precious capital on replacement plants when the time comes for replanting an exhausted field. Putting aside the ubiquitous corn and beans, which practically symbolize life itself in southern Mexico and Central America (Mayans refer to themselves as "Children of Corn"), the El Mozote economy, at least its cash component, was closely tied to the henequen plant and the various products derived from it.

El Mozote farmers cultivated henequen for its fiber, which they extracted from the cut leaves with a great deal of effort by hand, and with much less effort by machine, and then dried. The farmers bundled and sold this fiber, called *mescal* (not to be confused with the highly intoxicating southern Mexican spirit of the same name, also produced from henequen), or further processed it into rope *(lazos),* harvesting bags *(matates),* hammocks, and a variety of other goods. Some farmers grew henequen for mescal only, selling bundles of the dried fiber to intermediaries in El Mozote, Jocoaitique, and San Francisco Gotera. Other growers doubled as artisans and worked the fiber up into twine *(pita)* and the twine into the above-mentioned products. Landless households earned income during the dry season by extracting mescal for henequen growers, or they purchased mescal on local or regional markets and worked it up into finished products.

In this way, access to land and other resources (e.g., cattle) divided the population into economic categories. Favio Argueta, a native of El Mozote who moved to the town of Meanguera at the age of fourteen, described the situation as follows:

> The whole of the population of northern Morazán was composed of two sectors. One group which had its own work, which cultivated corn, cultivated basic grains and mescal . . . [or] that had cattle, little herds rather than large ones. The other part of the people, which was poor, lived totally from working extracting fiber from maguey . . . or from spinning the fiber. They made twine for lassos . . . and made hammocks and all that. That didn't provide the people any more profit than was necessary to more or less cover the most elemental necessities.

Peasants and artisans had to buy on credit when they had no cash on hand. Most communities, El Mozote included, harbored intermediaries who purchased products *adelantado,* paying 30 to 40 percent below market prices for future delivery. Poor peasants and artisans had a very difficult time improving their economic situations. Many men without secure dry-season work left between November and January following the corn harvest to pick coffee and cotton in the capitalist-dominated agro-export zones of the departments of Usulután, San Miguel, and others. The women and old people often remained in El Mozote to care for the small children and weave hammocks and other products to supplement the savings their husbands, sons, and brothers sent home or brought back. In the late 1970s, many people from El Mozote, like people throughout northern Morazán, were working seasonally on coffee plantations near Lourdes in the department of La Libertad, about twenty miles west of San Salvador. Many native inhabitants of El Mozote survived the massacre because they were picking coffee in Lourdes in December 1981; since they could not return to northern Morazán, they stayed in Lourdes for the remainder of the civil war.

INCIPIENT CLASS FORMATION IN EL MOZOTE

As we see, the range of options open to any household in plotting economic strategy was limited by the household's access to land. And land, in El Mozote as elsewhere in El Salvador, was unequally distributed. Various families owned upwards of 50 manzanas (1 manzana is equal to .7 hectares or 1.75 acres), a considerable amount of land by regional standards, though a pittance when compared to the massive plantations of the nation's wealthy oligarchs. José María Márquez, his brother Santos Márquez, his brother-in-law Israel Márquez, and various others fell into this category.[2] At the other extreme, El Mozote contained both poor families with only a manzana or two of dry, hillside land, and landless ones who owned only their house sites. These differences gave rise to a series of dependencies—common throughout northern Morazán—whereby landless and land-poor peasants rented land from the relatively land rich during the winter rainy seasons. Favio Argueta again: "The people rented land in two forms. Some people rented for a certain quantity of money, for fifty colones per manzana. There were people who paid half and at the end of the harvest paid the other half. Other people gave work in exchange for land rental. . . . to pay fifty colones one had to work a lot. It was very difficult. . . . They only gave him [the worker] the midday meal. He ate breakfast in his house and the employer gave him lunch."

As a result of two processes the land crisis became increasingly severe in northern Morazán in the decades before the civil war: population growth and the concentration of land in the hands of wealthier households through purchase from poorer ones. Fragmentation of land holdings was aggravated by legal stipulations that granted equal inheritance rights to each legitimate child. Unless parceled up earlier and camouflaged as a sale, the ten manzanas, for example, of a man or woman with four legitimate children was broken up after his or her death into four fields of two and one-half manzanas each. Illegitimate children, those whose fathers refused to inscribe them in the official municipal register, had absolutely no legal rights and inherited only in cases where the legal descendants demonstrated *"buena voluntad"* (goodwill) toward their siblings.[3] "Nolvo" stated that whereas in the 1930s the largest landowner in Meanguera possessed eight hundred manzanas, by the beginning of the war no one in the municipality owned more than two hundred manzanas.[4]

Government census statistics, though pegged at the municipal level, add to the story. Between 1961 and 1971 in northern Morazán, land under cultivation grew from 24,136 to 32,707 manzanas, representing an increase from 35.0 to 47.4 percent of the total area. But in Meanguera, which contained a higher percentage of potentially cultivable land, the farmed area as a proportion of total area increased from 59.1 percent to a whopping 91.2 percent over the same period. By 1971 only 577 of Meanguera's 6,615 manzanas were *not* under cultivation, according to the government's Third Agricultural Census (Flores Díaz 1980:47). This reflects, I believe, a situation in which a fixed land base was increasingly being cultivated and was still incapable of accommodating the growing northern Morazán (and more specifically Meanguera) population. By 1971 the average Meanguera farm had shrunk to only 4.9 manzanas, among the lowest in the region (El Salvador Ministerio de Economía 1974b:5).

The breakup of the few larger-than-average land holdings probably helped to alleviate the land crisis. However, a parallel process of concentration of land in the hands of wealthier farmers through purchase from poorer ones exacerbated it. The story of Rogelio Chávez provides a good example of this second process. Rogelio began in El Mozote as a poor landless peasant who rented land and grew corn. He supplemented his farming income by working as a hired laborer in trapiches, particularly that of Secundino Gutiérrez, his mother's first cousin. Trapiche workers inserted cut sugarcane into the wooden (iron after 1970) rollers of the mill, managed the ox team that provided the apparatus's motive power, cut wood for the furnace, and supervised the conversion of *guarapo* (cane juice) into *miel* (syrup), and miel into panela. For their work they were paid either cash or an amount of panela with an equivalent cash value.

In good years, when Rogelio's corn crop generated surpluses, he bought animals, and when the animals grew large, he sold them and began to buy land. He purchased his first five-manzana parcel in El Mozote in 1958, when he was thirty-five years old, and he continued to accumulate until he left the area in April 1981. At that time he owned twenty-five manzanas, which he had been planting in corn, henequen, sugarcane, and fruit trees. He and his wife, María, had one child after another, and his male children, as well as his sons-in-law, composed Rogelio's principal unpaid labor force. In the years before the massacre, Rogelio had also begun to modernize a previously inefficient beekeeping operation and was extracting twenty to thirty bottles of honey daily. "I was producing corn, beans, coffee, mescal, fruit, honey, everything," he said. "The only thing I had to buy was salt."

The self-sufficient household is a common peasant ideal, and Rogelio, through intelligence, hard work, and some luck, had come close to achieving it. However, there is another side to his story. For at the time he purchased that first five-manzana field, four families were living on it. "Where did they go?" I asked. "Some left for Honduras," he replied, suggesting that their departure had been voluntary rather than obligatory.

Rogelio had risen from the ranks of the landless workers to become a middle peasant, but his experience was far from the norm. Though some landless peasants accessed land through rental, and the vast majority worked up maguey fiber into fiber products, many people were unable to generate enough income locally to remain in El Mozote throughout the year. Poverty forced them to migrate seasonally to capitalist estates in the departments of Usulután, San Miguel, San Vicente, and elsewhere. As the men trickled back into El Mozote in January and February, they often brought with them money sent by friends and relatives who remained on the estates.

Other people, however, left permanently for Honduras before the Hundred Hours War of 1969, or for the cities and capital-intensive agricultural zones afterward. Municipal- or cantonal-level figures are unavailable, but at the departmental level Morazán experienced a net migration loss (the number of out-migrants minus the number of in-migrants) of 2,474 persons (2.01 percent of the 1966 population) to other departments, mainly San Miguel (37.9 percent) and San Salvador (29 percent), between 1966 and 1971 (El Salvador Ministerio de Economía 1974a:347–361).

Agriculture was the axis of the local economy, but El Mozote also developed into a dynamic center of petty commerce that attracted many peasants from surrounding hamlets to buy and sell. At least seven inhabitants of the village center owned small stores or dealt in cattle, henequen-fiber products, corn, and dry goods. Others dedicated themselves to carpentry, tile making, and sugar processing.

The incipient class distinctions—a variegated peasantry rather than polarized classes—assumed no clear and unambiguous political or ideological register. And the more accommodated groups were not all that wealthy when compared with peasants elsewhere in the country. The principal difference may have had less to do with ownership of luxury goods than with the location and type of housing owned. Only one or two households possessed automobiles, and since the town had no electricity, appliances such as televisions had little currency. With notable exceptions, the better-off families lived in the Plain, and shortly before the war over a dozen of them had constructed homes with concrete-block walls and concrete or mosaic-tile floors. By contrast, over 90 percent of the houses in Los González, La Chumpa, and elsewhere were one-room structures of *bahareque:* walls of mud plastered over a frame of interlaced bamboo, a baked-tile roof, and a dirt floor.[5] After housing, diet— the quantity and variety of food consumed and, in particular, the frequency with which meat was eaten—was an important index of family well-being. These differences in quality of life, though meaningful locally, were not great in any absolute sense. There's more than a grain of truth to the observation, made by an expatriate German who was long familiar with life in northern Morazán, that in much of the area the difference between being a "have" and being a "have not" "was whether or not you slept in the same room with your pig." Still, if Durham's prewar study of Tenancingo in Cuscatlán is generalizable to northern Morazán, a close relationship existed there between farm size and infant mortality, especially for households with less than two and one-half hectares (Durham 1979:85–86).

Another factor dampening potential social conflict was the fact that many of the wealthier El Mozote families had long histories of demonstrated leadership and personal sacrifice in the service of the community. If over the long run they benefited from the social and economic developments that they promoted, so did other people of humbler economic status. A listing of these developments makes it clear that, despite the agrarian crisis, El Mozote was a community "on the move" in comparison with many others in northern Morazán. Over the three decades from its founding in about 1945, the inhabitants had built a well-ordered adobe chapel and accompanying sacristy (locally called the *convento*, or convent) in which to house the priest during his infrequent visits; obtained a large, three-room brick schoolhouse from the government; constructed a *casa comunal* (community center); elected local representatives; and from the mid-1970s participated in an agricultural cooperative that developed projects in beekeeping, cattle raising, and henequen-fiber extraction.

HISTORY

By northern Morazanian standards El Mozote was a very young community at the time the war broke out, because it was founded only in about 1950 by people who moved into the Plain from La Guacamaya. The principal promoter of early settlement was Israel Márquez, a merchant and wealthy landowner who, it is said, tired of trekking to Jocoaitique for mass and sought to interest local peasants in constructing a church. They organized a fund-raising celebration and invited the parish priest of Jocoaitique, Santos Auxiline, an Italian with dubious knowledge of the Spanish language, who gave his blessing to the enterprise. Three years of fund-raising and donated labor resulted in the church—a large chapel really—in which the Atlacatl later interned the men and older boys on the morning of 11 December 1981.

The Márquez clan remained influential for the entirety of El Mozote's short existence before its ten-year abandonment after the massacre. All of the Márquezes were merchants and landowners: Israel, the patriarch; Alfredo, store owner and Israel's nephew; and José María, a large land-owner who became president of the cooperative, bought and sold cattle, and rented out land at the "reasonable" price of fifty colones per man-zana. José María is remembered as a good person who allowed people to gather wood on his property.

Of these three, Israel had the most power, which he wielded in a be-nign if not benevolent manner. For instance, Israel donated to the gov-ernment the land on which the school was constructed (probably with Alliance for Progress money). He also participated with others to con-vince the government to build an agricultural school in El Mozote. Until superseded by that of Marcos Díaz, Israel's store was the largest and best-stocked one in town, with nails, lumber, paint, and many other things; for years he kept it supplied with a team of sixteen mules that made the trip to and from Jocoaitique twice a week. He owned at least five houses in northern Morazán, a granary for corn storage, and a small sugarcane-processing facility.

Israel Márquez was the eldest son of Saturina Chicas and Francisco Márquez, both of whom were rural schoolteachers, by no means wealthy. Israel's economic success came only after his marriage to Paula Márquez (unrelated to him), who brought a large amount of inherited land to the union. Even as his fortunes improved, Israel retained a sense of humility that led him to share his knowledge and resources with others. He al-lowed customers without money to buy on credit (an established prac-tice in rural Latin America), donated medicine to people too poor to purchase it, and gave homes to his nephews and other people. Most telling is the fact that Marcos Díaz, the unwitting tool of the army who passed along the order for outlying residents to assemble in El Mozote before the massacre, learned the art of business at Israel's feet and, with Israel's blessing, founded a competing store out of a large home a mere hundred meters from that of his mentor. When war came to northern Morazán, Israel gave money, food, and cattle to the FMLN. Eighty years old in December 1981, he, too, was murdered by the Atlacatl soldiers.

Before leaving this discussion of Israel Márquez, it bears mentioning that he was also a doctor of the empirical variety. He read books about curing and made his own medicines, which he sold to the many people who came to him. His consultations were free. His medical practice was surreptitious because he was not licensed, but he attracted clients from all over the municipalities of Joateca, Meanguera, Villa El Rosario, and Jocoaitique. Often he sent his nephews to record the symptoms of sick persons and prescribe medicine for them, in this way sharing his medical knowledge as he did his knowledge of trade. If the problem was beyond them, he went himself. Israel often insisted that he knew everyone in El Mozote from the time that they were in the womb (because he assisted pregnant women) until they died, because everyone came to him for medicines.

Israel Márquez's illegal doctoring was appreciated in an area that was beyond the reach of institutionalized medicine, which was a consequence of both the peasants' poverty and the inadequacy of the state's public health system. Religion and education also suffered and sometimes failed through institutional neglect, whether of the church or the state, in northern Morazán. Hence, communities like El Mozote were left to resolve many problems by marshaling what money and raw materials they could and combining them in creative ways with voluntary labor. El Mozote may have been the region's most successful community in this regard.

The provision of schooling is a very good example. Before 1945 the only school nearby was in the hamlet of La Guacamaya, a lengthy walk away over footpaths that crossed a rugged gorge that was frequently swollen with fast-moving water during the rainy season. Children of families that resided in areas of La Guacamaya near El Mozote were unable to take advantage of even the meager two years of education that the La Guacamaya school offered. So El Mozote residents formed a ten-person directive, with Francisco Chicas as president and Israel Márquez as vice president, to seek a remedy. The directive acquired a piece of land below the Plain and put up a rudimentary structure, raising money through dances and raffles. Chicas then went to talk to the regional school delegate in Jocoaitique, who told him to conduct a census of school-age children. The census enumerated about seventy-five children, enough for the government to send teachers to the community. This school, named "El Jícaro" (the calabash tree) opened in about 1946, several years before the chapel, and it undoubtedly acted as a magnet drawing more peasant families to relocate closer to El Mozote.

El Jícaro remained the only local educational institution until a brick schoolhouse, constructed with government assistance, was opened on the Plain in the early 1970s, on land donated by Israel Márquez. With that event, the number of grades increased from two to three, and the number of teachers rose from one to three. Only people living close to the municipal centers, where schooling was offered through the sixth or seventh grade, had better possibilities.

El Jícaro was soon followed by the chapel, a much more substantial building that required a great deal of local organization and contributed money, materials, and labor. Like El Jícaro, the chapel was built without government assistance. Israel Márquez originated the idea. Israel and his *mozo* (hired hand), Juan Márquez Rodríguez, went door to door to explain the plan and solicit cooperation. At the time, people were traveling all morning on foot and by oxcart over dirt tracks to attend the Sunday services of the Franciscan priest, Santos Auxiline, in Jocoaitique. Since Jocoaitique was also the principal market town in northern Morazán for henequen-fiber products, grains, and other goods, visitors from outlying caseríos went there to buy and sell and to enjoy a bit of the excitement of town life, with its crowds of people, food stalls, and bars, as well as to discharge their religious obligations.

The length of the trip, which was particularly hazardous during the rainy season, and perhaps the prospect of acquiring the higher status that attaches to any community with its own church attracted people living in both El Mozote and La Guacamaya to serve on the board charged with church construction. The board raised funds through nightly rosaries paid for by local households. The group had to purchase lumber, nails, and other materials, but unpaid communal work groups produced the adobe bricks that formed the walls. Aside from the "master builder," Cruz Argueta, who was remunerated, construction labor and animals for hauling materials were donated. While men cleared the land, erected the frame, and laid adobe bricks, etc., women prepared the workers' meals. The church, named the Church of the Three Kings, was completed in

FIGURE 4 This baptismal font is one of the few surviving relics from El Mozote's Church of the Three Kings, destroyed on 11 December 1981 by the Atlacatl Battalion.

1957 or 1958 and was in regular use until the massacre. All that remains now of the burned and abandoned church is a low, thick ridge of melted adobe that marks the outline of the walls, and, leaning precariously in a rear quadrant, a stone baptismal font, discolored and pitted from over a decade of exposure to sun, wind, and rainfall. Later, the community added a one-room sacristy with a cut-stone floor, adobe walls, and tile roof. Though intended as a lodging for the Jocoaitique priest during his occasional visits to the community, the room was mostly used for storage. For twelve years after the massacre, the ruins of the sacristy preserved the remains of more than 140 Atlacatl victims.

For almost twenty-five years the Church of the Three Kings was the center of community ceremonial life, a ritual space where people from El

Mozote, Jocote Amarillo, La Guacamaya, and other hamlets assembled to worship God, Christ, and the saints; to celebrate baptisms, confirmations, and marriages; and to ease the souls of the deceased on their lengthy journey to the next world. However, the Church of the Three Kings remained without a resident priest, since the only priest in all of northern Morazán was based in Jocoaitique and usually visited rural villages like El Mozote only once or twice each year on locally important ceremonial days. For decades, *rezadoras* (female prayer sayers) were the principal resident religious practitioners. They played an instrumental role in wakes and other ceremonies for deceased persons, but they had no ecclesiastical authority to baptize, marry, or offer ablution.

Following Vatican II, Medellín, and the "preferential option for the poor," the Catholic Church responded to the paucity of priests in El Salvador by constructing in the late 1960s a number of centers for training lay catechists. Although a social and theological conservative—one is tempted to say reactionary—Father Andrés Argueta, the priest who replaced Santos Auxiline in the early 1960s, obediently sent young male peasants and artisans off to Chirilagua in San Miguel to attend Centro El Castaño, Centro Guadalupe, and Centro San Lucas, or to Jiquilisco, Usulután, to attend Centro Los Naranjos, where they were exposed to a progressive interpretation of the Bible and obtained practical knowledge in agronomy, animal husbandry, health, and cooperative development. After one or more two- to four-week courses, these catechists returned to their communities to partially fill the need for religious leadership, carrying out "Celebrations of the Word," organizing Bible study, and putting into practice the technical and community-development skills they had obtained. They did not, however, have the authority to baptize children, perform marriages, or offer ablution. When the state-sponsored repression intensified in the late 1970s, many of the catechists were singled out and killed. The survivors became refugees or joined the FMLN, where they served in combat squadrons, health brigades, logistics units, or the propaganda section.

El Mozote's catechist was José Carmen Romero, the brother of Daniel Romero, one of the local *mayordomos,* or fiesta sponsors. José Carmen trained as a catechist at Centro El Castaño, San Miguel, in 1970 with priests steeped in liberation theology, but on his return to Morazán, Argueta kept him on a short leash and gave him little opportunity to put his newfound ideas into practice. Some catechists in northern Morazán rebelled against Argueta's efforts to transcendentalize religion and to prevent its contamination by "foreign" social and political ideologies, and they eventually severed contact with him entirely. Another group of catechists was in complete agreement with Argueta and resisted efforts to politicize the church. Some of them even became informers for military and security forces, passing on information about alleged guerrilla collaborators in their communities. A third group of catechists attempted to maneuver between the extremes; they harbored progressive ideas but avoided either challenging Argueta's authority directly or doing things that might engender the disapproval of government security forces or local conservatives. This obviously placed limits on their practices. In my view José Carmen Romero fell into this category.

It was not necessary for El Mozote to have a priest in order to develop a vigorous ceremonial life. Even before the church had been completed, prominent men in the community selected 6 January (Three Kings Day) to be the community's *fiesta patronal* (patron saint day). For much of El Mozote's short history as a congregate community, Daniel Romero and Juan Márquez served as mayordomos, in charge of organizing *posadas* to obtain the money needed to purchase the decorations and fireworks and to pay the musicians and priest. In the *posadas,* area households served as overnight hosts for *estampas* (cloth banners printed with the image of a religious figure) and sponsored rosaries at which the attending public made contributions. The church garnered funds for the fiesta; the sponsors rose slightly in status and respect.

As population and trade grew, Three Kings Day developed into a real extravaganza that drew people from all over northern Morazán and from as far away as San Francisco Gotera. People came for the mass but also to enjoy the soccer games, rides, food stalls, gambling, fireworks, and dances that became constituent parts of the celebration. Recollections of Three Kings Day tend to subordinate religious ritual to the sheer excitement of seeing the Plain alive with people and color. Many traveling merchants and carnival people worked El Mozote into their "fiesta circuit," offering rides and games of chance and selling a variety of products that were not usually available locally. Former residents I talked to almost always mentioned the rides such as the carousel and especially the "umbrella," in which several dozen swing sets turned around a vertical axis and were propelled upward and outward by centrifugal force. And women seldom discuss the fiesta without describing their food stalls, which provided many households with a little extra income at the beginning of the dry season. The fiesta activities were concentrated on 5 and 6

January, but sometimes vendors remained until the seventh because, as one former resident told me, "the people didn't want to leave." Three Kings Day was fun, and it was profitable, too.

El Jícaro, the adobe church, and the new brick school were not the only community improvements coveted by nearby residents. In the mid-1970s El Mozote was chosen to be the recipient of an agricultural school, an *"escuela granja,"* that would train peasants in agriculture, carpentry, bricklaying, and other practical skills. According to eighty-nine-year-old Don Juan Evangelista Chicas, the school was to be a gift from the Venezuelan government to the government of El Salvador. Learning of these plans, the El Mozote Directive solicited the school from President Fidel Sánchez Hernández's minister of education, Rogelio Sánchez, during the period when Chicas was Meanguera's mayor, 1974–76 (he was the first municipal mayor from cantón La Guacamaya). Acceptance of the solicitude was made contingent on the community's ability to acquire five manzanas of land for the school. The directive selected a site near the brick school, at the foot of Cerro Cruz. Between them, Israel Márquez and his brother-in-law José María Márquez donated about a third of the land. The remainder was purchased with funds acquired from the sale of the old El Jícaro school site, which was expendable after the construction of the new brick school. The area was then measured by an engineer, and in 1978 two representatives from the Venezuelan Embassy arrived to approve the site. However, because of the deteriorating political situation in northern Morazán, construction was suspended. Eventually, according to one former resident, the authorities changed the school location to Zapotitlán, in the department of San Salvador.

El Mozote also had its own cemetery from which the spirits of the deceased passed on to the next life. The acquisition of a cemetery was a major accomplishment, the product of a nineteen-year struggle led by Don Juan Evangelista Chicas. Prior to its acquisition, relatives of the deceased confronted two unpleasant alternatives: they could lug the casket for miles over rugged, ravine-studded terrain to the Meanguera cemetery, or they could pay a hefty fine to the Arambala mayor for the right to a resting place in the Arambala burial ground. Poor people without the means to pay the fine often transported bodies clandestinely in the night to Tierra Colorada (in Arambala) bordering El Mozote in order to claim Arambala as the municipality of death. Having their own cemetery saved people in El Mozote and other hamlets time and money and obviated the need for such subterfuges.

THE AGRICULTURAL COOPERATIVE

Another major accomplishment, albeit one that benefited a minority of local households, was the establishment of an agricultural and stock-raising cooperative in 1975. Government extension agents, probably from DIDECO (General Direction of Communal Development, a government community-development agency), stimulated the formation of the cooperative. DIDECO personnel made an unsolicited trip to El Mozote to give peasants month-long training sessions in bricklaying and cooperative development. Local notables Israel Márquez (by then too old to work but still influential), José María Márquez, Daniel Romero, Alfredo Márquez, and two elderly brothers of the Chicas family, Juan Evangelista and Francisco, all signed on. The cooperative was formally installed on 23 May 1975 and was named, appropriately, the Asociación Cooperativa de Producción Agropecuaria "23 de Mayo" (Cooperative Association of Agricultural Production "23 May"), with the acronym ACOPAVEM.

José María Márquez became the first president of the co-op's board of directors. José Ramón Chicas was elected treasurer and Ignacio Chicas, an early immigrant from nearby caserío Los González, secretary. The first meetings were held at the home of Israel Márquez, where the members discussed how to raise capital. They decided to begin with contributions of fifty colones each in installments of ten colones monthly, an amount that was within reach of all but the poorest members. The money was transferred to a bank account in San Francisco Gotera and used as collateral to obtain loans with which to buy fertilizer (increasingly necessary to secure decent corn harvests in this overworked area) or cattle. Borrowers repaid the loans at the low interest rate of 6 percent to maintain the capital base. In essence, then, these El Mozote peasants wielded the cooperative like a lever to pry their way into the commercial banking system, which had historically been closed to them and impoverished peasants like them throughout the country.

The most optimistic project undertaken by ACOPAVEM involved the purchase of a motor-driven machine for extracting fiber from the henequen plant. Several such machines already existed in the area—in fact co-op treasurer Ramón Chicas owned one—but most fiber was extracted in a dirty, physically taxing, labor-intensive process carried out either by the owners of the henequen or, more frequently, by hired day laborers. Before the war mescal prices hovered around thirty-two colones per quintal (one hundred pounds), but after costs of production and hand processing were subtracted, the producer retained only fifteen colones.

Former co-op members disagree as to whether the machine was purchased through a bank loan or directly out of the co-op's capital base, but all insist that the co-op owned it free and clear and that it functioned for several years before the war and the exodus of members from the zone ended the cooperative experiment in El Mozote. Two people operated the gasoline-powered scraper, which members hauled from field to field in the bed of an oxcart. The field owner paid ten colones per quintal of mescal produced and also covered the cost of fuel and oil. Two workers using the scraping machine could produce about two hundred pounds of mescal daily, ten times as much as an equal number of manual workers pulling the leaves one by one through a pair of close-set wooden stakes *(estacas)* could produce in one day. The mechanical scraper did not significantly reduce the cost of fiber extraction, but it certainly facilitated the process and speeded it up.

It is worth noting that few communities in northern Morazán attained a comparable level of organization. Most of the half dozen northern Morazanian cooperatives that I have been able to document began as petty "revolving credit" associations; their members never accumulated the capital or developed the organizational and accounting skills necessary to move into the productive arena. The region's most successful cooperative, based in Joateca, expanded from 18 members in 1969 to 113 in 1980, when government repression forced many members to flee the area and it ceased operating. Cooperatives in Perquín (one), Jocoaitique (one), and Guachipilín (two) were of the "saving and credit" variety only. In the case of Jocoaitique, for instance, Father Argueta patronized a *cooperativa parroquial* (parish co-op) that assessed each member a quota of one colón monthly and used these funds to make small loans to associates based on their total capital contribution. Most contributors used the money to purchase fertilizer, though José Márquez, an El Mozote native (but a member nonetheless), said that he took out loans of five to ten colones only when there was an illness in the family and the necessity of going to San Francisco Gotera to consult with a private doctor. In 1975 Márquez pulled out of Argueta's organization and transferred his little stake to the newly formed cooperative in El Mozote.

THE LIMITS OF DEVELOPMENT IN EL MOZOTE

The accomplishments that I have discussed, which were propelled by a core of highly motivated peasants and petty merchants, contributed to improve the quality of life in El Mozote, albeit to a limited degree. Without leaving their community, the people of El Mozote could purchase most necessary consumer items, go to school, attend church, and bury their dead. I do not believe that this could have been said of any other hamlet in northern Morazán at that time. These services saved time and resources for everyone who lived within walking distance of the Plain. Those who lived farther away had to expend more time to shop, worship, and attend school. With its "main street" and the cluster of cement-block and tile-roofed buildings around the little plaza, El Mozote even looked like an embryonic municipal center, a far cry from the "typical" northern Morazanian hamlet, with its adobe and bahareque homes dispersed widely over the landscape.

Indeed, according to various former inhabitants, those who lived in the environs of El Mozote before the war were already thinking of themselves as "more civilized" and "more advanced" than peasants in La Guacamaya and elsewhere. Israel Márquez and other prominent figures shared the goal of developing El Mozote into a cantón politically independent of La Guacamaya, perhaps even a separate *municipio* with its own mayor, ANTEL (National Telecommunications Agency) office, and local bus stop. It is possible to read their protracted struggles as deliberate steps toward this end. Such a reading certainly would account for the tendency of former residents to remember the physical limits of the community as having encompassed not only Los González, La Chumpa, and La Polleta, but also Jocote Amarillo, La Ranchería, and other hamlets that are politically independent of El Mozote. Looking back over twelve years later, some former residents even remember El Mozote as having subsumed the *entirety* of cantón La Guacamaya and all the hamlets therein. They think of La Guacamaya as having been a dependency of El Mozote, rather than El Mozote as a hamlet within La Guacamaya, which was, in fact, the case.

El Mozote's social and economic progress nonetheless unfolded within an impoverished region that had been all but abandoned by the state. Even after small amounts of social investment during the 1960s and 1970s, transportation, health, and educational services remained third-rate, well below the minimum needs of the rapidly growing population. Northern Morazán simply wasn't a government priority. It contained no large commercial center; it was not an important coffee-growing zone; and the eroded highland soils and cool climate were not conducive to the production of cotton, an important postwar crop concentrated in the hot coastal plain of San Miguel and Usulután. Even cattle raising, along with commerce the principal means of capital accumulation for rich and poor alike in pre–civil war northern Morazán, generally remained small scale and unaffected by the modern technologies imported into Central America beginning in the late 1950s (Williams 1986:75–152). El Mozote and northern Morazán in general were part of the *tierra olvidada* (forgotten land), an economically backward region in one of the poorest and most economically backward departments of El Salvador. Low levels of local and regional capital accumulation determined that resolution of the fundamental problems confronted by the majority of the inhabitants would depend on social investment channeled through the state, and such investment was simply not forthcoming.

That El Mozote obtained its own school and saved its children a lengthy daily walk to Meanguera is a credit to the organization and persistence of the adult population, although the practical advantages of a primary school education should not be overestimated. In northern Morazán in the 1970s, only the children of the well-to-do, a small proportion of the population, advanced beyond sixth or seventh grade. In order to do so, they had to leave the area and board with relatives or in a boarding house in San Francisco Gotera or another city. Less than half the 1971 population aged 10 to 14 was even in school, and the proportion declined to a mere 4 percent for those children from 15 to 19 years, for the obvious reason that few municipal schools extended beyond sixth grade (El Salvador Ministerio de Economía 1974a:86, 91–93, 154, 157–158). The remainder of the department was not much better off. In 1971 all Morazán, 156,000 strong, contained only 19 people (of 7,703 nationwide) with post-secondary school educations, the fewest in the country (240). Census figures on housing stock, health, ownership of consumer durables, and access to various services such as electricity reinforce this dismal portrait. Long before the civil war, life was difficult in northern Morazán, a daily struggle—though not without its satisfactions and moments of levity—carried on amidst the ravages of poverty and disease. It was not, for many, a particularly satisfying existence, certainly not one that they would have defended had there existed reasonable prospects for improvement in the conditions of labor and material comfort.

When the social and economic projects designed and carried through by El Mozote's farmers and merchants are judged in this context, they appear all the more impressive, but also all the more futile: impressive for the energy, organization, and spirit of sacrifice that it must have taken to muster scarce resources; futile because such *proyectitos* (little projects) could scarcely address the fundamental scarcities of land and capital that are the bane of the rural poor worldwide. Cooperative or no cooperative, the land crisis continued apace as a rapidly growing population competed for a fixed, if not declining, land base. A common response in Morazán was to abandon the countryside for the capital-intensive agro-export zones of the south (Usulután, San Miguel) or for the urban centers of commerce and services, such as San Miguel and San Salvador. As noted above, by 1971 the department of Morazán had suffered a net loss through migration of 2 percent of its 1966 population (El Salvador Ministerio de Economía 1974a:347–361).

There is no reason to suppose that the agricultural cooperative stemmed this process to any significant degree. Members of ACOPAVEM were landowners, able to pay the ten-colón monthly dues. Few were wealthy, but almost all were among the more affluent sectors of the local peasantry and merchant class that cultivated maguey along with corn, sugarcane, and other crops. Furthermore, the growing mechanization of fiber extraction among co-op members and others was likely reducing the availability of dry-season work and forcing increasing numbers of poor peasants and rural laborers into seasonal, if not permanent, migration.[6] El Mozote, no less than northern Morazán in general, had become, if it had not long been, a cheap labor reserve for capitalist agriculture.

THE POLITICS OF REPRESSION AND

SURVIVAL IN NORTHERN MORAZÁN

By December 1981, civil war had definitively arrived in northern Morazán. The FMLN's "Final Offensive" of mid-January 1981 had failed to
bring a quick military victory in the last days of the Carter administration. Northern Morazán had been a war zone since October 1980, and
thousands of people, beginning with the town-based petty bourgeois
merchants and landowners, had already left the area for cities and refugee camps. Many hamlets, particularly in the municipalities of Torola,
Jocoaitique, San Fernando, and Villa El Rosario, lay abandoned. The
blackened frames of houses burned by the army during the offensives of
October 1980 and March 1981 spotted the landscape, and vines, weeds,
and wildflowers grew where formerly peasants had cultivated corn, beans,
sugarcane, and henequen. The relatives of people killed by military, paramilitary, and security forces marked the graves of their loved ones with
nameless crosses in order to protect themselves from possible reprisals
due to their association with the victims of political violence.

In this context the presence of about a thousand people living in El
Mozote and the surrounding area poses a problem. Why, given the rapidly
escalating danger, did they remain? What attraction—material, political,
ideological (or some combination of these)—prevented them from making the same decision as thousands of other northern Morazanians in
similar circumstances: to pull up stakes and flee for their lives?

Those who have written about El Mozote have advanced two diametrically opposed explanations for the presence of people in the area in December 1981. The first explanation maintains that El Mozote contained a large population of evangelical Protestants—trusting in God, politically neutral, having no truck with either government forces or the FMLN, but tolerating the presence of each to the degree necessary for survival. In this scenario, the inhabitants of El Mozote, or a large percentage of them anyway, were innocent beyond innocent. This view predominates on the Left and within the human rights community (Americas Watch Committee 1991:49; Danner 1993:54–55, 87, 101, 1994:17–19, 78–79, 99; FDR/FMLN 1982:13; McClintock 1985:309; Brown 1992:9).

An alternative view paints the inhabitants of El Mozote with a politically red brush. El Mozote, the U.S. Embassy in San Salvador informed the State Department on 31 January 1982, lay "in the heart of guerrilla territory" and its inhabitants had spent "most of the last three years willingly or unwillingly cooperating with the insurgents" (Hinton 1982a). The Greentree cable implied that as collaborators, the victims were in some sense responsible for their own deaths.

Members of the Salvadoran officers corp produced a version of events that attributed noncombatant victims to the FMLN's use of civilian homes as shelters from which to engage the Atlacatl in a pitched gun battle: "I do not have X-Ray vision, and I cannot see inside the house from which someone is shooting at me," Lt. Col. Domingo Monterrosa Barrios told Maj. John McKay, the assistant defense attaché, when queried about the event, "nor in those types of circumstances am I very disposed to waste my time trying to find out who else might be in the house" (cited in Danner 1993:113, 1994:122).

Still, this does not explain why so many civilians remained in the FMLN's principal operations zone, less than an hour's walk from the guerrilla command post and the Radio Venceremos broadcasting center in the hamlet of La Guacamaya. To explain that circumstance returns us, once again, to a choice between two alternatives: either the victims at El Mozote were religious fundamentalists, politically naive but also politically neutral, or the victims were FMLN combatants and/or collaborators.

We know now (many of us were pretty sure that we knew then) that the government's version, that the victims were guerrilla collaborators, was false. Forensic anthropologists excavating the El Mozote sacristy between October and December 1992 unearthed the remains of at least 143 persons in a primary burial. Seven were adults. The remaining 136 were adolescents, children, or infants, with an average age of 6 years (Kirsch-

ner et al. 1993:1). At least 43 skeletons displayed bullet wounds in the head
or thorax that could have caused death (Fondebrider, Bernardi, and
Doretti 1993:7). It was clear that some people were shot while lying on the
ground, because the bullets dented the stone floor after passing through
the bodies.

The human rights community and other interested parties would like
to obtain clear-cut answers about what happened at El Mozote, before as
well as during the massacre. But the reality of El Mozote was a very complex one that we will never fully fathom. The primary cultural and historical knowledge necessary for a reconstruction went to the grave with
the inhabitants, survivors such as "Chepe Mozote" (the wartime pseudo-
nym assigned to José Guevara, only nine years old at the time of the massacre) and Rufina Amaya notwithstanding. And besides, social science,
despite the claims of many of its practitioners, lacks an unequivocal
means of organizing and analyzing such knowledge so as to eliminate or
neutralize the subjective interests of the researcher. Nonetheless, I do believe that a case can be made that El Mozote's population was more politically diverse than has been previously portrayed, and that neither religious innocence nor collaborative guilt accounts for the activities of the
population during the years and months leading up to 11 December 1981.

EVANGELICAL PROTESTANTISM IN EL MOZOTE

Claims about El Mozote's evangelical community pervaded the first FMLN
broadcasts about the massacre aired on Radio Venceremos on 24 December 1981 and were disseminated in accounts of the massacre published
by the international press and human rights organizations (FDR/FMLN
1982:13; Americas Watch Committee 1991:49; McClintock 1985:309; Brown
1992:9; Rohter 1996:A4). For instance, on 11 January 1982, an article in *Der
Spiegel* (Bonn, Germany) accused government troops of murdering nine
hundred civilians, and then stated, "They [the victims] were Protestants
and believed themselves safe, for as members of the 75,000 strong evangelical community of El Salvador, the inhabitants of the district of
Mozotes [*sic*] considered themselves neutral" (Burns 1982). More than a
decade later, Mark Danner, in the most detailed attempt to reconstruct
the massacre produced to this date, asserted that El Mozote had been
"uniquely unreceptive" to guerrilla recruiters because "the hamlet was a
strong foothold of the Protestant evangelical movement" (1993:55, 1994:
19). According to Danner, "People had begun to convert as early as the

mid-sixties, and by 1980 it is likely that half or more of the people in El Mozote considered themselves born-again Christians; the evangelicals had their own pastor, and they were known—as were born-again Christians throughout Central America—for their anti-Communism" (1993: 55, 1994:19).

In different contexts, informants as varied as FMLN Comandante "Licho," political organizer "Nolvo," and American photographer Susan Meiselas (who accompanied Raymond Bonner on his trip to the massacre scene in early January 1982) asserted the presence of evangelicals in El Mozote. "Licho" was the most convincing witness: "Everyone knew there were many evangelicals in El Mozote," he told Danner, "and these people wouldn't support us. . . . Sometimes they sold us things, yes, but they didn't want anything to do with us" (Danner 1993:55, 1994:19). Meiselas implied that she could divine evangelicals from their appearance: "We saw about twenty-five houses destroyed around Arambala and Mozote. My strongest memory was this grouping of evangelicals, fourteen of them, who had come together thinking their faith would protect them. They were strewn across the earth next to this cornfield, and you could see on their faces the horror of what had happened to them" (1994:99).

It is somewhat surprising, then, to find that these views are not pressed upon visitors to El Mozote. Visitors neither see nor learn of the remains of a Protestant church with the size and "grandeur," not to mention the central location—just off the main plaza, a few meters from the casa comunal—of the Catholic Church of the Three Kings. And notwithstanding her testimony about the heroic death of a supposedly Protestant girl who, according to the soldiers who raped and killed her, continued to sing hymns even after being shot twice in the stomach, Rufina Amaya, in her role as guide, witness, and moral conscience to what occurred at El Mozote, consistently informs delegations of foreigners who solicit her views that the deceased were *both* Catholic *and* politically uninvolved.

Like Amaya, other former residents (some of whom have repopulated the hamlet) insist that El Mozote was overwhelmingly Catholic and are hard pressed to name more than a few Protestant families. In numerous conversations, survivors told me that El Mozote–area Protestants numbered between fifteen and twenty and resided in Tierra Colorada, a neighboring hamlet within the jurisdiction of Arambala. There a group of Seventh-Day Adventists worshiped in a small adobe church under the tutelage of their self-appointed minister, Telesforo Claros. Beginning in 1978, Adventist pastors from Mexico visited Tierra Colorada "to get to know the people" and to make more converts. They arrived on foot or by Jeep and stayed for a day or two. A lot of people attended the meetings, but most came from areas outside El Mozote. A few local men with serious personal problems saw the Adventist church as a means of personal salvation from the drinking, smoking, womanizing, and other vices that drained scarce economic resources and caused conflicts within and between families. But some, despite good intentions, were unable to put aside the *güaro* (distilled corn liquor), and they were expelled from the Adventist ranks.

Matilde Claros, who returned in February 1992 with her husband and children to her previous homestead in Tierra Colorada, asserted that the evangelicals could be divided into two categories: those who were sincerely convinced of the Adventist creed and those who were out to save their lives. Those in the second group were "recent arrivals" who gravitated to evangelical Christianity in the months before the massacre because of its politically neutral image.

The authorities treated practicing Catholics as anything *but* politically neutral. By the late 1970s the Catholic Church had been thoroughly tarred with the communist brush by the government, and Catholic catechists in northern Morazán were being systematically tracked down and killed by the army, security forces, and members of the Nationalist Democratic Organization (ORDEN), a nationwide paramilitary organization created in the late 1960s to provide "the eyes and ears of the security system at the grassroots level" (McClintock 1985:66). Many catechists did play key roles as political activists for the Popular Leagues "28 February" (LP-28) and the People's Revolutionary Army (ERP), the dominant FMLN group in northern Morazán. However, the authorities spread such a wide net that even conservative catechists were suspected of collusion with the "terrorists."

Consider the case of José Carmen Romero, the only formally trained and officially recognized El Mozote catechist. Throughout the period when progressive catechists were organizing Christian Base Communities in northern Morazán and preaching the "preferential option for the poor," Romero remained faithful to Father Andrés Argueta and his right-wing, transcendentalist interpretation of Catholicism.[1] Nonetheless, when rumors circulated that the army was looking for him in December 1980, Romero was forced to flee El Mozote for Arambala. He survived the massacre and later sought refuge in San Miguel, where he lives today.

The dangers associated with practicing Catholicism multiplied in

1981, when Rogelio Ponceele, a Belgian priest who arrived in La Guaca-maya to work with the ERP at the end of 1980, began to conduct services in El Mozote (López Vigil 1987:49–51). Radio Venceremos Director "San-tiago" (Carlos Henríquez Consalvi), who accompanied Father Ponceele into the zone from the capital, recalled that Ponceele's initial mass in El Mozote was held on 28 February 1981 to commemorate the fourth an-niversary of the 1977 massacre in San Salvador that gave rise to the founding of the LP-28, the ERP's popular organization. Ponceele also cel-ebrated masses in El Mozote on 24 March and 30 August of the same year. The priest remembered El Mozote as an attractive place:

> I had arrived so many times at this little town. . . . A well populated
> caserío with its little stores. In El Mozote it was even possible to drink
> a coca-cola! And when one comes out of the bush, after two months
> of not leaving from there, to drink a cold soda is like a dream.[2] I went
> there many times and celebrated mass. And the message was always
> about hope. . . . The people met, prayed, sang with "The Torogoces"
> [an FMLN peasant musical group]. It was nice to go to El Mozote.
> (López Vigil 1987:94)

Several people with whom I discussed these masses disagreed about the size and composition of the congregations. Santiago said that 150 to 200 peasants and no more than 10 guerrillas attended the services. Raquel, a church stalwart, stated that local inhabitants were afraid to be seen in the presence of armed combatants and that the majority of the generally small congregation was formed of ERP guerrillas from the La Guacamaya encampment. Less important than the numbers—Santiago and Raquel may, of course, have been referring to different services—is the fact that at least one of Ponceele's masses was broadcast over Radio Venceremos, which was regularly monitored by the army and assidu-ously studied by Lieutenant Colonel Monterrosa, the Atlacatl comman-der (Danner 1993:126, 1994:147).

Many El Mozote residents were scandalized by this turn of events. Prior to the broadcast, the ERP had maintained a low profile in El Mo-zote, avoiding open relations with collaborators to protect them from reprisals. Guerrillas entered the community at night or unarmed and in civilian dress during the day when they purchased goods from Marcos Díaz and other storekeepers. A public mass carried out by a priest who had abandoned his post in Zacamil, a working-class district of San Salvador, to accompany the guerrillas and their civilian entourage could be literally a death warrant for the entire community, or so many people believed. Local participation in the masses was less the issue than fear that the army would take Ponceele's presence there as proof that Catholicism in El Mozote had been given over to guerrilla Catholicism, to Marxism, communism, and all the other "isms" that threatened national security and capital*ism*. Breaking this dangerous identification by converting to the politically safer Seventh-Day Adventist religion was one available response. Even so, the number of converts was not large, according to the former neighbors of the Adventist minister, Telesforo Claros, nowhere near the "half or more of the people in El Mozote" asserted by Danner.

Few "convinced" Adventists died at El Mozote, but many Protestants *were* killed, according to Favio Argueta, a former catechist and ERP activist who worked in northern Morazán in the late 1970s, in the massacre at Cerro Pando on 13 December, which occurred as part of the same Atlacatl operation (cf. Tutela Legal 1991:55–57). Whether events at Cerro Pando and El Mozote became confused after the fact is uncertain. Of greater importance than the origin of the evangelical theory are its political implications. Many social scientists maintain that the widespread evangelical belief that God places rulers in power and only God can remove them leads most evangelicals to eschew oppositional politics (Annis 1987; Simons 1986; Stoll 1988, 1993:260–262; but cf. Lancaster 1988: 115–121). The repression of theological conservatives would therefore be counterproductive to a government confronted with a leftist revolutionary threat. When such repression occurs, as it sometimes does, it underscores the degree to which a government has lost its capacity to distinguish potential supporters from probable adversaries.

THE ERP AND CATHOLICISM IN EL MOZOTE

El Mozote is often written about as though the Atlacatl wiped out an entire community, killing everyone except for Rufina Amaya, "Chepe Mozote," and a few survivors who left on the eve of the massacre. This exaggerates what was, nonetheless, a horrible event. And those who write about the local peasants' having ignored several years of severe repression in northern Morazán out of a belief that they were insulated by their religious beliefs demean their intelligence. In reality, no part of northern Morazán was spared from the conflict of the late 1970s and early 1980s, although certain areas were affected more than others.

In northern Morazán, the hand of repression struck hardest in the rural areas of municipalities where the ERP had consolidated its organization of military committees and its civilian front group, the LP-28. The earliest centers of organization were El Progreso in Torola, Santa Anita in Jocoaitique, and La Laguna in Villa El Rosario. All were poor, dispersed, agriculturally based communities with minimal transportation, educational, and health services. They were also areas where Miguel Ventura, a progressive priest who entered northern Morazán in 1973, promoted Christian Base Communities through the medium of local peasant catechists.

With Father Ventura's arrival, the Church subdivided the Jocoaitique parish, which had previously encompassed all eight northern Morazanian municipalities, and created a new parish for Ventura with its center in Torola (see chapter 2, map 2). The Torola parish consisted of the municipalities of Torola, San Fernando, and Villa El Rosario. The Jocoaitique parish was reduced to Perquín, Arambala, Joateca, Jocoaitique, and Meanguera. Andrés Argueta remained in charge there.

Argueta was Ventura's uncle (his mother's brother) and played an important role in Ventura's decision to enter the priesthood. But the two were members of different generations and over the years had grown far apart ideologically. Argueta remained a traditionalist who sought to distance the church and his parishioners from politics (and thereby bind them all the more tightly to the system); he basked in the authority that accompanied his office and wielded that authority for personal enrichment, charging high fees for presiding at weddings and saint's day masses, and lower ones for baptisms.[3]

Miguel Ventura was trained in San Salvador in the seminary of San José de la Montaña with and by men who later dedicated their lives to (and often sacrificed them in the name of) bringing about progressive change: Ignacio Ellacuría, Jon Sobrino, Rutilio Grande, Armando López, and others.[4] Ventura was born into a family of merchant farmers in Yayantique, La Unión, and exhibited from an early age an organic connection with the country's rural poor. It could probably be argued that he had assumed concretely the "preferential option for the poor" long before he learned about it in seminary. Ventura opposed hierarchy and the elevation of the priest above the congregation, and he set about developing a Christian practice that reflected a more egalitarian set of values. He visited the most remote hamlets on a regular basis, presided over services without charge, and related with his flock as an equal rather than a superior. Given the differences in ideology and personal style, it was inevitable that uncle and nephew would clash (Ventura 1991).

The ideological conflict was also waged via the catechists sent by each priest to El Castaño, Guadalupe, Los Naranjos, and other church training centers. Several weeks each year Ventura went to El Castaño and taught classes to peasant trainees. On his return he regularly met with catechists in the Torola parish to consolidate the progressive ideology imparted at the training centers. By contrast, Argueta struggled to return progressively trained catechists to the conservative fold by monitoring their activities and pushing them toward politically acceptable ends.

As a result, Torola developed into a regional center of catechism and a place where catechists in Ventura's parish met to exchange ideas about community service and social and economic development, as well to discuss the Bible and interpret the word of God. The message of a New Society spread beyond Torola into Jocoaitique, and placed Argueta on the defensive. He responded by investing more energy in defending his domain. Conflicts between uncle and nephew became more frequent and increasingly intense.

In the mid-1970s, Rafael Arce Zablah, one of the founders of the ERP, introduced the idea of armed rebellion into northern Morazán. When Arce died in combat in 1975, responsibility for linking regional military committees to the urban ERP leadership fell to "Chele Cesar" (Santo Lino Ramírez) and "Balta" (Juan Ramón Medrano) (Medrano and Raudales 1994:66–77). The first northern Morazanians to join the ERP military committees were peasant catechists trained in El Castaño and linked to Miguel Ventura. In general, the ERP's popular base in northern Morazán developed in accordance with the strength of progressive Christianity: the areas of weakest progressive development were those in which the repressive forces were strongest and where Argueta had succeeded in consolidating his influence—above all, the municipalities of Arambala, Perquín, and Joateca.[5]

Although the municipality of Meanguera, where El Mozote was located, was part of the parish of Jocoaitique and was thus under Father Argueta's authority, the "preferential option for the poor" developed considerable influence there, promoted by Favio Argueta (no relationship to Father Argueta), "Felipe" (Andrés Barrera), and other catechists trained in El Castaño.[6] Progressive Christian work in Meanguera got a boost when Argueta was accused of collaborating with the sacristan in the Santa Catarina church located in the Meanguera town center to steal a valuable chalice. The chalice was returned, but the attempted theft alienated the population and Argueta abandoned the community to Ventura and catechists linked to him. In this way Cerro Pando, La Joya, and other cantones of Meanguera in Argueta's ecclesiastical domain became incorporated into the progressive Christian Base Community movement.

However, Argueta never lost control over El Mozote, which was situated at Meanguera's northern border with Arambala and was attended by a loyal catechist, José Carmen Romero, supported by his brother, Daniel, who served as a mayordomo. Neither man was ideologically conservative, but they respected Argueta and feared the consequences of challenging him. José Carmen, who "was in agreement with the changes [that accompanied liberation theology] but did not submit to them" (author interview with "Nolvo," 23 July 1993), left El Mozote for Arambala in December 1980, when rumors circulated that the army was looking for him. Daniel dropped discussion of social issues from his religious practice after his son, Atilio, who had joined the ERP, went over to the army in August 1981.[7] The progressive catechist Andrés Barrera, who attended El Castaño in 1970 at the age of thirty-four, occasionally preached in the El Mozote church, but his residence in La Guacamaya and identification with that "less advanced" area (see below) probably blunted his impact.

Miguel Ventura told me that before the war, he never appeared in person in El Mozote, which was too close to Argueta's Jocoaitique redoubt. Opportunities for him to do so ended in 1975, when Bishop Ramón Álvarez, a conservative in charge of the Diocese of San Miguel and Ventura's superior, reassigned him, probably at Argueta's request, to Osicala, located on the lower slopes of Cerro Cacahuatique south of the Torola River.[8]

In the late 1970s Favio Argueta of the town of Meanguera and "Nolvo" of La Joya became the ERP political organizers in the area of El Mozote. Both had kinship connections with residents there, but distance and other obligations limited them to occasional visits.[9] "Nolvo" was responsible for organizing the inhabitants in a huge territory that included the entirety of Cantón La Guacamaya, other sections of Meanguera, Agua Blanca and Calavera in Cacaopera, and the municipalities of Corinto and Joateca. The size of his territory impeded his work. Organizing work was also impeded by the rudimentary state of the transport system and, especially in El Mozote, by the absence of progressive Christian Base Communities, which might have served as seedbeds of political activism as they did elsewhere in northern Morazán, and more generally in El Salvador (Pearce 1986; Montgomery 1982). According to "Nolvo," the ERP recruited on the margins of El Mozote, but failed to penetrate the Plain, which was inhabited by the wealthiest and most influential families. By late 1981, he estimated that about forty men and women from El Mozote had integrated into ERP militias, civilian forces that carried out local operations. Compared to the widespread support obtained in La Guacamaya, Torola, Jocoaitique, and elsewhere, this was only a minor accomplishment for the ERP.

Few people were willing to directly risk becoming victims of repression by joining a militia, but many did collaborate by providing the guerrillas with food, labor, and money. A former combatant who worked in supply and who left El Mozote the day before the massacre reported that crews of up to thirty people labored in trapiches producing *panela* for the guerrilla army. Marcos Díaz regularly sold to the guerrillas, although he sold to the army as well. One informant said that Díaz liked the army but that he liked the guerrillas more. José María Márquez and Israel Márquez were dependable contributors of food and clothing. Many men and women in the community gave food—ten *atados* (about seven kilos) of panela or an *almud* (twelve kilos) of corn—when asked to do so. Socrates Ceballos, a member of the cooperative, even assisted in the clandestine excavation of a tunnel in Cerro Cruz intended to provide a safe refuge for local sympathizers in case the community was shelled by artillery or bombed from the air.

These actions, risky though they may have been, masked a range of political positions. Some survivors stated that they contributed because they believed in the struggle but were unable to take up arms due to advanced age, poor health, or family obligations. Others complied with requests because they feared the consequences of refusing. For instance, Ramón Gallegos, a wealthy peasant, complained to me that the guerrillas forced him to sell them a cow at below market price. He didn't want to, but he did it. The same people who helped the guerrillas like this also cooperated with the army during its frequent operations in the area. Thus a large (though indeterminate) proportion of the population of El Mozote felt squeezed *entre la espina y la espada* (between the thorn and the sword), and was only trying to "make out" or survive by taking what were considered necessary actions.

SURVIVAL

Because of the escalating violence in northern Morazán, many political conservatives had already left El Mozote as much as a year or more before the massacre, and some political radicals had joined the ranks of the guerrillas. About half the owners or residents of homes located in the Plain survived the massacre because they were not present in December 1981. As in the rest of the zone, the wealthier people went to San Salvador or San Miguel and the poorer ones to Honduras, San Francisco Gotera, or municipal centers such as Jocoaitique or Perquín, which were then guarded by detachments from the National Guard, the Treasury Police, and the army (Binford 1992). Several El Mozote merchants, such as Eloy Márquez, lived because they were away on buying trips; other residents were working in the northern mountains along the Honduran border sawing lumber or otherwise engaged in dry-season labor. Many people who abandoned their homes did so because they feared the ERP, which, despite its encampment in La Guacamaya and contacts within the community, remained a shadow organization for many people until after it seized control of northern Morazán during the Comandante Gonzalo campaign that began in June of 1982 (on that campaign see Villalobos 1982 and "Comandante Gonzalo . . ." 1982). But most were fleeing government repression or the threat of it. This last point is worth elaboration.

The El Mozote massacre was not the first massacre in northern Morazán, but was merely the first massacre that was widely enough reported to attract the attention of the international community. The carnage there began in 1976 with individual assassinations perpetrated by the National Guard, the Treasury Police, and death squads. The first massacres in northern Morazán—murders raised a power of ten—took place in early 1980, shortly before Napoleón Duarte entered the civilian-military junta and announced economic reforms in March of that year. Documentation of these events did not begin until prior to the signing of the 1992 Peace Accords, when the human rights commissions of Segundo Montes and of the Community Development Council of Morazán and San Miguel (PADECOMSM) compiled testimony relating to human rights violations. With the cease-fire and installation of the United Nations Truth Commission, many more people began to come forward and the magnitude of government repression became better known.[10]

According to testimony taken by the Human Rights Commission of Segundo Montes, 6 people were massacred in Villa El Rosario on 17 July 1979; several dozen (the numbers vary from 19 persons to 30 families) were killed and burned by the Treasury Police in Torola on 20 January 1980; in July of 1980 more than 20 people met their deaths in Los Golondrinas, a hamlet in cantón Zapotal of Jocoaitique. Several massacres were perpetrated during the first big military invasion of northern Morazán, which took place in October 1980. The largest of these occurred at Villa

Table 1   Massacres in Northern Morazán, 1980–81

Hamlet, Municipality	Date	# Victims	Party Responsible
1. La Guacamaya, Mean.	11/80	15	?
2. Villa El Rosario, V.E.R.	1/20/80	?	Civil Defense
3. Agua Blanca, Cacao.	3/10/80	20	Atlacatl Bat.
4. Flor Muerto, Cacao.	4/22/80	20	Atlacatl Bat.
5. Azacualpa, Torola	10/80	12	?
6. Villa El Rosario, V.E.R.	10/5/80	15–25	Hammer and Anvil Bat.
7. Villa El Rosario, V.E.R.	10/12–16/80	100	Atlacatl Bat.
8. La Guacamaya, Mean.	10/13, 24/80	18	Atlacatl Bat. and Arce Bat.
9. El Tule, Torola	12/19–20/80	10–20	Atlacatl Bat.
10. Los Golondrinas, Joco.	1980	40–50	?
11. Villa El Rosario, V.E.R.	1/20/81	20	Atlacatl Bat.
12. Agua Blanca, Cacao.	3/10/81	20	Atlacatl Bat.
13. Flor Blanca, Cacao.	3/10/81	20	Atlacatl Bat.
14. Flor Muerto, Cacao.	3/16/81	31	Atlacatl Bat.
15. Villa El Rosario, V.E.R.	7/81	22	Atlacatl Bat.
16. Flor Muerto, Cacao.	12/8–12/81	20	Atlacatl Bat.
17. Cerro El Ortiz, Cacao.	12/12/81	8–10	?
18. El Junquillo, Cacao.	12/12/81	50–55	?
19. El Mozote, Mean.	12/11–13/81	1,000 (est.)	Atlacatl Bat.
20. El Mono, Aram.	11/82	11	Civil Defense

Source: Human Rights Archives of the Human Rights Commission of Segundo Montes.
Note: Three cantones of Cacaopera—Agua Blanca, El Junquillo, and Guachipilín—lie north of the Torola River. The town of Cacaopera and four additional cantones under its jurisdiction lie south of the river.

El Rosario, where about 100 people were shot to death (see Mena Sandoval 1991:204). And on 12 March 1981, over 40 women and children at El Junquillo were bayoneted to death by soldiers under the command of Capt. Napoleón Medina Garay, a psychopathic killer known to northern Morazanians as "the butcher of Junquillo" (López Vigil 1991:274; United Nations 1993:66–68). I have listed only a few of the massacres that occurred in northern Morazán between January 1980 and December 1981 in table 1. Inhabitants of El Mozote, located less than an hour's walk north of the FMLN command post at La Guacamaya, did not have to receive notice of every atrocity to know that the area of Morazán north of the Torola River was becoming a very dangerous place in which to live.

The army punished Andrés Barrera, the La Guacamaya catechist who frequently preached in the Three Kings church, by murdering thirteen members of his family. He testified before the Truth Commission in 1992 as follows:

> On the thirteenth of October 1980, well-armed, uniformed soldiers of the Atlacatl and Arce Battalions entered Cantón Guacamaya in the Jurisdiction of Meanguera of the Department of Morazán. All the victims mentioned above [in the document] were slaughtered with light arms and machine gunned, and after being assassinated were brutally reduced to ashes in the homes where the acts occurred. Among the victims were men, women, children, and a pregnant woman. The remains were buried three days after the massacre.

The October massacre in Villa El Rosario, the largest massacre prior to that in El Mozote, was denounced by Feliciano García and three other persons on 28 July 1992:

> On 16 October 1980 at 12:30 P.M., soldiers of the Atlacatl Battalion and other battalions of the same units entered Villa El Rosario and captured, among others, the youth Feliciano García. The youth and the rest of the captured persons were led to the plaza of the stated community, where they were obliged to arrange themselves in a file. They [the army soldiers] threw them to the ground face down and pointing at them with their rifles and with bayonets at the back of the neck, submitted them to vigorous interrogations and forced them to admit to the accusations. In said plaza there were around two hundred captured men of distinct ages. Some of them attempted to flee and were immediately assassinated by the soldiers. Of the rest, some were liberated after nine hours of tortures, and others were assassinated. Feliciano García was liberated at 3 P.M. the same day, badly bruised.
>
> More than one hundred of the two hundred men who were captured with Feliciano García were assassinated. The soldiers forced their victims to dig their own graves, where they were assassinated after being badly beaten and tortured. (Denunciation by Amadio Carillo, Nemesio Carillo, Lorenzo Hernández, and Feliciano García, 28 July 1992, Archives of the Human Rights Commission of Segundo Montes)

Table 2   Killings by Military and Security Forces in Northern Morazán

Time Period	# Massacres	# Victims	Mean Victims	Other Killings	Total Victims
1980	10	265	29.4	142	407
1981 (Jan.–Nov.)	5	113	22.6	60	173
1981 (Dec.)	4	1081	218.0	3	1084
1982–1991	1	11	11.0	109	120
Total	20	1470	73.5	314	1784

Source: Calculations based on material in the Human Rights Archives of the Human Rights Commission of Segundo Montes.

Accounts like these could be multiplied many times over, since for each massacre in table 1, testimony was taken from at least one (and in some cases six or seven) witnesses, who were present during the incident or came along shortly afterward. Few of these human rights violations were denounced during the years in which they occurred. Given this history of widespread human rights abuse, it is clear that the massacre at El Mozote was *not* an aberration. Massacres, even if of modest proportions by comparison (and there is certainly nothing modest about the wholesale torture and murder of a hundred, or even ten, unarmed people), were regularly occurring features of life in northern Morazán for about two and one-half years before the human rights catastrophe that accompanied Operation Rescue. And these massacres were preceded by numerous killings and disappearances on a smaller scale. This material provides evidence for McClintock's (1985:299) contention that "[i]nitially, the execution of counter-terror after October 1979 differed little from that under the Romero government; the difference was essentially one of scale."

Table 2 summarizes the results, by no means complete, of my effort to gauge the level of killing on the part of the military and security forces in northern Morazán during the course of the war, with particular emphasis on the period from 1 January 1980 to 30 November 1981. The massacre at El Mozote and other Operation Rescue massacres have been categorically isolated in order to examine the level of violation against the right to life prior to December 1981. This table indicates that the first 23 months of the 1980–81 period resulted in 580 victims, of whom 65 percent, or 378, were killed in 15 massacres (defined here as the collective murder of 10 or more persons).[11] Of those 15 massacres, 7 occurred in the municipality of Cacaopera and 5 in Villa El Rosario.

Witnesses blamed the Atlacatl for 10 massacres, despite the fact that 6 of the 10 occurred before March 1981, when the Atlacatl entered into active duty following its training by a U.S. military training team.[12] The battalion had established such a widespread reputation for brutality that witnesses giving testimony in 1992 about acts that occurred at the beginning of the preceding decade blamed the Atlacatl for brutal and inhumane acts carried out before it had even been formed. By the end of the war more human rights violations were attributed to the Atlacatl than to any other military unit (United Nations 1993, app. 5).

Until December 1981 El Mozote escaped the mass violence that shook the municipalities of Villa El Rosario, Jocoaitique, Torola, Cacaopera, and the southern and western sections of Meanguera. Danner even claims that El Mozote escaped incidents of war-related violent death altogether, which I have found to be untrue. He portrays El Mozote as an island of placidity in a tumultuous sea of violence and social conflict:

> Only the month before [the massacre], soldiers had come during an operation and occupied El Chingo and La Cruz, two hills overlooking the town, and though the people of El Mozote could hear mortars and scattered shooting in the distance, the soldiers had not bothered them. In the crazy-quilt map of northern Morazán in 1981, where villages "belonged" to the government or to the guerrillas or to neither or to both, where the officers saw the towns and hamlets in varying shades of pink and red, El Mozote had not been known as a guerrilla town. (1993:54, 1994:17)[13]

But if El Mozote "had not been known as a guerrilla town," a position held by the Left as well, how are we to account for the fifteen (minimum) murders and assassinations that occurred there between January 1980 and early December 1981? Discussions with current and former residents of El Mozote and with former ERP activists who worked in the zone indicate that these killings were carried out on the one side by the army, security forces, and paramilitary groups linked to them, and on the other side by the ERP in its campaign to eliminate *orejas* (informers).

The first major act of violence in El Mozote took place in February 1980, when security forces captured three young men in Meanguera. The agents took the captives to the El Mozote cemetery, where they killed them, burned their bodies, and left the charred remains in the open as a

warning to the inhabitants of La Guacamaya, according to several informants. On the 28th of February, rockets lit up the sky from hamlets
throughout La Guacamaya as the ERP formally announced its presence
on the third anniversary of the massacre in the Plaza Libertad following
the government's 1977 electoral fraud. Later that year military personnel
accused Nicolás Márquez, a traveling salesman, of supplying goods to the
guerrillas and warned him to leave the region. When he failed to do so,
he was picked up and assassinated in the plaza of Jocoaitique while in
town to register the sale of a steer. Also in 1980 the brothers Francisco
and Eulogio Márquez Chicas were killed by the Armed Forces in separate
incidents. Over the course of the following year Mercedes Pereira was
disappeared, also in Jocoaitique, and the army killed José Rufino Claros,
husband of Raquel Romero, during an operation in Jocote Amarillo.
With the exception of the young men from Meanguera, all of these victims were El Mozote natives.

The ERP blamed local informers for *señalando* (pointing out) peasants and workers in El Mozote and elsewhere, and responded with a regional campaign to eliminate them. Many of the informers had joined
ORDEN and exploited the power of the position and their contacts in the
military to personal advantage. The first people killed by the ERP, according to informants, were Anacleto Claros, accused of being an in-
former for the military, and Juan Márquez, who was innocent of wrongdoing and died in the grenade blast that took Anacleto's life. Various
informants also mentioned that Onofre Vigil, Luís Márquez, Eustacio
Vigil, "Moncho" Márquez, and "Chango" Chicas were also killed by the
ERP, as were Mateo Romero and his son Santos Romero, José Baldome
Orellana Márquez, Chepe Pascal, and Doroteo Pérez. In some cases the
ERP warned accused informers to leave the region and gave them an opportunity to do so; refusals were met with summary executions, which
were publicly rationalized at meetings or on handbills. Some degree of
investigation of the cases usually preceded judgment. Nonetheless, it is
clear that in such a confused and tension-ridden social climate, mistakes
were made and excesses were committed; some ERP operatives eliminated not only informers, but alleged thieves, cardsharps, and other socially marginalized persons. Not one of the assassinations mentioned
here found its way into the files of either the Truth Commission in
1992 or the Human Rights Committee of El Salvador, Nongovernmental
(CDHES-NG), a point that raises questions about the accuracy of the generally accepted figure of 75,000 war-related deaths produced by Tutela

Legal, Americas Watch, and other human rights organizations. The actual toll was probably substantially higher.

The contest between government-linked forces and the ERP was repeated in virtually every community in northern Morazán during 1980 and 1981. One result, as might be anticipated, was the inculcation of a climate of fear that affected all civilians, the politically uncommitted as well as those who had taken and were defending sides. No one was immune from the violence. An argument with a neighbor, a conflict over a debt, or an insult made under the influence of *güaro* might lead the aggrieved party to tell a soldier, a guardsman, or a government official that person X or Y was engaging in suspicious behavior. That could be enough to seal one's fate, since government forces seldom sought to investigate the charges, and "innocent until proven guilty" was not a principle recognized by the military, security forces, or ORDEN civilian irregulars.

Fear spurred a large-scale exodus of people from northern Morazán to refuges in Honduras and elsewhere, to displaced-persons camps in El Salvador, to major regional cities such as San Francisco Gotera and San Miguel, and to San Salvador. The flight began in early 1980 but intensified after a massive military operation in October 1980 that lasted twenty-two days, involved two thousand army and security-force troops, and was accompanied by intense artillery bombardment of the conflictive areas. Government forces committed at least three massacres during the operation. The poor inhabitants of most rural areas were forced into the municipal centers, which were guarded by detachments from the army and security forces as well as civilians organized, often against their will, into Civil Defense units similar to the Civil Patrols that still exist in rural Guatemala.

The National Commission for Assistance to the Displaced Population (CONADES), a government agency created to deal with displaced persons during the war, estimated that as of December 1981 (prior to the El Mozote massacre), 29,790 Morazanians had been displaced from their homes by the violence, almost half (14,092) from municipalities in northern Morazán (CONADES 1982). Eighteen months later, the numbers had swollen to 75,734 for the department and 28,298 for northern Morazán (CONADES 1983).[14] By June 1983 five displaced-persons *asentamientos* (settlements) existed in the vicinity of San Francisco Gotera. They contained almost six thousand people, a number of whom were from El Mozote (Americas Watch Committee and Lawyers Committee for International Human Rights 1984:39). As discussed in chapter 3, Todd Greentree and Maj. John McKay interviewed several of these people (which ones are unknown) on 30 January 1981 during their investigation of the massacre for the U.S. Embassy (Danner 1993:103–105, 1994:106–108).

As a result of government repression, the FMLN response to it, military invasions, bombings, and other conflict-related threats to life and limb, most of the people living in El Mozote elected to abandon the community before December 1981. Table 3 summarizes the results of fourteen genealogies, compiled from interviews with former residents. Shelli McMillen, my field assistant, and I asked informants to enumerate family members living at the time the massacre occurred. Each genealogy focused on the descendants of a founding patriarch and matriarch, and encompassed three to four generations.[15] Overall, 29 percent, or 168 of the 586 people included in the sample, died in the massacre at El Mozote. Nine others were victims of government repression before the massacre; many of them were captured and killed while away from the community, in Jocoaitique, Perquín, or elsewhere. At least 10 additional people died in war-related violence following the massacre, usually in combat while fighting on the side of the FMLN. If these figures can be taken as representative, then 70 percent of the prewar inhabitants had either deliberately abandoned the community because of the deteriorating political situation (the majority) by the time the Atlacatl Battalion arrived or were absent because they were working elsewhere (a minority). Some left in 1980, a year or more before the massacre; others fled hours or even minutes ahead of the invading troops.[16]

Though about a third of the prewar El Mozote residents were killed, losses varied widely among different extended family units. Three of the fourteen extended families in the sample lost less than 10 percent of their members; in one case everyone survived. At the other extreme fall three other extended family units, in which more than 60 percent of the members were slaughtered. Thus, while all survivors have been deeply affected by the deaths, and everyone lost relations of some degree in this highly endogamous community, some lost more than others.

The point can be illustrated by examining the genealogies of the extended family units of two brothers (figs. 5 and 6): TM (no. 2 in table 3) and NM (no. 4 in table 3). Although TM's extended family unit suffered six deaths during the war—one person assassinated by the army in October 1980, three more murdered in the massacre, and two who died fighting to overthrow the regime—each of his six children left some descendants. Compare this to the tragic fates of NM and Catalina, whose line is

Table 3 Genealogical Survey of Sample of Former El Mozote Residents

Extended Family Unit	# Members in Unit	# Members Living in Dec. 1981	Total Mozote Massacre Deaths	% Mozote Massacre Deaths	Before Mozote Massacre	After Mozote Massacre
			Estimates of % Dying at Mozote		Other War-Related Deaths	
1. JSC	48	48	25	52.1	0	2
2. TM	43	41	3	7.3	1	2
3. EM	35	34	13	38.2	2	0
4. NM	23	23	14	60.9	0	0
5. MAO	27	27	10	37.0	0	0
6. RC	88	84	30	34.1	0	0
7. FC	61	54	4	7.4	1	3
8. JCR	41	37	13	35.1	2	0
9. FA	29	25	16	64.0	0	0
10. JAD	28	25	16	64.0	0	0
11. CM	29	28	8	28.6	0	2
12. EM	71	65	7	10.8	1	0
13. VM	71	64	9	14.1	2	0
14. JEC	33	31	0	0.0	0	1
Total	627	586	168	28.6	9	10

Source: Based on interviews conducted by author and Shelli McMillen in 1993.

survived only by Anastacio and his five children, and by one orphaned child left by Maximino. Should Anastacio return to resettle El Mozote, he will have to do so without the assistance of his three brothers, whose remains probably lie somewhere beneath the grassy surface of the gently sloping area between Cerro Cruz and Cerro Chingo.[17]

THOSE WHO REMAINED

Given the high levels of repression in the region in 1980 and 1981, which included more than fifteen killings in El Mozote, and the exodus of two-thirds of the community's inhabitants, why, then, did *anyone* remain? And what of the political leanings of those who did? Fear was pervasive among the inhabitants, especially after the army operations of October

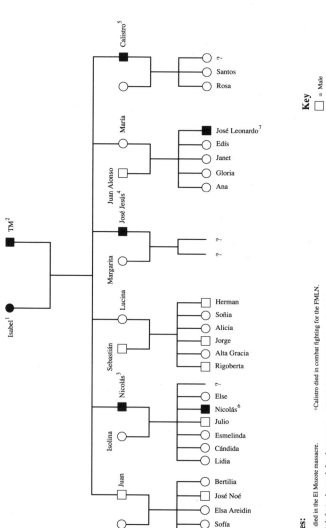

Key

☐ = Male

○ = Female

■ or ● = Deceased

Notes:

[1] Isabel died in the El Mozote massacre.

[2] TM died of natural causes before the massacre.

[3] Nicolás Sr. was assassinated in Jocoaitique 30 October 1980 by the army while obtaining a document required to sell a steer.

[4] José Jesús was killed by the Atlacatl in Arambala on 10 December 1981.

[5] Calistro died in combat fighting for the FMLN.

[6] Nicolás Jr. was one year old when he died in the El Mozote massacre; he was being cared for by Daniel Romero.

[7] José Leonardo died in combat fighting for the FMLN.

FIGURE 5 Genealogical chart of descendants of TM and Isabel.

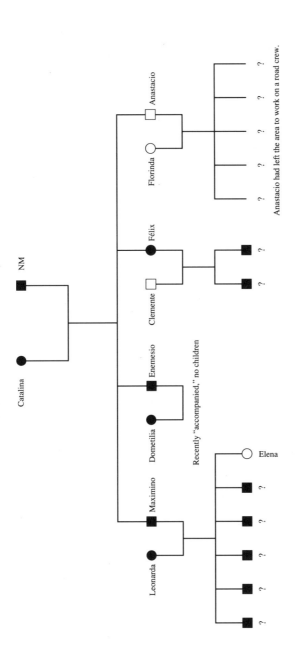

Note:
All deceased persons died in the El Mozote massacre.

FIGURE 6 Genealogical chart of descendants of NM and Catalina.

1980 and March 1981. The military frequently bombarded La Guacamaya from artillery positions in Osicala south of the Torola River, La Planta in Jocoaitique, and Quebrachos, Meanguera. An occasional shell overflew the target area to fall near houses on the outskirts of El Mozote. The hamlet's school shut down after the 1980–81 school year, and in August 1981 an air force bombing left a gaping hole in one of the building's walls.[18] Also, soldiers entered El Mozote on various occasions en route to "search-and-destroy" missions in La Guacamaya. The troops solicited food and information from inhabitants but otherwise tended to leave them alone. Most of the captures and disappearances took place outside the community center or on its periphery. A few people were grabbed and murdered, even in broad daylight, but the majority of the politically "undecided" population had no way of knowing whether or not the accusations that the victims had collaborated with the guerrillas were merited, since the ERP maintained a low profile there. In my view many residents were waiting the situation out and hoping that things would improve. No one—army, ERP combatants, civilians—could have predicted at that time that the Salvadoran civil war would endure for another ten years, that more than 75,000 people would be killed (and 7,000 disappeared), or that the war would end with the signing of United Nations–brokered Peace Accords between the government and the FMLN.

It was risky to stay, but we must recognize that it was risky, a different sort of risky, to leave. Where to go? What to do? How to live? Home, family, relationships, land, and history were tied to El Mozote. In most cases to abandon the area meant to cut oneself off from an established life and to start again with few resources in a strange place—to become a "displaced" person or a "refugee," terms that reference both movement and loss. To minimize these losses many of the people who fled El Mozote entrusted relatives with their homes, animals, and other possessions. The caretakers understood that eventually the owners would return to reassume their lives. Some people, to avoid the risk of material losses, chose not to leave at all.

In April 1981 Rogelio Chávez of La Ranchería went to Lourdes in La Libertad to earn money for the spring corn planting. His wife, María, followed in September with other members of the family. They left the property in the care of two sons and several sons-in-law, all of whom were killed in the Chávez house in La Ranchería. Marcos Díaz's mother pressured him to leave, but he stayed because he accepted an officer's promise that nothing would happen, and also because he had no one to mind the store in his absence. Matilde Claros, who lived in Tierra Colorada, was reluctant to abandon home and animals despite rumors of a possible massacre. She was preparing to go to the Plain one day when her husband, Fernando Rojas, confronted her with a choice: "Stay if you want," he said, "but the children go with me." The whole family left just ahead of the soldiers. They met up with other civilians and crossed the Sapo River at Las Pilas, then ascended into the hills on the other side toward Rancho Quemado, northeast of Perquín. From several miles' distance they watched dozens of *zopes* (turkey vultures) circle over the community. "If you had stayed," he told her, "you probably would have died."

A most surprising encounter occurred between Shelli McMillen and Susana, a woman who lost her Aunt Ermelinda and two cousins (Ermelinda's children): Alejandro, who was mute, and Roberto, who was deaf. (Deaf, dumb, incapacitated, mentally retarded—the old, infirm, and handicapped received no more consideration from the Atlacatl than did the wholesome of body and mind.) Susana stated that she had tried unsuccessfully to convince Ermelinda to leave. Susana was afraid of both the soldiers and the guerrillas since "both killed people," though she feared the army less because "one can talk to them with trust."

"But how can this be?" Shelli asked. "The soldiers killed over a thousand people here." Susana became very passionate and angry, and cried through the next part: "The soldiers warned people to leave Morazán, but they didn't because they didn't want to leave their *things*. People are more important. I don't have my things anymore, but I have my life."

Fear of abandoning their meager possessions, their "things," and taking off for parts unknown was one reason people stayed. The FMLN guides who offered to lead people to safe zones refused to allow them to take with them farm animals and other bulky possessions. Another related reason was that some of the most influential and respected people in the community—Israel Márquez, José María Márquez, Santos Márquez, and Marcos Díaz—also stayed and, of course, died. Among the wealthier store owners, only Alfredo Benítez, who was on a buying trip, survived. Had Israel (then eighty years old), José María, and especially Marcos Díaz taken flight, they surely would have had company. With valuable property, much of it perishable (stock) or at least destructible (homes, tools, domestic animals), El Mozote's petty bourgeoisie had the most to lose by abandoning the area. Wealth was an adhesive, binding them to hearth and home; through its effect on them, it bound others as well.

Finally, several informants stated that they were discouraged from leaving by the guerrillas, who were, at the time, poorly armed and supplied, and were desperately in need of the goods and labor that local civilian collaborators provided and the food and manufactured goods (e.g., clothing and shoes) that local merchants like Marcos Díaz sold to them. After the militarization of northern Morazanian towns in late 1980, it became impossible to openly purchase food, clothing, and medical supplies in bulk without being suspected of collaboration. The situation in Perquín, an important market town about five miles northwest of El Mozote, was the norm throughout the zone in 1981 and 1982. Heriberto, a peasant and woodcutter, spoke to me on 7 October 1992 of his experience during the period:

> Those who came to Perquín from outside to purchase goods were placed under suspicion. For that reason we couldn't go there to buy. People living close to the town purchased because they were seen all the time. . . . So you had to walk confidently into town in order to buy what was needed to treat your children's fever or your own fever. If you arrived in Perquín and began to purchase two injections of something, such as penicillin, there would be other people next to you watching what you were buying, and if they saw that it was a lot, immediately they would run to the Armed Forces and tell them that "so and so is buying so many injections. What do they use them for? They use them for the guerrillas." And then would come the repression.

Fear, suspicion, and a high level of surveillance in the towns limited ERP access to goods through legal channels, especially after October 1980, when much of the formerly clandestine network of the ERP integrated into the FMLN guerrilla force. For this reason I cannot completely rule out the possibility that ERP commanders made a strategic decision to limit organizing in El Mozote to keep supply channels open. The decision not to organize Azacualpa (in the cantón of San Fernando) in the late 1970s might have served as a precedent.[19]

Days before the massacre, however, the FMLN did attempt to warn civilians to leave the area and provided guides to lead them to safety. The FMLN received ample warning of the coming invasion from its intelligence section, which could scarcely miss the movement of thousands of troops and tons of war materiel over the road from San Miguel (Danner 1993:66, 1994:47). Some former combatants even claim that the troop movements and plans, including those to massacre the civilian population, were passed to them by agents within the military; others say that a massacre was only considered a possibility. Whichever the case, "Nolvo" and several other organizers toured the community and warned many of the remaining inhabitants that their lives would be in danger if they remained. In the process, "Nolvo" gathered up members of the local militia and other civilian collaborators from throughout the region, some eleven hundred by his estimate, and marched north across the Sapo River to Rancho Quemado. Yet many people remained unconvinced (and some failed to receive the message). On 23 July 1993 "Nolvo" told me that, confronted with the "contradiction between the position of the Armed Forces [channeled through Marcos Díaz] and our [FMLN] position," they elected to stay.

It is hard to avoid the conclusion, reached by others as well, that the people who died at El Mozote were the least *decidido* ("persuaded," "convinced," but meaning, in this context, "politically committed"), as it is often put in northern Morazán. Some of them favored social change and might even have agreed that armed revolution was the only way left to achieve it, but they had not taken a firm stand. The political situation in the country—and particularly in conflictive areas—had become increasingly polarized, the alternatives for action narrowed to a few: leave the area for the cities or for refuge; actively support the government and seek its protection; or go into the hills with the guerrillas. Prior to the massacre, about 70 percent of the prewar inhabitants of El Mozote left; several dozen of these had enlisted in the ranks of the ERP or supported the government. Those who did none of these things were murdered. To be cold and analytical about it, and using all the advantages that hindsight offers, we could say that those who died misread the situation. Fear of the unknown (or of the known poverty that awaited them), fear of leaving hearth and home and the small stake that they had built up, and an exaggerated trust in the wisdom of the local elite kept them waiting too long.

INVESTIGATION AND JUDGMENT

The killings by the army have traumatized the Salvadorean people. One is very cautious about rising up against the government when one has seen bodies of people sawed in half, bodies placed alive in battery acid or bodies with every bone broken. I saw all those things last year. And I know who did it, and so do the Salvadorean people. So now we will wait and just try to survive, but we will remember.
　　　　　　　　　　　　—Leonel Gómez, quoted in McClintock, *The American Connection*

In a curious way something that everyone knows at some level has a shadowy existence until the moment when it steps boldly onto the stage.
　　　　　　　　　　　　—James Scott, *Domination and the Arts of Resistance*

The United Nations Truth Commission report, *From Madness to Hope,* was released on 15 March 1993 (United Nations 1993); the report placed on center stage the real dimensions of human rights violations in El Salvador during the civil war. The shock value of the report did not derive from the number of cases discussed, for the commission investigated only a small percentage of the murders and assassinations carried out between January 1980 and July 1991, the period covered in the investigation. Nor did it derive from the horror of the events depicted, for horrible events had for many years received ample coverage in national and international media. In fact, El Salvador, second perhaps only to Guatemala in Latin America, had acquired a reputation for horror worthy even of Hollywood treatment, as in Oliver Stone's frenetic, overblown *Salvador,* a revved-up cinematic counterpart to Joan Didion's cynical book by the same name (Didion 1983).[1] In the early 1980s "El Salvador" (or "Salvador"), as these titles suggest, stood in a metonymic relationship with murdered nuns, headless bodies, and mangled corpses. And most people, certainly most people in El Salvador, were very clear about who was responsible for them, even if they weren't publicly saying so for the reasons stated above by Leonel Gómez.

The significance of the Truth Commission's report lay in the commission's official status and accepted neutrality as a product of a United Nations–brokered agreement between the government and the FMLN signed in Mexico on 27 April 1991. The commission was made up of three persons appointed by Javier Pérez de Cuellar, secretary general of the United Nations, and its mandate as spelled out in the Peace Accords was to carry out "the investigation of grave acts of violence occurring since 1980, whose mark on society reclaims with great urgency public knowledge of the truth" (FMLN 1992a:18). The commission members—former Colombian president Belisario Betancur, former Venezuelan foreign minister Reinaldo Figuerado, and an American professor of law from George Washington University, Thomas Burgenthal—were given wide latitude in determining which of the estimated 75,000 deaths and other violations to examine. The commission began work following the signing of the Peace Accords, and with the help of 20 assistants it interviewed more than 2,000 Salvadorans and investigated 22,000 denunciations of human rights abuses during the war.[2] After an intensive six-month study the commission attributed 85 percent of the violations to the Armed Forces; it judged that another 10 percent were the responsibility of death squads made up of anticommunist groups within the Armed Forces, members of intelligence services, and members of the Salvadoran oligarchy whose aim was to exterminate the opposition; the commission assigned the remaining 5 percent to the FMLN (United Nations 1993:41–42, 139).[3] The Truth Commission report dispelled the shadowy world of official denunciations, alibis, and whitewashes, and verified what Tutela Legal, the Human Rights Committee of El Salvador, Nongovernmental (CDHES-NG), Amnesty International, the Americas Watch Committee, the Lawyers Committee for International Human Rights, and other so-called "leftist-oriented" human rights organizations had been saying all along.

In addition to fixing responsibility, the Truth Commission recommended that the guilty parties be declared unfit to hold public office for ten years and banned for life from occupying public security or national defense posts; it recommended the dismissal of military officers involved in committing assassinations, covering them up, or hindering their investigation; and it also recommended a total restructuring of the judicial system, the military, and the police. The judicial system was particularly singled out and accused of being "incapable of taking action against those responsible for abuses." Pardon for offenders was considered indispensable, but "this pardon . . . should not be a formal one, limited to the non-application of sanctions, but should be based on the rectification of past experience" (United Nations 1993:185–198).

Of course, past experience can hardly be rectified if the parties to the process cannot agree about what happened. Only in exceptional circumstances, usually where there was a combination of overwhelming evidence with strong and persistent international pressure, did the military admit culpability. In those rare cases the High Command, the government, and the U.S. Embassy (hardly an objective force) expended enormous efforts to contain inquiry to soldiers in the lowest possible ranks—rogues, they argued, who were "out of control" and transgressed the military mandate to respect the rights of civilians (e.g., El Salvador Ministerio de Cultura y Comunicaciones 1987:50). This has been more or less the situation in every case where a conviction of some sort was obtained: the murders of Rodolfo Viera, head of the Agrarian Reform Institute, and of American Institute of Free Labor Development workers Mark Pearlman and Michael Hammer on 4 January 1981; the rape and assassination of three U.S. nuns and a Catholic lay worker on 2 December 1980; the massacre at San Francisco in 1988; and the killing of six Jesuits, their housekeeper, and her daughter by members of the Atlacatl Battalion at the University of Central America on 16 November 1989, during a nationwide FMLN offensive (Americas Watch Committee 1991; United Nations 1993:44–50, 60–65, 151–155). In each of these cases, the intellectual authors of the crimes got off scot-free because they were protected by their peers, supported unconditionally by conservative politicians and oligarchs, and shielded by an inept, frightened, and generally right-wing judiciary. What rectification, then, indeed what clarification, might we expect in the case of the El Mozote massacre? The victims at El Mozote were poor peasants, artisans, and petty merchants rather than prominent intellectuals or foreign religious workers. And unlike the massacres at the Sumpul and Lempa rivers, where many of the civilians fleeing military sweeps survived encirclement operations and could later testify to the troops' actions, the Atlacatl was relatively successful in eliminating witnesses at El Mozote. About a thousand people were slaughtered during the three-day operation, but only fourteen people provided declarations in the court case, and few of those who testified were eyewitnesses to the events.[4] Among them only Rufina Amaya had been captured by the military and then escaped (Tutela Legal 1991:69).[5] Even if there were a few eyewitnesses too afraid to testify—and research indicates that this was indeed the case—the survival rate could not have exceeded 1 or 2 percent. From a purely technical point of view, the Atlacatl Battalion did its job well.

Almost eleven years after the massacre, the remains of El Mozote's one-room sacristy were excavated by an internationally known team of Argentine forensic archaeologists who specialize in the investigation of human rights violations. Before describing the conclusions reached by the specialists and some of the evidence on which those conclusions were based, let me set the scene—political and otherwise—in which this work unfolded.

POPULAR ORGANIZATIONS AND THE JUDGMENT OF EL MOZOTE

The archaeological work was the product of a two-year struggle waged by inhabitants of northern Morazán, including El Mozote survivors and relatives of victims.[6] Three events set the stage for the pursuit of justice in the El Mozote case: (1) the return of former inhabitants of the El Mozote area from refuge in Colomoncagua, Honduras, to northern Morazán between November 1989 and March 1990; (2) the San José Accord on Human Rights, signed by the government and the FMLN in Costa Rica on 26 July 1990; (3) the Peace Accords signed in Mexico City on 16 January 1992. The San José Accord led to the creation of an independent U.N. human rights verification team in El Salvador and opened up political space for civilians to protest human rights violations. When the Mexico City Accord terminated the war on 1 February 1992 and initiated a ten-month period of demilitarization, the political space widened further. Out of the negotiations came the Truth Commission, empowered to investigate a broad range of past violations.

However, investigation of the El Mozote massacre began long before the creation of the Truth Commission, and it was initiated and advanced not by an international commission but by northern Morazanian peasants whose relatives, friends, and neighbors had been ruthlessly cut down in December 1981 by the soldiers in the Atlacatl Battalion. Officials in the Catholic Church had long known about the case but had taken only weak action. Shortly after the massacre, Father Gerardo of San Francisco Gotera informed Archbishop Rivera about the atrocity, but all Rivera did was to call a meeting with political parties. Bishop Ramón Álvarez, who headed the San Miguel diocese responsible for ecclesiastical affairs in Morazán, could not be depended upon for assistance as he was (and remains) an army chaplain with the grade of colonel. One priest described Álvarez to me as "a bishop who is not a bishop but . . . is a government functionary in the structure of the church."[7] Álvarez maintained silence throughout the war about human rights violations, unless, of course, the violations were alleged to have been committed by the FMLN.

The repatriation of refugees, many of them El Mozote survivors, from Colomoncagua between November 1989 and March 1990 restored a critical mass of potential witnesses, including Rufina Amaya, to the area in which the massacre had taken place. Peace talks, which were broken off following the bombing of the offices of the National Federation of Salvadoran Workers (FENASTRAS) by unknown right-wing elements in October 1989, were renewed a few months after the November 1989 FMLN offensive. A settlement was on the horizon, and with it the possibility of a blanket amnesty that would rule out the investigation of extant human rights cases like that of El Mozote. Only two years earlier, in October 1987, the Duarte-led government had declared an amnesty that led to the release of four hundred untried political prisoners the following month but also threatened to close the books on most political crimes committed by government forces (Amnesty International 1988:5, 13). Members of a region-wide human rights commission formed in May 1990 were understandably worried about the declaration of an even broader amnesty law that would wipe out all possibilities of obtaining justice in the El Mozote case. They decided to preempt the process and move the case forward as quickly as possible.

However, northern Morazanians could not do this without assistance. They resided in a war zone under FMLN control and were being treated by the government as guerrilla *masas:* harassed, threatened, arrested and beaten, and still occasionally disappeared and assassinated, although much less frequently than in the 1980–83 period (see chapter 8). At first, Father Esteban Velásquez made entreaties to the Company of Jesus (Jesuits) with the idea of linking the El Mozote massacre to the Jesuits' murder, then approaching its first anniversary. Differences in the timing, size, and location of the killings were offset by some interesting parallels: each occurred during a major military operation (offensive in the El Mozote case, defensive in the Jesuit one), each was carefully and systematically planned, and each was carried out by the Atlacatl Battalion—one massacre at the beginning of the decade, the other at the end. What better symbol for El Salvador's "decade of war"? Also, Velásquez, who entered northern Morazán "illegally" in 1987 after abandoning his post in the capital, was personally disturbed by the international attention given to the Jesuit case and the absolute dearth of interest in the El Mozote massacre. During an interview in June of 1993 he stated, "It seemed sad to us that there might be such an effort as was being made in the Jesuit case, the enormous solidarity and the legal efforts of every type of organization, and the absolute lack of force in cases such as El Mozote. Specifically, as a Jesuit I felt a moral obligation, since I was in Morazán, to ensure that the same effort that was being made in the Jesuit case might be made for the [El Mozote] case."

But his efforts led to naught. No suggestion emanating from northern Morazán received a positive response from the Jesuit hierarchy in El Salvador. The Company of Jesus even refused to use the occasion of the first anniversary of the Jesuit massacre, 16 November 1990, to solicit public support for the investigation of the El Mozote massacre. Having been denied assistance by the Jesuits, who had their own human rights agenda, popular organizations in northern Morazán then contacted various humanitarian organizations; ultimately they decided to turn the case over to Tutela Legal, the human rights office of the Catholic archdiocese of San Salvador: they decided it was reputable, efficient, and less politically stigmatized than CDHES-NG, COMADRES (Committee of Mothers and Relatives of Political Prisoners, Disappeared, and Assassinated of El Salvador "Monseñor Romero"), and other Salvadoran human rights advocacy groups.

However, Tutela Legal officials were concerned about the possible impact on the organization's reputation of working on a case initiated by popular organizations that the government and U.S. Embassy viewed as composed of FMLN *masas*.[8] After a number of discussions with representatives from northern Morazán, Tutela Legal Director María Julia Hernández committed to the case on the condition that Tutela Legal would play a completely autonomous role; the organization was unwilling to take the political heat that would accompany formal collaboration with northern Morazanian popular organizations. This may have been the only way to win Tutela's interest, but it was not "correct," according to Velásquez: "We respected their criteria, but they never appeared correct to us. They were afraid to stain their hands with the organizations that represented the people, who had convoked them and taken the initiative. This had nothing to do with leadership or personalism but was about how to most effectively aid the community, and for that reason we accepted it" (author interview, San Salvador, 10 June 1993).

However, Velásquez acknowledged that, once committed, Tutela Legal "dedicated itself completely, absolutely, and totally" to the case. Hernández assigned the case to two of the organization's young, gifted, and most dedicated lawyers. They visited northern Morazán, still a war zone that could be entered only by passing three military roadblocks. Assisted informally by the human rights commissions set up by the region's grassroots movements, the lawyers gathered testimony from witnesses and survivors of the El Mozote massacre residing in Segundo Montes, Jocoaitique, Perquín, and elsewhere. As a result of the arrangement, Tutela Legal received most of the public credit in the investigation. But without the labor of human rights workers in northern Morazán, who located witnesses, arranged for them to meet the lawyers, surveyed the massacre sites, and carried out myriad other tasks that could only be accomplished by residents with an intimate knowledge of the social and geographical landscapes in this war zone, the investigation would not have gone forward as it did. It also would likely have stalled without the negotiations, protests, and demonstrations employed by area residents to maintain pressure on the judge who handled the case to keep the process moving along.

Tutela Legal filed the initial brief on the El Mozote case on 26 October 1990 before Judge Federico Ernesto Portillo Campos, of the Second Court of First Instance in San Francisco Gotera. Portillo received the denunciation, opened an investigation (which judges in El Salvador are empowered to do), and began to take testimony. Five witnesses, including Rufina Amaya, braved the military roadblocks into San Francisco Gotera to testify in court. Other witnesses followed later. The judge attempted unsuccessfully to limit the number of witnesses and employed other stratagems in order to hinder the investigation, but under the institutional prodding of Tutela Legal and public pressure from civilians residing north of the Torola River, the investigation proceeded.

However, the case stalled when Tutela Legal raised the issue of bringing in an experienced forensic team to supervise the recovery of physical evidence. At the time the nation still lacked any competent forensic archaeologists, despite the thousands of people interred in mass graves following the massacres of the early 1980s. But, then, qualified forensic investigators might have uncovered "uncomfortable" facts that would have reflected badly on the military, the government, and the U.S. administrations that had defended them against charges of massive human rights abuses. Tutela Legal's lawyers knew that skeletal material recovered from a bungled excavation, as shocking as that material might be, would be useless for clarifying the circumstances under which the victims had died.

In May 1991 Portillo responded positively to the Tutela proposal of providing credentials to Argentine and U.S. scientists so they could work with the Truth Commission. But soon thereafter he deferred the request to Supreme Court President Dr. Gabriel Mauricio Gutiérrez Castro, who tabled it for months without taking action (Tutela Legal 1991:74; United Nations 1993:124). Gutiérrez Castro's behavior eventually earned him a rebuke from the Truth Commission, which recommended that he be retired along with the remainder of the Supreme Court (United Nations 1993:125, 189). This was only one of a variety of tactics employed by the government between July 1991 and 13 October 1992, when the first spadeful of earth was removed, to prevent the exhumation or, alternatively, to have it carried out by incompetent or partisan agents.

For instance, Judge Portillo claimed during the spring of 1992 that El Mozote had been mined by the FMLN, and he refused to allow the forensic work to begin until the area had been "swept clean" of ordnance, since he did not want to be held responsible for accidents that might occur. He suggested that the army do the job. But Tutela Legal rejected the proposal with the argument that the FMLN had not mined the area and that the army's real object in entering El Mozote would be to sweep up, not mines, but evidence left there by the Atlacatl over a decade earlier. Eventually the two sides compromised and FMLN troops, then encamped at six sites in northern Morazán while they awaited demobilization, inspected the area under the supervision of a United Nations Observers Team (ONUSAL). Not a single mine was located.

Even after the area had been declared mine free, Judge Portillo continued to delay in providing official endorsement that the Argentine forensic team could serve as "expert advisers" to the Truth Commission, deferring to his superior in San Salvador. In response, over two hundred people from northern Morazán protested in the streets of San Francisco Gotera. Following a desperate phone call from Portillo to Gutiérrez Castro, the Argentine archaeologists received their authorization the following day.

Inspection of the massacre sites began on 27 May 1992, with the participation of witnesses, Judge Portillo and his assistants, Tutela Legal lawyers, human rights observers, and ONUSAL representatives. During weekly walking tours over several months, survivors pinpointed nine sites around El Mozote (and many other sites in other hamlets) alleged to contain a substantial number of remains. Father Michael Brown, who assisted Tutela Legal, described one such excursion:

> We followed the witnesses on foot to La Joya. Only María Julia Hernández and the judge had the privilege of riding mules. We descended from the road into a valley divided by a river. Once sparsely populated and bountiful in agricultural harvest, it was now abandoned and overgrown. The hot morning sun beat down on our heads as we followed the witnesses to the sites of the massacre. . . .
>
> The witnesses showed us where they had encountered and buried the dead. At each site, they gave us the names and ages of the dead, or as many of them as they knew and could remember. In one location, a witness testified that he encountered and buried 16 victims, including his pregnant wife and young children. A simple wood cross marked the location of their grave. Burned and fallen timbers and broken, red clay tiles marked what was once their home.
>
> . . . This day, the judge suspended the proceedings at about 2:45 P.M., saying that we were all tired and that it was going to rain. Antonio and David [the Tutela Legal lawyers] protested that there were six more grave sites in the area, but to no avail. The judge simply refused and walked away. Antonio and David took it as a sign of his lack of interest in pursuing the truth. . . . We were to return to Morazán the next six weeks, visiting the many sites of the massacre. (Brown 1992:6–7)

THE SACRISTY EXCAVATION

The forensic team elected to begin the exhumation with the sacristy next to the El Mozote chapel (fig. 2, no. 13), as it was accessible, it was well preserved, and it held out the best possibility of yielding a large amount of evidence. When the Atlacatl Battalion burned the building, the tile roof had collapsed and the adobe walls had fallen or had been pushed in. By October 1992 the sacristy, Israel Márquez's home, and most of the other body-laden sites exposed to the elements were covered with thick vegetation. Thus before the work of excavation could even begin, small trees and shrubbery had to be removed with machetes, and the corners and entrance way of the structure identified. The Argentine archaeologists laid out the site in twenty squares of 1.5 square meters each.

The top eighty centimeters of material, which consisted of a clay-like soil of decomposed adobe, yielded no bones and few artifacts (Fonde-brider, Bernardi, and Doretti 1993:1–2). Below this layer the crew struck roof tiles. At this point Judge Portillo called for a halt to the work, saying that nothing significant had been or was likely to be found. But at the insistence of the archaeologists, work continued. Just below the tiles the excavators encountered the first human bones. As they dug deeper, eventually reaching the sacristy's stone floor, and extending the excavation from the perimeter of the building toward the center, progress was slowed by the need to uncover, clean, catalog, and eventually remove a dense mass of scrambled osteal material: crushed skulls; broken femurs and tibiae; disarranged ribs, carpals, and metacarpals; and thousands of bits and fragments that were identifiable only by specialists, if at all. As we shall see, however, rather than being evenly dispersed around the interior the skeletal remains tended to be concentrated in zones.

Word that human bones had been struck spread quickly, and the national and international press descended like a pack of coyotes to pick, metaphorically, at the dry white remains. El Mozote's dead were being resurrected after ten years in the tomb, and the sacristy was thrust upon the stage, where it became the setting for a series of public performances. Under the tent erected to protect the site from the elements and shield the workers from the sun, the young Argentines (Mercedes Doretti, Luis Fondebrider, Patricia Bernardi, and Claudia Bernardi) supervised an all-male crew from the Salvadoran Institute of Legal Medicine (which alternated with another crew from the Commission of Criminal Acts). The forensic workers dug, photographed, taped, cataloged, explained, and supervised, their demeanor measured and serious, emanating respect both for the dead whose remains were being brought into the light and for the local peasants who hovered just outside the rope barrier around the sacristy, observing the disinterment. The Salvadoran assistants varied in their responses. Some took their work as seriously as the supervising archaeologists, while others, clearly unaccustomed to physical labor and perhaps resentful at having to engage in it, kept up a running banter that frequently overstepped the bounds of propriety and highlighted their pro-government position on the reasons for the massive deaths.

At one point during the excavation of the sacristy, workers uncovered a piece of green cloth of the type used in the skirts or blouses worn by peasant women. The reaction of the workers was recounted to me in July 1993 by Gloria Romero, who monitored the disinterment on behalf of the Human Rights Commission of Segundo Montes:

[W]hen they encountered this cloth they all began to laugh . . . those of the government's Institute of Legal Medicine. They began to laugh among themselves: "Ahhh, here are the 'children.'" They thought that there were the [remains of] guerrillas because it was the same green cloth [used in uniforms], but it was of another kind. This, then, was the mentality of this type. But suddenly a sheet of paper like this one [which she was holding] was dug up. A part of it was badly burned. Curious, they began to read it. What could it be? A little notebook of the children who went to the school. And then suddenly there appeared a piece of a very small child of maybe seven years. How sad it was, with a part of its leg with a little shoe made of rubber with five patches. . . . They had patched it with nylon. And [the child had] a little horse in his little pocket, a little plastic horse that was one of the toys that they had. This they found in his pants' pocket.

When all this was dug up people protested and the workers quit screwing around. Then, suddenly, they came upon a woman who was pregnant. You could see that in her death throes she tried to give birth. That's what it was; it was nothing else.

And how did the government workers react to what they saw?

Those of the government institute tried to laugh, but there were always people who protested [this behavior], not among them, but people who were working with the Argentines. This was really important because afterwards one no longer heard so much talk or so much joking. The work continued in a more formal manner.

Judge Portillo arrived each day in a white station wagon, part of a caravan of officialdom that made the trip into the guerrilla-occupied highlands from the departmental capital of San Francisco Gotera. He set up chairs and a table in the shade, and had two young female assistants to attend to his needs. He wore a gaudy white cloth vest with the word *juez* (judge) stenciled on it in blue. From this comfortable rearguard area, Portillo shouted orders to his charges or made periodic incursions into the excavation to inspect the latest find or receive instruction from the forensic experts. When questioned by the press, he often intoned the official views that the victims had been guerrilla fighters who died in combat or that perhaps they were civilians who had died in a cross fire between the contending sides. In at least one press interview, overheard by

FIGURE 7 These skulls and the bones surrounding them represent but a fraction of the massive amount of osteal material uncovered from the sacristy at El Mozote by Argentine forensic anthropologists in October–November 1992. The 31-square-meter sacristy yielded 117 articulated skeletons; nonarticulated matter upped the number of individuals represented to a minimum of 143.

Gloria Romero and shared with me in July 1993, Portillo stated that "he could not say for certain that the remains were those of humans."

The rope barrier partitioned off an inner arena of serious scientific labor from an outer zone of observation. Inside the ropes, the El Mozote massacre was the subject of the science of archaeology, realized by meticulous description, cataloging, classification, and mapping of artifacts (bones, projectile fragments, spent cartridges, bits of clothing, coins, shoes, eyeglasses, combs, hairpins, crucifixes, mirror fragments, and so on) in three dimensions (see Fondebrider, Bernardi, and Doretti 1993:5 for a complete list of artifacts). "Truth," couched in the form of hypotheses, best guesses, and probable sequences, would be the end result of quantification, comparison, and analysis. On the other side of the ropes, photographers jockeyed to secure the best camera angle, especially when something they found striking was being unearthed. They sought truth in a different way, in images intended to perplex, shock, and disturb: a shoe with a bone extending out of it, smiling skulls, a huge jumble of disarticulated bones, bits of clothing sticking to white ribs, a child's toy amidst a miscellany of skeletal material. Their truth manifested an immediate, known quality that predated their arrival at El Mozote; for them El Mozote was a medium through which they gave material form to their personal visions of horror, as they searched for that one image that could sum up what the massacre meant. Even so, for most of the journalists and photographers, El Mozote could be little more than a punctuation mark, a story they would milk until it played itself out. Even *Sixty Minutes,* the U.S. television melodrama that masquerades as serious investigative journalism, produced an El Mozote segment, arranging for Raymond Bonner and Susan Meiselas to revisit the site of the crime they had reported on and photographed more than ten years earlier (*Sixty Minutes* 1993). For maximum impact (or the highest possible ratings?) the producers held up the broadcast for months until the Truth Commission released its report in mid-March 1993.

Also standing around the rope barrier on each day that I visited the sacristy site were area residents. Some, I knew, were survivors who escaped death because they had left the zone days, weeks, or months beforehand. Others were local peasants who stopped in at the sacristy on their way home from the fields. With their *cumas* (curved knives used in agricultural work) at their sides, they stood in the hot sun and silently contemplated the slow, deliberate process by which with dental picks and brushes the workers in the pit removed the dirt, a particle at a time, to reveal more bones and associated artifacts. No one, least of all the press, so enamored of officialdom (the judge) and expertise (the archaeologists), thought to ask them ("the common people," referred to in northern Morazán as *la base,* "the base," or *las masas,* "the masses") what they thought.[9] In fact, only protests by human rights officials overcame the judge's efforts to prevent local inhabitants from observing the recovery up close.

By 17 November 1992, more than a month after the beginning of the excavation, the preliminary work at the sacristy—which is to say the work involved in recovering the skeletons and associated nonskeletal material—had been completed. The archaeologists transferred a minimum of 117 "anatomically articulated human skeletons" from the 4.6-by-6.9-meter (31.74 square meters) sacristy to a laboratory in Santa Tecla (Nueva San Salvador), near the capital, where it was subjected to further study by the Argentines and four U.S. forensic scientists: Robert Kirschner, forensic pathologist; Clyde Snow, forensic anthropologist; Douglas Scott, archaeologist and ballistics specialist; and John Fitzpatrick, orthopedic ra-

FIGURE 8 Local peasants observe the exhumation of remains from the sacristy of the Church of the Three Kings in El Mozote in October 1992. Judge Federico Ernesto Portillo Campos sought to bar viewers from the site, but rescinded in the face of protests by human rights groups based in northern Morazán and in San Salvador.

diologist. Laboratory examination increased the number of individuals represented to 143 that could be typed by age and sex, though Snow (1993:5–6) argued for 146. However, the great density of osteal material (an average of 4.6 skeletons per square meter), combined with the destructive effects of fire (possibly spawned by an incendiary device) and the impact of falling tiles, make it likely that the actual number of dead interred in the sacristy was even greater; as Snow observed, "[I]t is very likely that some skeletons were so completely destroyed by the fire that they have not been recovered" (5–6).

All but 7 of the 143 skeletons for which there was adequate skeletal material for sex and age estimations were identified as children and adolescents between the ages of 0 (newborn) and 16 years.[10] The average age was 6.1 years. Of those in this category, 44 percent were male and 56 percent were female (61 males, 76 females). Six of the 7 adult skeletons were females, with the oldest an estimated 42 years. (The seventh was a 50-year-old male.) One of the women (labeled no. 33 for want of other means of identification) was pregnant in the third trimester (Kirschner et al. 1993:1; Snow 1993:6). The predominance of children in the sacristy and the near absence of adult males effectively destroyed the High Command's contention, repeated whenever the issue was brought up, that El Mozote had been a guerrilla encampment and that the deceased were FMLN combatants killed in a pitched battle with the army.[11]

As the evidence against this hypothesis mounted, the right-wing press proposed an equally preposterous theory, earlier alluded to by Atlacatl Battalion commander Domingo Monterrosa in a conversation with John McKay (U.S. Defense Attaché's Office, confidential cable to Defense Intelligence Agency, cited in Danner 1994:203–206), that excused civilian deaths as lamentable "collateral damage" resulting when the Atlacatl sought to root out the guerrillas from the houses in which they had taken refuge. Here is the *Diario de Hoy* (1992c) version:

> According to residents, a terrorist camp of the FMLN functioned in El Mozote and for three days, at the beginning of 1981 [*sic*], a confrontation began when soldiers of the Atlacatl Battalion were informed that two soldiers had been kidnapped.
>
> The soldiers moved in the direction of the place to rescue their comrades, obliged the sentinels to flee, and those [the sentinels] according to guerrilla tactics went down into the center of the camp and hid among old people, women, and children.
>
> The terrorists holed up in what had been a religious center and from there opened fire against the troops, producing a confrontation that lasted three days, that, according to residents, gives an idea of the magnitude of the resistance that the army encountered.
>
> This was the way in which the death of children and women might have been produced, said a local inhabitant.

Meanwhile, Salvadoran government officials offered their own speculations. On 23 October, Supreme Court President Gutiérrez Castro emphasized that El Mozote was the object of "an impartial judicial procedure," to which he added that the remains of fifty-seven persons (to that date) had been discovered "in the ruins of a church presumably destroyed during combats when the peasant locality was occupied by terrorists of the FMLN in the twelve years of war, according to testimony of subversive leaders" (cited in *Diario de Hoy* 1992a). Meanwhile, even after the forensic experts concurred that the available evidence pointed overwhelmingly to a massacre, Juan Mateu Llort, director of the Salvadoran Institute of Legal Medicine, continued to provide an alibi for the Atlacatl Battalion. He admitted that the Atlacatl had committed "an inhuman act since they knew that the area was inhabited by many children," but without a shred of evidence, he rejected the possibility of a massacre: "I discard the possibility of a massacre in cold blood and in this case history will judge me if I am wrong, but I'm stubborn and I maintain as I have since the beginning of the investigation that it was a confrontation" (cited in *Diario Latino* 1992:16).

The task of clarifying what exactly did lead to the deaths of the sacristy victims was complicated by the great density of skeletal material (the bodies piled two, three, and four deep in the compact space) and the damage wrought, probably postmortem, by a very intense fire and the collapse of the heavy tile roof. On the other hand, the fallen roof did help to preserve the remains by preventing the entry of large animals that would have consumed the soft tissue and disturbed the in situ setting. Because so much skeletal material stayed together, even if layered over other similarly articulated skeletons, the archaeologists could confidently assert that the sacristy was a "primary burial": either the people died within it or their bodies were deposited there before the soft tissue had decayed (Fondebrider, Bernardi, and Doretti 1993:3).

Ascertaining the causes of death was a more problematic operation, though careful study of the ballistic material and its spatial relationship to the skeletons provides the basis for a reasonable hypothesis. The archaeologists recovered 245 spent cartridges, all intact, and 263 projectile fragments. The pattern of dispersion of the projectile fragments corresponded to that of the osteal material. Hence, a 10-square-meter area that contained 70 percent of the skeletons and 80 percent of the concentrations of bone matter also contained 60 percent (159) of the fragments. And the second- and third-ranked areas of skeletal concentration (15.4 percent and 14.5 percent respectively) were also the second- and third-ranked areas in numbers of projectile fragments (15.2 percent and 10.6 percent respectively) (Fondebrider, Bernardi, and Doretti 1993:6–7). The remaining fragments were dispersed elsewhere in the building. Finally, the archaeologists located many fragments in direct association with bones or beneath holes in clothing that was in contact with the remains. In some cases the bullets had passed through bones and dented the stone floor beneath. Based on the analysis of this material, the team concluded that "at least 43 individuals received discharges from firearms

that could have caused their death" (head and/or thorax) and stated that
the evidence suggested that another 24 had been shot in the arm, leg,
and/or pelvis (7).

Most of the spent cartridges were encountered in either the doorway
or the southwest corner of the interior, whereas the vast majority of the
projectile fragments were in the central area, in association with the largest concentration of skeletal material. Based on these patterns of dispersion and association, the forensic team concluded that the assassins were
"located in the entrance way and the southwestern part of the interior of
the house, shooting from or toward the interior of the habitation, mainly
in the direction of the central squares . . . [where] 85% of the skeletons
and 75% of the projectile fragments were found" (8). That some of the
victims were strangled, drowned, knifed, or bludgeoned to death cannot
be ruled out, but forensic experts found neither signs of knife marks on
the skeletons nor fractures with cranial depressions of the sort that result
from the impact of a blunt instrument (Kirschner et al. 1993:2). Considering the length of time that had transpired since the massacre and the
state of the skeletal remains, many of which were totally destroyed and
most of which were damaged by fire and the weight of the collapsing roof
and walls, one could hardly conceive of stronger evidence that something
horrible had taken place in the priest's visitation chamber next to the
Church of the Three Kings in caserío El Mozote, cantón La Guacamaya,
municipality of Meanguera. Kirschner et al. (1993:2) summed up the evidence: "There is no proof to support the argument that the victims, almost all small children, had participated in combat or had been trapped
in a crossfire between contending forces. On the contrary, the evidence
supports decidedly the conclusion that they were intentional victims of a
massive extrajudicial execution." And the forensic archaeologists concurred: "All the information indicated points to the idea of a massive
crime, where there is no evidence that could sustain the possibility of a
confrontation between two parties" (Fondebrider, Bernardi, and Doretti
1993:11).

Yet only after ballistics specialist Douglas Scott cleaned and studied
the 245 spent cartridges could the Atlacatl Battalion be materially linked
to the massacre, albeit circumstantially. Scott (1993:8) found that all but
1 of the cartridges came from OTAN 5.56 mm shells, which are used exclusively in the M-16. The 34 cartridges with a grade of conservation sufficient to permit microscopic analysis were fired from 24 different firearms, suggesting, by extrapolation, the participation of a large number of

people in the massacre. All of the m-16 cartridges were stamped with the letters "LC," identifying their site of manufacture as Lake City, Missouri. Over 90 percent bore a 1978 date. The latest date was 1981.

The m-16 has been the standard infantry weapon of the U.S. Army since the Vietnam War. It was also the weapon supplied to the Atlacatl Battalion when U.S. military advisers trained and outfitted the unit in El Salvador in early 1981 (Danner 1993:61, 1994:38). At the time of the El Mozote massacre regular army troops (the Atlacatl Battalion was an "immediate-reaction" battalion, the Salvadoran equivalent of the U.S. Special Forces) and the National Guard were equipped with the German-made g-3; the National Police used the .38 Smith and Wesson revolver and the U.S. m-1 carbine (McClintock 1985:328; English 1984:409). In 1981 the fmln had very few M-16s. Had the fmln received m-16s through its international contacts, as was later alleged to have been the case (United States Department of State 1985:33), those weapons would have been Vietnam-era models, and it is reasonable to think that they would have been accompanied by Vietnam-era ammunition as well, which Scott showed was clearly not used at El Mozote.[12]

On the basis of the foregoing evidence I suggest the following scenario to account for the material discovered in the excavation: In small groups children and a few women were taken out of the home of Alfredo Márquez, where they had been confined since early morning on 11 December 1981, and were marched to the sacristy. On reaching the small building they were forced to enter and were shot down by their escorts from within the interior or from the doorway. As one group was killed, another followed, escorted by a different group of soldiers. This would account for the large number of different firearms employed. Some individuals may have been killed outside the sacristy—strangled to death or stabbed in soft tissue areas that left no marks on the bones, thus partially accounting for the nightmarish cries recorded by Rufina Amaya: "Mama, they are killing us," "they are strangling us," "Mama, they are sticking us with knives." Or the voices that haunt Amaya may have come from children being murdered by other groups of soldiers elsewhere in El Mozote, probably within the home of Alfredo Márquez or in its vicinity.[13] The discovery of a large number of gunshot victims in the sacristy does not discredit Rufina Amaya's personal testimony, but reinforces it, amplifies it, and underscores the importance of carrying out additional archaeological and forensic work at El Mozote to clarify just exactly what did transpire, as well as to recover the remains of the deceased so that they can be given a proper burial. But as we shall see, there is tremendous resistance on the part of the government to doing that.

The reports of the various forensic experts were published as appendices to the Truth Commission report and thus played an important role in sustaining the commission's conclusions about El Mozote and, by implication, about other cases in which military and security forces were accused of having carried out wanton killings that they then sought to cover up. But how was this report, replete with testimony and conclusions that so damaged the image of the military, received?

THE GOVERNMENT RESPONSE

Response to the Truth Commission report followed political lines: ringing accolades from the Left, venomous critiques from the military and from the Right.[14] To political conservatives in El Salvador and the international community the report was biased toward the FMLN; it was unfair, partial (since it examined only a sample of the violations), and inaccurate. And it had no legal standing in El Salvador since its authors were foreigners of questionable integrity (*Diario de Hoy* 1993f). Dr. Ernesto Alfredo Parada, the law faculty dean at a private university in El Salvador, judged the Truth Commission report "an affront to the State of Right, to ethics, politics, and civilized good fellowship of Salvadorans" and asserted that "the so-called Truth Commission comes to be a group of three persons, in the style of the inquisition, which always seeks dishonor and public shame . . . for El Salvador and Salvadorans" (cited in *Diario de Hoy* 1993c). Supreme Court President Gabriel Mauricio Gutiérrez Castro, criticized in the report for having impeded the El Mozote investigation, rejected the commission's recommendations as "a clear and open meddling in the internal affairs of the country" (cited in Centro Universitario de Documentación e Información 1993a:6).

High-ranking officers such as Col. René Emilio Ponce, Gen. Juan Rafael Bustillo, Col. Orlando Zapeda, and others indicted by the Truth Commission for gross human rights violations were no less vehement in their condemnations. Ponce opined that the conclusion "misrepresents the historic reality and makes accusations lacking in foundation and objectivity, affecting negatively the process of pacification supported by all sectors of the citizenry" (cited in Centro Universitario de Documentación e Información 1993a:7). Bustillo, accused in the report of helping to plot the Jesuit murders, turned the report on end by portraying the indicted officers as the real victims, and he threatened that government and FMLN peace negotiators would have to answer because they "compromised our names" (cited in *Diario de Hoy* 1993b). Thumbing his nose at the report's recommendations that figures implicated in human rights violations not be allowed to serve in public office for ten years, Bustillo shortly thereafter announced himself the National Conciliation Party's presidential candidate for the March 1994 elections, though he later withdrew his candidacy.

Col. Julio César Grijalva, commander of the First Infantry Brigade, called everything about the report "an offense against the Salvadoran people" and said it "places all Salvadorans in the same plane of madness that gives impulse to the communists to attempt to seize power by force of arms, death, and destruction. If to combat communism is madness, then we prefer to continue being mad" (cited in *Diario de Hoy* 1993d).

Finally, on 24 March 1993 the Armed Forces released its official response to the Truth Commission. It criticized the report as unjust, incomplete, illegal, unethical, partial, and disrespectful. The military blamed the FMLN for having provoked the war and touted its own role as the nation's savior:

> The Armed Forces is proud of having fulfilled its mission of defending the people and creating a favorable atmosphere, as it demonstrated in its actions over the entire course of this tragic and dark period of our history, for pacification and the preservation of our democratic and republican system, which it accomplished at the cost of its blood, as well as sacrifices and hardships endured by its faith in God and a tireless spirit of service to the Nation. (cited in *Diario de Hoy* 1993e)

The preceding comments draw from but a few of the dozens of articles, editorials, and commentaries critical of the Truth Commission report that appeared in the conservative press between 16 March and 30 March 1993. The toxic cloud of rhetoric unleashed by spokespeople for and defenders of the military and the judiciary formed itself around the main poles of right-wing ideology: God, Nation, and Property, with the military institution portrayed as the principal defender of all three. Called to public account, perhaps for the first time in its history, the Right denied the accusations, dismissed the mountain of supporting documentation, and vilified the accusers as "an inquisition," "meddlers," "biased," etc. The immense rage evinced by the invective can best be understood, I think, if we consider the source: this is the same hatred and rage that, compounded with fear (of the organized peasant and worker), motivated the atrocities for which the Right was now being held responsible before the Salvadoran citizenry and the international community.[15] It may also be viewed as the mimesis between the brutality and hatred attributed to supposedly "communist" workers, peasants, priests, etc., on the one hand, and the exploitative relations of production, which often sustain a semifeudal character in El Salvador, on the other (Taussig 1987: 134). In the culture of terror of late-twentieth-century El Salvador, no less than in the Ecuadorian Amazon during the late-nineteenth- and early-twentieth-century rubber boom, "the epistemological, ontological, and otherwise philosophical problem of representation . . . becomes a high-powered medium of domination" (121).[16]

President Alfredo Cristiani found himself in a dilemma. He had no intention of implementing the report's recommendations, but he could not reject out of hand the results of a commission that his own negotiating team had helped to create and behind which his government stood. Instead of condemning the report, he embarked on a campaign to prevent its recommendations (which were supposed to be binding on both the government and the FMLN) from being put into effect. Hence on 14 March, the day before the Truth Commission report was due to be released, Cristiani went on television and radio to lobby for a blanket amnesty. This plea followed strenuous efforts on his part to prevent the report's publication. His allusion to the potentially "destabilizing" impact of the report was a clear signal that his government was under pressure from a military that it did not fully control. Shortly after the document was made public, Cristiani presented his Amnesty Law before the Legislative Assembly, which passed it on 20 March with the votes of legislators representing the Nationalist Republican Alliance (ARENA), the Authentic Christian Movement (MAC), and the National Conciliation Party (PCN). Christian Democrats abstained, while the Democratic Convergence voted against it (Centro Universitario de Documentación e Información 1993a:8). With the amnesty in place, the work of exhumation at El Mozote ceased.

OTHER EXCAVATIONS

However, before mid-March, when the above-mentioned events transpired, two additional sites had been excavated, in whole or in part, at El

Mozote. To complete the record, I will discuss them briefly. The second excavation was opened in January 1993 at the site of the remains of a home owned by José María Márquez (fig. 2, no. 14) and lived in by his daughter, Sofía Márquez. The house was located about fifty meters east of the sacristy. Llort's Institute of Legal Medicine team was digging through "an undisturbed geological formation" in the patio area when Roger Heglar and Charles Cecil, forensic anthropologists from California, showed up and pressed the excavation into the area where the house itself had stood.[17] Neither man was a competent speaker of Spanish, and this inhibited communication with human rights monitors from Tutela Legal, Segundo Montes, and other organizations, who did not speak English. Did this site, too, provide evidence of victims? Both Gloria Romero of the Human Rights Commission of Segundo Montes and one of the lawyers from Tutela Legal said that it did. Romero stated in our July 1993 interview that

> Yes, there were a lot. . . . you see there was a concentration that was without doubt a number of babies, because they had little tiny bracelets that are put on children soon after they are born. . . . There were three or four of these little bracelets, a concentration of them. And there were safety pins for babies' diapers. All these concentrations were at that site, almost at the door of José María's house, in the first part of the house, and in the majority [of the house] they found concentrations of the long hair of women.

Human bones were located too, "a large quantity," most of them badly burned, probably from the explosion of a very powerful incendiary device. Cecil agreed. He told me that he and Heglar identified eighty-six "cranial clusters," representing a lot of individuals, although the fragmentation was so great that he was unable to estimate how many individuals the clusters might have represented. Cecil said that the locations of the clusters and the small number of spent cartridges suggested that the people were dead when they were placed in the house; the condition of the remains made it appear that afterward a powerful explosive device generating great heat was tossed in (cf. Eisner 1993). However, by this time El Mozote was no longer news. The big story, that of the sacristy, had broken, and few members of the press, national or international, bothered to make the trip from the capital to observe the second excavation.

The excavation of José María's house was completed on 25 January 1993. Then Heglar and Cecil directed the institute's workers for several more days at the home of Benita Díaz (fig. 2, no. 18), where, according to the testimony of witnesses, the owner and her children were killed and buried by the Atlacatl. The anthropologists recovered the headless skeleton of one very large man before they returned to the United States on 28 January to fulfill other commitments. Cecil and Heglar planned to return in the spring, but they were never called back. Someone later came and retrieved the tools, and without an active site the United Nations officers assigned to guard the area retired. The skeletal and other material recovered from the homes of José María Márquez and Benita Díaz was taken to the Institute for Legal Medicine laboratory in Santa Tecla, and though Heglar later faxed a report on the Márquez site to El Salvador, no report of the findings there was ever made public or sent to Tutela Legal, to the Human Rights Commission of Segundo Montes, or to any other interested party.

The unannounced cessation of archaeological work at El Mozote and the absence of reports from the last two sites provide additional evidence that the government has no commitment to clarifying the events that transpired there during Operation Rescue. (The irony in the name grows the more one reads about this case.) We have seen how it took a combination of committed and fearless survivors, a well-oiled regional human rights organization, the assistance of a high-profile organ of the Catholic Church, and pressure from the United Nations to move the case forward. But after the FMLN demobilized in December 1992, northern Morazanians faced new and daunting challenges: the imminent return of mayors and the reconfiguration of regional power; growing problems of physical survival as emergency rations provided by humanitarian organizations during the war were reduced and the population was reintegrated into the capitalist-dominated national economy; and the difficulties and conflicts that attend the process of transforming hierarchically based military-style organizations into popular and democratic ones (Cagan 1994; Binford 1993a, in press). In the future loomed perhaps the largest challenge of all: that of preparing for the March 1994 elections in which the FMLN would compete openly for power through the ballot box. Responding to the new situation sapped personnel and resources from the regional human rights lobby. For most people, surviving the present and preparing for the future assumed higher priorities than clarifying the past.

Then, in June 1993, the Company of Jesus sent Esteban Velásquez, a key figure in prosecuting the El Mozote case, back to Spain to "reflect" for a few years, punishing him for having violated orders when he abandoned his post in the capital and arrived without permission in northern Morazán in 1987 to take up the preferential option for the poor. The Human Rights Commission of Segundo Montes began to train community-level human rights monitors, and leaders of sectors within the Left, including the ERP's Joaquín Villalobos, agreed to retreat on some human rights demands in order to obtain economic resources from the government.[18] All this meant that whereas people continue to look to clarify the past (the relatives of the war dead can hardly do otherwise), they have been propelled by economic and political contingencies to direct most of their attention and energy toward crafting the future. Few people with whom I spoke agree with the amnesty, but, lacking an effective means of opposition, they are resigned to accepting it.

Still, I agree with Father Velásquez that the exhumations should continue, if not to contribute further to clarification of the massacre, then at least to recover and provide a decent burial to the many hundreds of people whose remains are scattered in common graves in fields, trenches, and beneath destroyed homes. At least seven sites remain to be excavated at El Mozote, not to speak of burial sites in Jocote Amarillo, Cerro Pando, La Joya, and other hamlets that fell within the Atlacatl's zone of operations. Buried under the broken and fragmented roof tiles and the decomposed adobe bricks of the Israel Márquez house lie, according to Rufina Amaya, the skeletal remains of dozens of adult women forced into the building and shot down in groups of twenty. Likewise, beneath the surface of the foundation of the adobe home of the merchant Alfredo Márquez quite likely lie more children, perhaps even those of Rufina Amaya, who were strangled, stabbed, and shot to death. "If the exhumations continued in Nueva Trinidad and the Sumpul after the amnesty," Father Velásquez asked on the eve of his departure for Spain in June 1993, "why aren't they going to continue with the exhumations at El Mozote?"[19]

A REFORMED MILITARY?

The El Mozote massacre occurred toward the end of a cycle of death-squad killings, massacres, and scorched-earth operations that left tens of thousands of Salvadorans injured and dead. In the ensuing years, particularly the years following 1983, massacres and death-squad killings declined in number. After the war the Truth Commission, which carried out its investigation in a climate relatively free of intimidation, also noted the decline in politically motivated killings. Eighty percent of the 5,682 homicide complaints processed by the commission took place in the three years from 1980 to 1982; the remaining 20 percent of the homicides were spread over the following nine-year period. On this basis the authors defined "a first period characterized by collective executions and killings, compared with a second phase in which the repression was more selective" (United Nations 1993, Vol. 2, Appendix 5:17).

The U.S. Embassy and State Department pointed to this decline as proof that the Salvadoran military was becoming "professionalized" and had been won over to the need to respect civilian life. For instance, consider the following postwar statement by Elliot Abrams—the assistant secretary of state for inter-American affairs from 1985 to 1989 and the Reagan administration's consummate apologist—justifying the administration's role in covering up many of the most egregious military and death-squad violations: "You cannot make a human rights argument for abandoning the Salvadoran government in the early 1980s and permitting a Liberation Front victory. When the Carter administration left office [January 1981], there were roughly 800 death-squad killings a month, and by extremely hard work we reduced that by 95 percent. That's a pretty good achievement" (quoted in Krauss 1993c). It wasn't nearly as good an achievement as Abrams claimed, and it was accomplished at the cost of billions of dollars in military and economic aid that prolonged the war and took tens of thousands of additional civilian lives. Though human rights advocates employing different counting methodologies acknowledged that political murders declined during the Reagan years, they also argued that abuses remained unacceptably high and that the State Department's rosy conclusion was not warranted.

But what interests me here is less Abrams's assertion that human rights in El Salvador improved under Reagan than the manner in which he couched the assertion. Like many administration apologists, Abrams assumed that a correlation existed between human rights performance, which I equate here with the level of human rights violations, and the level of "respect for human rights." For Abrams and many others, a reduced number of human rights violations perpetrated by an identifiable group is evidence that its respect for human rights is on the rise. "Respect" involves "consideration, courteous regard," according to *Webster's New Universal Unabridged Dictionary* (1983, p. 1542), and we might think of "respect for human rights" as the "consideration" on the part of an individual or group to extend (or to deny) to other individuals or groups the same rights which they feel justified in claiming. Most people would, if they could, claim for themselves the full range of rights internationally recognized in Protocol II of the Geneva Convention, the Universal Declaration of Human Rights, and other documents of the kind (IDHUCA 1986).

However, it is also clear that many people apply the human rights mandate in a discriminatory fashion, restricting full application to people "like themselves" and denying human rights to others, whom they categorize as Other and therefore as undeserving. For instance, U.S. citizens of European descent often respond to the arrival of African Americans into the neighborhood, Chicanos into the school system, or Palestinians into the country with efforts to keep "those people" out. Conventionally, then, difference is often acceptable only when it is circumscribed by sameness, i.e., the minor differences among individuals who recognize one another as holding membership in the same category (e.g., middle- or upper-class European American males, for instance). In the case of El Salvador, we have seen that historically the bourgeoisie and the military have never accepted, even abstractly, the fundamental equality of peasants with plantation owners or workers with bankers (see chapter 3).

These considerations lead me to differentiate between two components, frequently confused, of human rights: one component, "human rights performance," refers to human rights practices and is, theoretically, measurable; the other component, "human rights conceptions," must be inferred from speech and action. Human rights performance can be operationalized and then empirically measured through the collection of evidence about human rights violations: homicide, torture, forced relocation, etc. The larger the number of violations attributed to a group during an interval of observation, the worse the human rights performance and, by implication, the lower the respect for human rights. But human rights performance need not rise and fall with the level of respect for human rights, since the number, type, and intensity of violations can be influenced by many factors other than the "conceptions" that underpin them. Institutional barriers, opportunity, the possibility of retaliation, access to weapons of destruction, and other factors can prevent one group of people from acting out fantasies of discrimination, injury, and destruction that derive from the very low esteem in which it holds another group.

In El Salvador the U.S. government adopted the public position that an improving human rights performance on the part of the military indicated that the Salvadoran government was bringing the military "under control" and that military officers had developed a new conception of human rights; however, I will argue in this chapter that the attitudes of the military officers had not changed and that their behavior was, above all, a strategic concession to the Reagan administration, related to U.S. funding of the Salvadoran war effort. The implication for atrocities such as the one that took place at El Mozote is obvious: insofar as the military continues to interpret citizens exercising their rights as terrorists attempting to destabilize the system and undermine the fatherland, restraint in the use of repression will depend on factors *external* to the military institution itself. If those external factors (international pressure, press coverage, conditionality of economic and military aid, etc.) are absent, other El Mozotes could occur.

THE DEBATE OVER COUNTING

The widespread acceptance of the empirical model among government officials and the public channeled much debate over human rights in El Salvador into numerical contests: what counted as a violation; how violations were to be categorized and attributed; whose numbers were more accurate, and so on. Human rights advocacy organizations systematically sought to broaden the human rights debate by scrutinizing the institutional and noninstitutional arrangements that contributed to human rights violations, impeded their investigation, or covered them up (e.g., Americas Watch Committee 1991; Amnesty International 1988; CDHES-NG 1986). But because the Reagan administration manipulated a view of human rights that corresponded to the commonsense beliefs of the press and public, the performance model ("Human rights performance is improving if the numbers are decreasing") dominated public debate (cf. Americas Watch Committee 1984b).

The Reaganite approach to human rights dovetailed with the U.S. public's proclivity—reinforced by U.S. press coverage—to think of the world's non-Western peoples in predominantly numerical terms, as masses of humanity rather than as complex combinations of unique individuals speaking different languages, worshiping different gods, and struggling with variations on the same capitalist system that oppresses and alienates the majority of people in the West. Congress and the public were willing to accept that a reduction in the number of political murders (incorrectly attributed to extreme groups of the Right and Left rather than the government) represented real progress. Only following the killing of priests, nuns, and American citizens—"civilized" people like Us or at least enough like Us to matter—was the empirical approach put aside. And then the embassy and State Department attributed these crimes to "renegades" or "deviants" beyond institutional control and put some pressure (though never enough) on the Salvadoran government to find and punish the guilty parties. The pressure, however, seldom involved actual cutoff of military and economic assistance, and even when it did, the aid was soon restored.[1] On the Salvadoran side, investigations, when undertaken, *never* implicated the crimes' intellectual authors (Americas Watch Committee 1991:89–106; United Nations 1993; Lawyers Committee for Human Rights 1989:17–36; Special Task Force on El Salvador 1990; Doggett 1994).

Press coverage reinforced the distinction between the cheapness of peasant lives and the value attached to middle-class urban ones. Between 1980 and 1983 there occurred in El Salvador an absolute minimum of 297 collective killings of 5 or more people committed by the military, security forces, and paramilitary groups linked to the military (ORDEN, Civil Defense) (United Nations 1993, app. 5:19). Yet the international press devoted 50 articles to the assassination and funeral of Archbishop Romero and only 44 articles to 16 rural massacres that occurred in 1980 and 1981 (app. 3:42–43).[2] I do not accept that every bit of the difference can be adequately accounted for either by the archbishop's high international prestige or by the remoteness of the locations in which the rural massacres occurred.[3] If the sites where the assaults took place had been so isolated and militarized as to prevent the entrance of the press or the exodus of witnesses, then the massacres would not have been reported at all.

LOW-INTENSITY CONFLICT DOCTRINE AND HUMAN RIGHTS

According to both U.S. officials and Salvadoran military officers, the improvement in human rights performance occurred when the Salvadoran military adopted the low-intensity conflict approach being promoted by the U.S. Military Mission to El Salvador and by the Southern Command in Panama. Thomas Pickering, U.S. Ambassador to El Salvador from 1983 to 1985, explained low-intensity conflict doctrine as the "integration of military operations, civilian defense, and economic development" (cited in Manwaring and Prisk 1988:224). A more cynical (and more accurate) definition, however, is that "[l]ow-intensity conflict . . . is that amount of murder, mutilation, torture, rape, and savagery that is sustainable without triggering widespread disapproval at home [in the United States]" (Michael Klare, cited in Nelson-Pallmeyer 1989:32).

Low-intensity warfare is total war fought simultaneously on all fronts: economic, political, and military (Barry 1986; Nelson-Pallmeyer 1989). The strategy emphasizes winning the trust of the civilian population, whose active collaboration is thought to be the key to eradicating the guerrilla threat. To win the people's allegiance, the government must provide what, in essence, the insurgents have promised to provide: "El Salvador came to represent the most important effort to apply the lesson of Vietnam: namely, it takes development and democracy, not just military force, to root out revolution. If a war was needed to defeat the FMLN, just as essential was a campaign to reform the feudal institutions and redress the political, social, and economic inequalities in El Salvador to quench the rebel fires forever" (Schwarz 1991:7).

U.S. advisers urged their Salvadoran protégés to lure the FMLN's non-combatant civilian supporters into the government fold by supplying them with food, shelter, health, education, and, of course, "security." This meant accompanying government propaganda about El Salvador's newly hatched democracy—the first ostensibly free elections were held in March 1982—with programs that actually improved lives. In theory, recipients of government assistance would then distance themselves from the guerrillas. Once socially isolated and deprived of peasant-based intelligence, supply, and logistical assistance, FMLN guerrillas would become easy targets for eradication by government forces (Schwarz 1991:7–10).

The strategy rested on two assumptions. First, U.S. military strategists expressed confidence that additional training and the assistance of U.S. advisers would bring the Salvadoran military "under control," i.e., that despite its lurid history of distrust of and brutality toward the peasants, the Salvadoran High Command would adopt low-intensity warfare strategy and act on it (see Waghelstein in Manwaring and Prisk 1988:279). The magnitude of the task should not be underestimated. It consisted of nothing less than a total makeover of the military institution and its personnel, rather like insisting that an adult who had grown up speaking one language and acting according to one set of cultural assumptions internalize a completely different language and way of being—and rapidly, in a matter of months or, at best, a few years. In this case the language was the language of human rights, and the new way of being entailed government treatment of its historic enemies (workers and peasants) as its dearest friends and, insofar as the war came increasingly to be seen as one fought over "hearts and minds," its potential saviors. A large dose of imperial pretentiousness was required for the U.S. government to believe that the officers' corps, and to a lesser extent the oligarchy, would willingly adopt the American advisers' recommendations at a time when the nation was immersed in a bloody civil war in which, from the perspective of elite military officers, businesspeople, and government officials, civilization—or, what is the same thing for them, their livelihoods and property—was in the balance (Schwarz 1991:38–39). The gringos weren't doing the dying, as every Salvadoran on both sides of the political divide knew. So what gave them the right to call the shots? (The reply, of course, is money.)

Second, low-intensity warfare theorists assumed that memory could be detached from history and that workers and peasants would, if treated more humanely, come to view this newly "professionalized" and "respectful" military as somehow different from the one that only a few years before had tortured, raped, and massacred its way across the countryside with complete impunity. In essence, the military planners took it for granted that mostly illiterate peasants could be programmed to respond, like rats in a Skinner box, to whatever mix of stimuli an investigator selected. Memories, even memories of pain and suffering, don't stay with rats for very long. The Skinner box provides a particularly appropriate analogy in that B. F. Skinner, the Harvard behavioral psychologist, argued that positive reinforcement (analogous in this case to land, health services, schools, etc.) invokes the desired bar-pressing behavior (collaboration) in the rat (Salvadoran worker/peasant) with more consistency and over a more prolonged period than negative reinforcement (threats, captures, disappearances). El Salvador was, then, a laboratory, "an ideal testing ground," as Benjamin Schwarz noted, "in which to demonstrate the effectiveness of low-intensity conflict doctrine" (Schwarz 1991:1; cf. Barry 1986:4).[4] And analogous to Skinner's rats, Salvadorans, especially poor Salvadorans, were the U.S. military scientists' expendable subjects.

THE WOERNER REPORT

The Woerner Report prepared the ground for the introduction of low-intensity conflict doctrine to El Salvador. The Pentagon dispatched Gen. Fred Woerner to El Salvador in 1981 at the request of Napoleón Duarte, president of the civilian-military junta. Woerner's orders were to develop a national military strategy for El Salvador and a military assessment for the United States and to outline a security-assistance program by which the United States could aid the Salvadoran government in its counterinsurgency campaign (Woerner in Manwaring and Prisk 1988:115). According to Gen. Wallace H. Nutting, commander-in-chief of the U.S. Southern Command from 1979 to 1983, Woerner "produced a force development program, key to the problem, which has provided the basis for the whole security assistance program since then" (Nutting in Manwaring and Prisk 1988:114). Woerner wrote that a military victory would take up to five years and require an investment of as much as $300 million. At the time, embassy officials thought this an unnecessarily bleak (and expensive) assessment, but it pales when compared to the reality of a twelve-year war with a $6 billion price tag—and no military victory (Schwarz 1991:2–3).[5]

The Woerner Report emphasized the need for a larger, better-trained army to counter the guerrillas. Guided by Woerner's recommendations, members of the U.S. Military Group drew up a campaign plan, called the National Plan, and implemented it in 1983 in the departments of San Vicente and Usulután. The National Plan was the first systematic effort to combine large-scale military operations to clear conflictive areas of guerrillas, social and economic assistance, and civil defense, which are at the core of low-intensity warfare doctrine (Barry 1986:53; MacLean 1987:21). According to Col. John D. Waghelstein (cited in Manwaring and Prisk 1988:223), the National Plan "placed emphasis on civic action and developmental projects behind a security screen," with the object of developing popular support for the government.

Eventually the Salvadoran High Command also endorsed the principles of low-intensity conflict embodied in the National Plan and the more ambitious "United to Reconstruct" Plan that followed. Salvadoran colonels and generals became avid spokespersons for "democracy" (by which they meant elections) and "development" (i.e., civic action), and they publicly acknowledged the importance of popular support to defeat the FMLN (see interviews with Salvadoran officers in Manwaring and Prisk 1988:171, 213, 215, 219, 221; Schwarz 1991:22). In December 1987 Defense Minister Carlos Eugenio Vides Casanova emphasized the need for "complete support to the democratization process" and "a profound and truthful position of respect from the high command and, accordingly, from all the Armed Forces toward human rights and all the Salvadoran people" (Vides Casanova in Manwaring and Prisk 1988:218–219). Col. René Emilio Ponce, later accused by the Truth Commission of complicity in the Jesuit murder (United Nations 1993:44), commented that

> one of the most significant advancements made during these past years has been to create an image of ourselves in the eyes of the international world as a respecter of human rights and a terminator of abuses inflicted on the people by government authorities. We must face the fact that we were, at one time, responsible for the brutalities and ill-treatment imposed on the citizens of the country. I repeat, the support and impetus given to the democratic process and the socioeconomic reforms were essential. (cited in Manwaring and Prisk 1988: 215)

Even Col. Domingo Monterrosa joined the parade. By the time he was appointed commander of the Third Brigade in San Miguel on 25 November 1983, "he talked not like some kind of butcher but like an American. He was completely full of this idea of conquering hearts and minds" (Salvadoran journalist Lucía Annunziata, cited in Danner 1993:125, 1994:142).

By 1985 the government was arguing that the war had been turned around and that the FMLN was on the wane. They assigned credit to the popular government created through elections in 1982 and 1984, land reform, reform of the banking and credit systems, professionalization of the military and security forces, and implementation of new military strategies (small-unit tactics, greater mobility of forces, long-range patrols) that disrupted rebel supply lines, impeded troop buildup, and kept the FMLN on the run.

However, claims of imminent victory proved to be inaccurate. The FMLN was in trouble in 1984–85, but its difficulties were less the product of a groundswell of popular support for the government—which never materialized despite post-election propaganda—than of a stepped-up government bombing campaign and air mobile assaults that prevented large-scale FMLN troop concentrations and took a tremendous toll among civilian supporters. By 1986 the FMLN had made the transition from a war of position (large units defending territory) to a war of movement (small-unit guerrilla warfare) expanded to previously untouched areas of the national territory. The revised strategy successfully neutralized government advantages in troop strength and U.S.-supplied materiel, and the civil war remained stalemated for its duration (Binford 1992; MacLean 1987; Harnecker 1993:252–274; Villalobos 1986).[6] Had the government actually solidified a base of support among the peasants and rural workers, the FMLN strategy of guerrilla warfare and dislocation of forces would have failed because small FMLN guerrilla teams organizing and fighting on unfamiliar terrain (areas outside the "traditional" conflict zones) would have been easy prey for enemy agents and regime loyalists.

THE SALVADORAN MILITARY AND HUMAN RIGHTS

To understand why the government did not develop a popular base, we need to briefly revisit Ponce's claim that "one of the most significant advancements made during these past years has been to create an image of ourselves in the eyes of the international world as a respecter of human rights and a terminator of abuses inflicted on the people by government authorities." Ponce didn't say that the Salvadoran military and security forces *really* respected people's human rights; he stated, frankly and unambiguously, that they had created "an image" that they were doing so. Between the image and reality lay a yawning chasm.

Human rights improved only in the eyes of those who were *predisposed* to find improvement and, even then, only when compared to the massive bloodbath that characterized the 1980–82 period: the massacres at El Mozote, Sumpul River, Lempa River, Las Hojas, and numerous other atrocities, complemented by a tidal wave of assassinations carried out in cities and countryside by military units, security forces, and those linked to them (ORDEN, the Civil Defense, etc.) in the state security apparatus. By late 1983 the crude methods of repression had largely accomplished their purpose. The popular movement had been crushed or forced underground, and much of the countryside had been transformed into a virtual free-fire zone. Civilian survivors of military operations joined the guerrillas, fled conflictive areas for displaced-persons camps or the anonymity of crowded urban space, or left the country (see chapter 6). Had military and security forces continued the "scorched-earth" campaign, they would have encountered fewer potential civilian victims.

When the junta consented to sponsor elections for a Constituent Assembly in 1982 in preparation for the general elections in 1984, continuing open repression of peasants and workers suddenly became counterproductive. It doesn't look very "democratic" when body dumps are overflowing and the international press is inundated with reports that whole villages have been wiped out to the last man, woman, and child by government forces. And since the Reagan administration needed to present El Salvador as a nascent democracy in order to justify to Congress and the American people the much higher level of funding called for in Woerner's "force development program," it pressed hard on the Salvadoran government to reduce civilian body counts. Through four presidential certifications administration officials argued that the situation was improving, though mounting evidence of military involvement forced the administration to "gradually moderate its denial that any abuses emanated from the Salvadoran army and the security forces" (Americas Watch Committee 1991:120; cf. Burkhalter and Neier 1985).

In December 1983, Vice President Bush visited El Salvador and lectured the top thirty-one military leaders of the High Command on the importance of bringing the death squads under control. His was a fortuitous selection of audience, considering that the U.S. Embassy had tenaciously defended the military institution against accusations of complicity in death-squad murders. Following the Bush visit, death-squad murders "serendipitously" entered a steep and prolonged decline, which greased the congressional wheels for an equally steep and prolonged increase in U.S. military and economic aid. "If a whisper in the ear of the right military officer could so greatly reduce the flow of blood spilled by the death squads," Americas Watch wrote in 1991, "there can be little doubt as to where the murderers got their orders" (p. 24).

However, a new pattern of human rights violations emerged to replace the earlier pattern of assassinations, massacres, disappearances, and macabre tortures (usually preceding homicides). The new pattern, initiated in about 1984, combined the following elements: indiscriminate bombing and shelling of the civilians who remained in conflictive areas; indiscriminate capture, torture, and imprisonment; systematic destruction of homes and crops; and forced relocation of noncombatants. Not one of these forms of repression was new to El Salvador or to the conflict; all had taken place during earlier stages of the war. But from late 1983 they increased in frequency as functional elements of the low-intensity warfare strategy introduced, managed, and financed by the United States government. For that reason, I have treated them as a new pattern of violation.

My argument, then, is that the shift in the pattern of human rights violations was a response to strategic military and political concerns. Contrary to administration officials, the Salvadoran government, and some members of the press, I find little evidence for the claimed internal reorganization of the military institution, the subordination of that institution to civil society, or even the ideological conversion by the officers' corps toward a more humanitarian perspective on the poor. Rather, the High Command was convinced to adopt the low-intensity conflict approach by the failure of scorched-earth policies to eliminate the FMLN, by U.S. control of the war's purse strings, and by an accumulation of negative press reports that jeopardized further U.S. funding—all *external barriers* that affected the empirical register of human rights performance but had absolutely no impact on the ideological register of human rights attitudes or the social register of the relationships that underpinned those attitudes. It should become clear, too, that official claims about low-intensity conflict doctrine seek to conceal the fact that low-intensity conflict practice "uses terror and repression to intimidate or punish, cosmetic reforms to pacify or disguise real intent, and disinformation to cover its bloody tracks" (Nelson-Pallmeyer 1989:42).

In the following sections I take up briefly two aspects of the pattern of human rights violations that emerged from 1983 and to some degree persisted until the end of the war: the bombing campaign and systematic torture.

The Bombing Campaign

A key feature of low-intensity conflict strategy was to keep the rebels on the run and to prevent them from massing large-scale forces. To this end the United States trained long-range reconnaissance patrols to penetrate guerrilla-controlled areas, pinpoint the location of guerrilla camps, and transmit the information to higher officials, who organized helicopter-based assaults or called in bombing missions. Once the guerrillas and their supporters had been forced out of an area through a combination of shelling, bombing, and ground operations, low-intensity warfare doctrine called for the areas to be repopulated with "strategic hamlets" (as employed by the United States in Vietnam) defended by Civil Defense patrols composed of loyal civilians armed by the military. The repopulation strategy was attempted unsuccessfully between 1983 and 1986, when first the National Plan and then the United to Reconstruct Plan were put into operation.

The Reagan administration renovated the Salvadoran Air Force following its virtual destruction during an FMLN raid on Ilopango Air Base in September 1982 by supplying planes and helicopters (mainly subsonic A-37 jets, O-2 spotter planes, and Huey UH-1H transport helicopters), armaments (2.75-inch rockets, machine guns, and bombs of 250-, 500-, and 750-pound size), and pilot training (Hatfield, Leach, and Miller 1987: 13; LeMoyne 1985b; Williams 1985). By 1983 the air war was underway. The military strategy enjoyed a few successes (e.g., López Vigil 1991:381, 401–413), but the FMLN's shift to small units and dislocation of forces in 1984–85 eliminated large guerrilla troop concentrations and deprived the military of its number one target. Air force and artillery units were relegated to shelling and bombing that stubborn core of civilians who refused to abandon their homes in conflictive areas through countless land invasions. Unable to cripple the guerrillas directly with the air war, the military sought to make life so miserable for civilians in FMLN-controlled areas that they would be forced to flee to the cities and displaced-persons camps, where they could be politically neutralized and controlled. In essence, the Salvadoran High Command pursued an updated, high-tech, and infinitely more deniable version of the same "empty-the-sea" strategy that precipitated the massacres of the early 1980s.

In 1984–85 aerial assaults supported by large-scale military invasions forced civilians to flee on *guindas* (organized retreats). After the army retreated from the operations zone and the survivors returned to their villages in Chalatenango, Cabañas, northern Morazán, the Guazapa area, San Vicente, and elsewhere, they found their houses destroyed, fields burned, and domestic animals slaughtered (e.g., Metzi 1988; Schaull 1990; Americas Watch Committee 1986:32). The air force even attacked displaced persons who had assembled in conflictive zones to receive medical attention or food from the International Red Cross, the only institution allowed to administer assistance there during most of the 1980s (Americas Watch Committee and Lawyers Committee for International Human Rights 1984:45–51).

Many such incidents were investigated by the international press (e.g., Cody 1983; Dickey 1983; cf. the press summaries in Americas Watch Committee 1986:5–24) and hardly any by the Salvadoran press (United Nations 1993, app. 3). But many more went unreported or were reported only long after the fact because they involved small numbers of people and occurred in conflictive areas into which journalists and human rights monitors seldom ventured. In liberal journalistic parlance, the accusations could not be "confirmed."

Embassy and State Department personnel generally dismissed allegations by claiming that bombing civilians was contrary to Salvadoran government policy. "The policy is, you don't bomb villages, you don't kill civilians," an unnamed American official told James LeMoyne in July 1985 (LeMoyne 1985b) in response to refugee accounts of indiscriminate attacks on villages. When confronted with irrefutable evidence, U.S. officials attributed the attacks to accidents or claimed that they were carried out by individuals who were violating the policy (Americas Watch Committee and Lawyers Committee for International Human Rights 1984:115).

On a more insidious note, the State Department, well into 1984, sought to impugn the testimony of bombing/shelling victims by arguing that because guerrilla *masas,* or noncombatant supporters, were "intermingling with and [in] support of the armed insurgents," they were "something more than innocent civilian bystanders" (Schell 1984). In other words, civilians were fair game!

This position dovetailed nicely with that of some field officers in the Salvadoran army (see below), but flew in the face of the definition of "civilians" and the list of protections they were entitled to under international treaties to which both the United States and Salvadoran governments were (and remain) signatories. "Civilians," according to the 1949 Geneva Convention, are persons who do not bear weapons and thus take no active part in the hostilities; though civilians render moral, political, and material support to one side or the other, their lives and possessions are to be respected. In international law, the killing of civilians is *murder* (see Americas Watch Committee 1984b:30–45; IDHUCA 1986:109–116).[7]

By making the FMLN's noncombatant supporters responsible for their own deaths, the embassy sought to justify its exclusion of civilian victims of military operations in guerrilla-controlled zones from the casualty statistics that it released to the public in its weekly "grim-gram." But as Americas Watch (1985:132–133) pointed out, the embassy *even lacked a category by means of which to assign responsibility to government forces* had it agreed that they had perpetrated human rights violations. It parceled out responsibility for human rights abuses among five categories: "guerrillas," "possibly guerrillas," "far right," "possibly far right," or "unknown assailants."[8] Absent the civilian deaths in guerrilla-controlled zones and in the context of the real decline in death-squad murders that began in November 1983, the human rights situation took on an increasingly rosy hue, *numerically speaking.*[9] By the time Napoleón Duarte took office in June 1984 following an April election runoff, the Reagan administration could claim that only the intransigent FMLN "terrorists" stood in the way of the consolidation of democracy in El Salvador. Meanwhile, dozens of rural peasants were being blown up and machine-gunned with impunity.

Rather than improving, the circumstances, the form, and to a lesser degree the locale of the human rights violations changed in response to changing military strategies and war technologies: fewer tortured bodies by the roadsides, more testimony about air attacks that were "difficult to confirm." When journalists did visit (at their peril) guerrilla-controlled zones, victims of the air war had already been buried, and correspondents had to make decisions about who and what to believe: the denials emitted with clockwork regularity by the High Command and its patron, the U.S. government; or the accusations of government complicity in civilian deaths made by the FMLN, its supporters, and the supposedly "leftist" human rights lobby. The best many journalists could do was to outline their dilemma. For instance, James LeMoyne[10] of the *New York Times* wrote on 18 July 1985, "Most reports of air attacks come from battlefields where army ambushes and guerrilla mines make access for reporters all but impossible. Witnesses are usually highly partisan. Government officials universally defend the air force. Much testimony condemning bombing comes from peasants who identify themselves as rebel supporters" (1985b).

For LeMoyne and other liberal correspondents, the victims were no more believable than the victimizers. By virtue of their "even-handed treatment" journalists insinuated that hundreds of peasants involved in dozens of incidents separated widely in time and space could have conspired to mislead the international press about the circumstances under which their friends and relatives had been dismembered by the flying "death squads" that supplemented land-based troops. In this way the mainstream press participated in the "war of images, ideas, and deception" that is as much a part of low-intensity conflict as the "war of bullets and bombs" (Nelson-Pallmeyer 1989:5).

Even so, by late 1984 enough reports of air force bombing of civilians had accumulated to spur President Duarte to action. In September he issued orders that future air strikes be authorized by the chief of the Armed Forces staff, and he limited air raids to circumstances in which Salvadoran combat troops were "in contact with the enemy; are attacking fixed installations of the enemy; and to interdict enemy supplies or troops" (cited in Americas Watch Committee 1985:10). However, Salvadoran military officers continued to deny that civilians lived in northeastern Chalatenango, the Guazapa Volcano, northern Morazán, and other areas under day-to-day FMLN control. And they were not shy about stating as much to the foreign press.

The same month that Duarte ordered the air force to respect civilian lives, Major Murcia of the Atlacatl Battalion described Los Llanitos, where the army had committed a massacre the previous July, as a region totally controlled by the guerrillas. He explained that all nonguerrillas had left the villages. "There is no peaceful life there," Murcia told James LeMoyne, "there are no people in this zone" (LeMoyne 1984). Over a year later, when the press accused the government of "bending rules" on air attacks (never of breaking them) by destroying civilian houses, military spokesperson Colonel Aviles opined, "The good people, the people not with the guerrillas, aren't there" (LeMoyne 1985a). Given these attitudes, it is not surprising that civilians remained targets of planes and artillery. Even foreign journalists and prestigious visitors were fired upon; Mayor Gus Newport of Berkeley, California, came under attack while en route to visit Berkeley's Salvadoran sister city, which was located in a conflictive zone in Chalatenango (Americas Watch Committee 1985:25–26, 35).

Rather than recount the experiences of foreigners, I will refer to a summary of the testimony of NA, a fifty-year-old peasant who fled Joateca in northern Morazán following an army operation that began on 28 March 1985. Better than dozens of facts and figures, NA's story illustrates what was at stake for civilians in the air war:

> He was a farmer and had lived in the outskirts of Perquin, Morazan until late October 1984. He . . . testified about the army operation [in Perquín] on October 18, 1984. First an explorer plane came and then an A-37 bombed the zone and the houses, forcing people to run out. He jumped into a ravine where it was hard for the children to follow; debris and garbage fell into the ravine from the impact of a bomb that went off in the next instant. The bomb fell very close to his two children. His son, Modesto, 4, was killed; he recognized him by the remains of his pants. His daughter, Maria, 5, was killed and her remains were too scattered to recover. His wife, Fidelina, 30, was killed at the same time. (Americas Watch Committee 1985:16)

That Modesto's young frame was so pulverized that he could be recognized only "by the remains of his pants" and that María's remains "were too scattered to recover" was probably the consequence of a direct hit from a 500-pound or 750-pound bomb. A 500-pound bomb that explodes on impact creates a crater approximately 50 feet in diameter and 15 feet deep (see fig. 12). Northern Morazán was bombed less intensively than northeastern Chalatenango or the strategic guerrilla redoubt of Guazapa, fifteen miles north of the capital. Still, the majority of peasants in that area with whom I have discussed the war speak with the authority born of repeated traumatic experience of the characteristics of the different types of aircraft employed by the air force and the effects of the armaments they discharged. The majority can also recount at least one personal story of close escape, if not a more tragic one in which a friend or relative was badly wounded or killed while washing clothes, planting corn, or, ironically in one case, placing flowers on the grave of a departed loved one. In testimony gathered toward the end of the war, northern Morazanians denounced thirty-nine air force bombings and machine gunnings between 1982 and 1991 (see table 5 below). However, I suspect that the more numerous near misses and "minor" violations (destruction of crops and homes) would not have seemed serious enough in retrospect to warrant reporting (cf. United Nations 1993, app. 5:7).

In 1987 the government claimed that political deaths had declined from eight hundred per month in 1980 to only twenty-two per month between September 1984 and August 1985 (El Salvador Ministerio de Cultura y Comunicaciones 1987:30). The U.S. Embassy basically concurred (United States Embassy 1986a, 1986b). However, if the government and the embassy had counted civilian deaths that occurred during Salvadoran military operations in conflictive areas among the "political deaths," they would have arrived at figures over 500 percent higher (Americas Watch Committee 1985:39). True, fewer civilians were killed and wounded in air attacks in the mid-1980s than during earlier ground sweeps, but by the time the United States provided the resources for the air war, the number of civilians in conflictive areas had declined precipitously, and those remaining quickly learned to take defensive measures to protect themselves (Americas Watch Committee 1986:5).

The air war continued at a diminished level until the signing of the Peace Accords in 1992, even though the FMLN's deployment of SAM-7 ground-to-air missiles acquired from Nicaragua's Sandinistas "inspired" Salvadoran pilots to curtail their bombing missions in areas of guerrilla control. When I first undertook fieldwork in northern Morazán in June 1991, about six months before the war's end, many peasants, particularly those residing outside municipal centers, flew homemade white flags from tall poles or trees next to their houses in hopes that the air force would recognize and respect their civilian status.

Torture

The Truth Commission stated that between 1980 and 1982 torture generally served as a grisly and painful prelude to murder: "More than constituting practices in themselves, [tortures] are elements that are added to the scene of executions, increasing their brutality" (United Nations 1993, app. 3:9). In the mid-1980s the role of torture changed to conform with the needs of low-intensity conflict strategy. Military and security forces subjected captives to sophisticated tortures that left few marks in order to extract information and obtain signed and videotaped confessions that could be published in newspapers and broadcast on television to discredit the resurgent popular movement. As in the case of bombing and shelling, journalists confronted two parties with diametrically opposed versions of the truth: state functionaries denied that captives were tortured or that confessions were coerced (e.g., El Salvador Ministerio de Cultura y Comunicaciones 1987:50), while victims horrified the press with narratives of brutality and mistreatment and of pain and suffering.

María Teresa Tula became active in COMADRES (Committee of Mothers and Relatives of Political Prisoners, Disappeared, and Assassinated of El Salvador "Monseñor Romero") after her husband was arrested during a strike at a sugar mill. (He was assassinated by government agents while in custody in June of 1980.) In May of 1986, as punishment for her work with COMADRES, she was on two occasions abducted, while pregnant, by males in civilian dress, forced into a car, blindfolded, and taken to an unknown location, where she was interrogated and tortured. During her first capture Tula was beaten, choked, threatened with death (a gun was placed to her temple), raped by two men, cut on her stomach, and told by her captors that they were going to torture her children in front of her:

> This went on for three days and three nights. After they administer all of these psychological tortures, you get to a difficult point. They tell you that they are going to kill your whole family. They told me that they had my sister and my children and they were going to kill them all. When they tell you that, you prefer that they kill you instead of your whole family because you have already been living through torture. These are the kinds of moments you don't wish on anyone, not even your worst enemy. (cited in Stephen 1994b:134)

Several days later Tula was unceremoniously dumped in Cuscatlán Park (in midtown San Salvador); she was dazed, her clothing "torn and full of blood" (cited in Stephen 1994b:135). Fortunately, the fetus was unharmed.

But a few weeks later she was seized again, this time by nonuniformed members of the Treasury Police. They robbed her of her belongings and took her, blindfolded, to their headquarters, where she was kept in custody for twelve days before being remanded to Ilopango Prison. Her inquisitors told her that her husband had been a terrorist and that her case was a real problem:

"We haven't decided what we are going to do with you yet. We don't know yet if we are going to kill you, mess you up for the rest of your life, or have you disappeared."

When they said this, I felt cold. Goosebumps spread all over my body like one long wave. I couldn't even imagine everything they could do to me. All the horrible things. (cited in Stephen 1994b:143)

Her statement strikes at the heart of the relationship: the absolute power of the inquisitor, the powerlessness of the victim. "Torture," as Kate Millett (1994:35) explains in *The Politics of Cruelty*, "is all hierarchy intensified, magnified, brought back to its archetypal and most brutal level, the archaic pairing of master and slave." The captor's calm meditation on Tula's future communicated in the most horrific way that he was the master and she was his slave.

The Treasury Police did not kill María Teresa Tula. They forced her to remove her clothing; they fondled her, drugged her, beat her on the legs, back, and elsewhere, and subjected her to the *capucha* (a rubber or plastic hood tied over the head and frequently containing lime, powdered insecticide, or some other toxic substance that wreaks havoc on the respiratory system). They interrupted the tortures with offers of money, security, and a new life overseas if only she would cooperate, confess, and implicate others: "I had to endure five days and nights of tortures nonstop. They didn't beat my baby inside, but they beat me everywhere else. They were trying not to leave any permanent marks. Before, they used to leave people all swollen and purple with chemical burns and burns from electric shocks. Now they are more careful" (cited in Stephen 1994b:151).

Finally, she was forced to sign a blank paper. This was a confession, drafted "in accordance with the political needs of the government" (CDHES-NG 1986:29). Although no lawyer or judge was present, it was legal under Decree 50, the "special enabling legislation" (Millett 1994:52) found in virtually all national security states. Decree 50 permitted the authorities to hold people suspected of having committed crimes against the state for fifteen days before allowing them access to legal assistance or formally charging them.[11]

María Teresa Tula's experiences reflect those of hundreds of other political prisoners whose testimony was analyzed and discussed in *Torture in El Salvador*, published in September 1986. Released in the United States and generally ignored by the mainstream press, *Torture in El Salvador* was researched and written inside Mariona Prison by the Human Rights

Committee of El Salvador, Nongovernmental (CDHES-NG), and distributed in the United States by the Marin Interfaith Task Force of Mill Valley, California. The circumstances that led to its production commenced with the arrest, torture, and false imprisonment of five members of CDHES-NG in May 1986. Following their incarceration they worked with the Committee of Political Prisoners of El Salvador (COPPES) to take testimony from 433 of the 434 prisoners remanded to Mariona between January and August 1986. Mariona is a men's prison exclusively, so all of the prisoners were male and 85 percent came from rural or agricultural zones (CDHES-NG 1986:79).

CDHES-NG explained how the military and security forces employed a deliberate, one might even say "scientific," combination of physical, psychophysical, and psychological tortures to force confession and engender collaboration with them: "[E]ach and every technique has been elevated to the level of a skill. They have become experts in evaluating the degree with which each type of torture must be applied, and the manner of conducting the interrogation process" (CDHES-NG 1986:19).

Prisoners arrived at Mariona after being subjected to an average of 19 different tortures: 8 physical tortures, 5 combined physical/psychological tortures, and 6 psychological tortures. Almost three-quarters of the prisoners testified that they had been struck in the head, 81.7 percent were hit in the thorax, and almost 20 percent in the testicles. Half were forced by their captors to engage in exercise to the point of collapse; 40.2 percent were asphyxiated, and 18.7 percent received the capucha. Smaller percentages were victims of more "creative" tortures, such as the "airplane," reported by 44 (10.2 percent) of the 433 informants. "This type of torture," the CDHES-NG (1986) explained, "consists of tying the person's hands and feet, or thumbs, with the hands behind the back, and suspending him, causing intense pain and dislocation of different parts of the body" (50). Almost 10 percent received the "hammock": "The hammock is done by two people, who take the victim by his hands and feet, swinging him in such a way that he strikes the wall, then throwing him with great force upon the floor" (50).

Sixty-six prisoners (15.2 percent) had been threatened with rape, though only two testified that they were actually sexually violated (see table 4). Had the survey been conducted in Ilopango, where women were imprisoned, the incidence of rape would have been very high indeed (cf. Stephen 1994b:161). Like María Teresa Tula, most captives were also threatened with death (94 percent) and with harm to their families (76

Table 4   Percentages of 433 Mariona Prisoners Subjected to Each of 40
Forms of Torture

Physical Tortures	%	Psychophysical Tortures	%
Blows to the head	74.1	Blindfolded	98.8
Blows to the ears	51.7	Kept awake	89.4
Blows to the thorax	81.7	Stripped of clothing	58.0
Blows to the abdomen	76.2	Denied food and water	63.7
Blows to the back	58.4	Fed spoiled food	47.1
Blows to the extremities	56.6	Denied use of bathroom	60.0
Blows to the testicles	19.6	Given drugs against will	46.7
Forced to stand	79.4	Sexually violated	0.5
Unspecified injuries/wounds	13.1		
Immersion in water	17.1		
Asphyxiation	40.2	Psychological Tortures	%
Strangulation	46.9		
Capucha (hood)	18.7	Threatened with rape	15.2
"Airplane"	10.2	Threatened with death	94.0
"Horse"	19.4	Threatened with harm to family	76.0
"Hammock"	9.7	Simulated assassination	71.4
"Piñata" (suspended, beaten)	16.6	Verbal aggression	94.2
Prolonged exercise	50.6	Others tortured within hearing	63.5
Electric shocks	13.6	Tortured with animals	6.2
Burns	11.8	Kept in isolation	77.3
Use of other apparatus	32.6	Accused by false witness	34.9
Bound, handcuffed	94.2	Other psychological tortures	24.7

Source: CDHES-NG 1986:82.

percent); over 70 percent testified that the captors simulated their assassination by shooting off a gun next to their heads, by taking them to a ditch where they were told that they were going to die, or by some other manner. Considering the epidemic levels of death-squad murders in the late 1970s and early 1980s, perpetrated in large part by the military and security forces, such threats were undoubtedly taken seriously. CDHES-NG (1986) concluded, "The essence of torture has not changed. It has taken root within the State security apparatus, to the point where it has become a structural practice and is not subject to change" (14).

In the early 1980s horrible tortures and mutilations (acid burns; severed limbs, tongues, and ears; gouged eyes) preceded (or followed) assassination in order to leave ghastly scenes that would convince the living to eschew oppositional political activity (United Nations 1993, app. 5:19). To this end, the results of torture had to be made public and visible. However, Duarte's 1984 electoral victory and the rejuvenation of the popular organizations that his election enabled established a different context for torture. Beginning in the mid-1980s torture became more systematic and moderated. It functioned to instill fear in captives and to extract a confession from them that would "neutralize, destroy, or eliminate all forms of political opposition by identifying them as militants, or sympathizers, collaborators, or believers in the armed opposition" (CDHES-NG 1986:25).

The accused were tortured slowly during the fifteen-day "grace" period permitted under Decree 50 (until its expiration in October 1987). Those administering the interrogations learned to cause pain (and even permanent disability) with less visible evidence so that the "democratic" government could plausibly argue that members of the military and security forces were bound by the Armed Forces Code of Conduct, which supposedly ensured "respect for such rights in all actions engaged in by the Armed Forces, particularly the arrest and treatment of political prisoners" (El Salvador Ministerio de Cultura y Comunicaciones 1987:45).[12] Just as it covered up the El Mozote massacre and other massacres and killings, the U.S. Embassy collaborated in this charade when it dismissed reports of systematic torture and accepted as legitimate many of the confessions manufactured by the government and signed under duress by political prisoners (Hatfield, Leach, and Miller 1987:21; Americas Watch Committee 1991:130).

Unlike death-squad killings, the incidence of torture did not change significantly following Bush's December 1983 visit to El Salvador and his chat with the High Command. For instance, Americas Watch asserted that political deaths declined 40 percent, from 1,910 to 1,130, between 1985 and 1986, but that arrests—a major occasion for torture—increased 47 percent, from 2,846 to 4,193, during the same period (Americas Watch Committee 1987:7–8, 68). According to the Truth Commission, the incidence of torture declined a mere 15 percent from the 1980–83 period to the 1984–90 period, but four of the seven years between 1984 and 1990 registered higher incidences of torture than either 1982 or 1983. Furthermore, more tortures were reported in 1989 than for any other year of the civil war.

Of course, no numerical summary should be allowed to substitute for individual testimonies. It is crucial, therefore, that we keep in mind that

Table 5 Human Rights Violations Reported to the Truth Commission by
Northern Morazanians, 1980–91

Years	# Reports	Assassinations	Disappearances	Destruction/ Robberies
1980–81	144	207	1	5
1982–83	53	54	1	3
1984–87	85	35	4	1
1988–91	54	12	3	3
Total	336	308	9	12
(%)	—	(48.5)	(1.4)	(1.9)

Source: Human Rights Archives of the Human Rights Commission of Segundo Montes.

each of the 433 Mariona prisoners lived a history as terrifying and painful
as the one recounted by María Teresa Tula. However, the U.S. government, the liberal press, and to a large degree the U.S. public simply refused to take seriously the words of the persecuted among El Salvador's
popular classes—the peasants, workers, displaced, slum dwellers, and
the unemployed—against those of Salvadoran military officers, embassy
spokespersons, and State Department functionaries.

Finally, it is important to note that many peasants and rural workers
were "informally" tortured in the course of military operations without
ever having been arrested, charged, and incarcerated. The military killed
fewer people during ground operations, but regularly threatened, beat,
and robbed civilian inhabitants of conflict zones suspected of collaborating with the FMLN. Low-intensity conflict strategy ideals notwithstanding, the treatment meted out by Salvadoran military operatives vacil-
lated, often unpredictably, from one extreme to the other. The friendly
Dr. Jekylls who presided over the distribution of food, candy, and bal-
loons and provided medical care (a military dentist pulling dozens of
rotted teeth) during civic actions were quite capable of turning into cruel
Mr. Hydes who tortured peasants suspected of smuggling materiel, hiding arms, or providing the guerrillas with food and information. And
though rural dwellers developed a variety of self-defense mechanisms to
reduce the likelihood of falling victim to military violence, the preva-
lence of accounts of seizure, accusation, and torture in northern Morazán indicates that they were often unsuccessful.

Captures	Tortures	Bombings and Aerial Machine-Gunnings	Total Violations	Mean Violations Annually
34	14	0	261	130
26	12	9	105	52
118	16	15	189	47
39	7	15	79	20
217	49	39	634	53
(34.2)	(7.7)	(6.2)	(99.9)	—

THE MILITARY AND HUMAN RIGHTS IN NORTHERN MORAZÁN

Table 5 documents the changing character of human rights violations in northern Morazán. Almost 80 percent of the 261 violations reported for 1980 to 1981 involved assassinations. The percentage would have been much higher had I included massacres in the table (see table 1). Following Operation Rescue of 7–17 December 1981, and more rapidly in the post-1983 period, assassinations declined and were replaced by captures, tortures, and bombings. The decline of total annual human rights violations to 52 during 1982–83 (from 130 in the previous two-year period) is related to the FMLN's military ascendance and a weakened Salvadoran army that made fewer forays into the area. The following period (1984–87) shows the situation at the height of the "low-intensity" warfare policy, during which the decline in assassinations (to about 9 annually) was accompanied by a tremendous rise in captures and tortures, which came to account for 71 percent of the violations. It is important to note that the vast majority of captures also involved torture, a fact not reflected in the log of violations from which this table was constructed, but one that becomes clear on reading the details of the individual testimonies. The pattern of violations is similar to the pattern that resulted from analysis of "indirect sources" by the Truth Commission (see chap. 6, note 2).

The figures are only partial, particularly as regards noncapital offenses. Many men and women captured, interrogated, and tortured by the army on one or more occasions failed to testify before human rights monitors or the Truth Commission. And had every person who was robbed or whose home was burned during military sweeps actually complained to the Truth Commission, the human rights files in northern Morazán would contain hundreds or thousands of denunciations rather than the meager dozen enumerated in table 5.[13] Qualifications aside, I do believe that, as regards violations against the person (capture, torture, assassination) and total violations, the material provides a useful gauge of the changing pattern of human rights violations over the course of the 1980–91 period.

Reporting is probably most complete for the years between 1988 and 1991, by which time visitors and international aid organizations (Doctors without Borders, Aid in Action, the World Lutheran Foundation, Voices on the Border, and others) were providing services and sponsoring projects in northern Morazán. Also, most municipalities in the zone had by then established human rights committees linked to PADECOMSM (Community Development Council of Morazán and San Miguel), formed in April 1988, or to the Human Rights Commission of Segundo Montes (Binford 1992). The committees gathered denunciations of abuses and passed them to offices in San Salvador; workers there shared the information with the press and communicated it to a network of supporters in Europe and North America. The international presence in northern Morazán, Chalatenango, and elsewhere did not prevent abuses, which continued to the end of the war, but did serve as one more check on the military and a resource for local human rights monitors.

THE GODS OF WAR

Christopher Lehmann-Haupt (1994) regards human rights violations in El Salvador as a lamentable product of the "gods of war," thus assigning responsibility for them to an abstract cosmic force beyond the domain of human control. But northern Morazanians who suffered the depredations know from personal experience that those "gods of war" are human beings who dwell in San Salvador and in Washington, D.C. The experiences of two northern Morazanians illustrate this.

Marcos is a fifty-three-year-old peasant agriculturist (about five feet two inches in height) who has the chiseled musculature of an athlete and the strength to shoulder a hundred-pound bag of newly harvested corn and carry it four kilometers from his field on the steep slopes of Cacolote

Hill to his modest adobe home in cantón Azacualpa, San Fernando. But despite his impressive physical ability, Marcos is frequently unable to work due to the excruciating pain of the migraine headaches that began shortly after the severe beating about the head that he was given by army troops in the San Fernando church over a twenty-four-hour period one day in the late 1980s. Over the course of several months in the fall of 1992, when I lived in San Fernando, Marcos little by little used up my entire supply of Tylenol 3 tablets, which provided him with temporary relief, and he then requested more of this "miracle drug."

Doña Lola is renowned in much of northern Morazán for her work as a Christian organizer, midwife, and general counselor, and as an unremitting and fearless advocate for the poor. One late afternoon during the summer of 1992, Doña Lola and I drank cup after cup of her thick, strong Perquín coffee and discussed the cultivation and processing of the coffee plant, about which she is a veritable mine of information. A thunderstorm tormented the hills that sheltered the patio of the ruined coffee-processing plant next to her home. With each jagged bolt of lightning that irradiated the surrounding crests, our conversation abruptly ceased as Doña Lola closed her eyes, bowed her head, and involuntarily flinched in anticipation of the coming thunder crack.

"What's wrong, Doña Lola?" I asked her. "Does the thunder remind you of the bombs dropped from A-37s or Push-Pulls?"

"No," she replied, "it sounds just like the explosion of artillery shells lobbed by the army from Osicala [more than twelve miles south]."

Lola knew that the thunder was harmless, and her reflexive response to it was, I suppose, a residual product of numerous bombardments and close calls with death. Also, Doña Lola had been captured three times by the army and accused of being a guerrilla sympathizer; she was tortured on two of those occasions. Now her blood pressure is chronically low, and she periodically experiences dizziness and fainting spells that confine her to bed for days or even weeks at a time.

Marcos and Lola share with many other northern Morazanians the physical and psychological scars resulting from twelve years of being shot at, bombed, threatened, tortured, beaten, and robbed by military, security-force, and paramilitary units. A 1991 survey of the 1,769 families in Segundo Montes City (refugees who fled northern Morazán for Colomoncagua, Honduras, in 1980 and 1981 and returned to construct a new community beginning in late 1989) noted that, apart from the "general causes" of poor health related to underdevelopment, such as malnutrition, contaminated water supplies, and environmental contamination, there existed more specific war-related causes, including "prolonged stress, frequent submission to tense situations such as forced evacuations, bombings, the death of family members, handicapped family members, etc." According to the authors, "A strong relationship was found between exposure to stress and general state of health": "Some of the people interviewed related that after fleeing from the army their bodies kept shaking, and it is frequent to encounter among the hypertense, people who saw their entire family assassinated, or to find women with heart problems who lost all of their children in combat" (IDEA 1992:35). Seventeen percent of Segundo Montes residents told surveyors that they were either chronically ill (12 percent) or handicapped due to wounds received in the war (5 percent). I warrant that the percentages would be higher among those thousands of civilians like Marcos and Lola who weathered the entire war in northern Morazán.

In this chapter I have argued that it makes more sense to speak of a changing pattern of human rights violations by government forces after 1982 than of an improved human rights performance. Instead of eradicating entire communities during messy ground operations, the military shelled and bombed civilians in order to force them to leave FMLN zones of control. It destroyed houses, fields, and forests necessary for the peasants' survival; and at opportune moments, it captured civilians and forcefully relocated them away from areas where they were thought to represent political problems. Disappearances and assassinations leading to mutilated corpses along roadsides decreased; however, the use of torture to intimidate and to extract confessions increased.

I conclude that repressive institutions are capable of mitigating levels of cruelty according to their directors' assessment of the costs and benefits involved. The military's "respect for human rights" did not change in the 1982–84 period, and claimed improvements in its human rights performance were questionable as well. In the mid-1980s the High Command merely substituted one pattern of abuse with another pattern in order to create the image, as Colonel Ponce noted above, that they were democrats. The U.S. Embassy, State Department, and others politically *predisposed* to accept this image cynically ignored the massive counterevidence generated by human rights advocacy organizations and denied that violations of human rights occurred, or, alternatively, they admitted that such acts occurred but denied that they were human rights violations (arguing that the civilian victims were FMLN masas and therefore legitimate military targets); described the violations as "excesses" rather than a basic component of the High Command's strategy to win a military victory; or argued that arbitrary arrest and torture represented an "improvement" over the scorched-earth policies of a few years earlier.[14]

It took the brutal killing of six Jesuits—fair-skinned intellectuals of predominantly European descent, people with whom Europeans and European Americans could identify—at the University of Central America on 16 November 1989 to bring home to the international community that respect for human rights had not improved in El Salvador. Planned by the High Command and executed by elements of the Atlacatl Battalion, the operation occurred toward the end of a decade that had been ushered in by the assassination of Archbishop Oscar Arnulfo Romero, on 24 March 1980 (cf. United Nations 1993:44–50; Special Task Force on El Salvador 1990; Doggett 1994; Whitfield 1995). Representative Joseph Moakley (Democrat, Massachusetts), who headed an investigation into the massacre of the Jesuits, concluded,

> We are convinced that the military's contribution to the problems of human rights and a paralyzed judicial system are not caused by a few renegade officers; they reside at the heart of the Armed Forces as an institution. Decades of power, tempered only by the need to maintain a working alliance with wealthy landowners and businessmen, have created an upper echelon within the armed forces that too often find deference to civilian authority neither necessary nor desirable. The tanda system has insulated many senior military officers from responsibility for their own actions, harming discipline, undermining morals and eroding professionalism. As a result, the armed forces remain unwilling to police themselves, and only accept the right of others to do so when enormous pressure is applied. (Special Task Force on El Salvador 1990:54)

The Salvadoran military entered the postwar period as a better-armed and better-organized killing machine than it had been at the beginning of the war but little changed in terms of its conception of the popular classes. In 1991 the Rand Corporation's Benjamin Schwarz wrote in a study of low-intensity warfare and El Salvador contracted by the U.S. Department of Defense that "American policy in El Salvador has perforce added immeasurably to the Salvadoran armed forces' political weight and resources. The military is larger, stronger, and more autonomous than at any time in its history, and it has not relinquished its self-appointed role as a bulwark against subversion" (1991:69).

In this context it is important to point out that the Achilles heel of the peace process was the refusal of the government to agree to the FMLN's proposals for a thoroughgoing demilitarization of Salvadoran society. The Peace Accords mandated a 50 percent reduction in the size of the military, from 63,000 to 31,500 troops, but this force level is still over three times larger than the number of troops—10,000—that composed the Salvadoran Armed Forces in 1979 (IDESES 1993:11). Some human rights offenders were ordered purged from the military following the September 1992 release of the Ad Hoc Commission report, but the limited nature of the investigation (only 240 of 2,203 officers were interviewed by the commission and 102 were recommended for transfer, demotion, or release), the lack of cooperation on the part of the Armed Forces, government resistance to carrying out the recommendations, and the vituperative outcry raised against investigators by military officials bespeak the institution's fortress mentality and its unwillingness to admit culpability in a time of peace for crimes committed during the civil war (Centro Universitario de Documentación e Información 1992a; IDHUCA 1992a).

In early January 1993, when President Alfredo Cristiani had for the umpteenth time attempted to annul the Ad Hoc Commission mandate by transferring to posts abroad some officers accused of human rights violations and leaving others untouched to serve out their careers at home, *El Salvador Proceso* editorialized,

> This signifies that the Armed Forces retains sufficient power to block the purge or, in the best of cases, to ensure that it is carried out when and how it [the military] decides. In other words, the reduced group of military chiefs that controls the army has veto power over the decisions of the president of the republic and, for that reason, the Armed Forces continues being, in fact, a discussant [in the matter], which is openly unconstitutional. With this power structure, the overthrow of the State is unnecessary, since the president of the republic is a prisoner of the Armed Forces. (Centro Universitario de Documentación e Información 1993b:2–3)

The purge of the military was eventually completed, though long after the sixty days mandated in the Peace Accords. However, the possibility that any of the officers named by the Ad Hoc Commission (or the Truth

Commission) might be tried for war crimes was removed by passage of the Amnesty Law (see chapter 7). Again, as in the past, impunity ruled.

The Armed Forces suffered a significant loss of prestige as a result of the public airing of the role of so many high-ranking officers in the planning and execution of grave human rights violations. But this may be a mere temporary setback, a less-than-fatal wound to a powerful institution that can be expected to attempt to assume its position at the head of society whenever popular struggles again threaten capitalist "order" and the beams of the international spotlight are redirected elsewhere. In September 1992, CDHES-NG archives contained the names of 176 officers "systematically involved in grave violations of human rights" (1992:3–4); many of the officials named were overlooked by the Ad Hoc and Truth Commission reports and now occupy positions of great authority in the supposedly "purified" and "professionalized" military.

The U.S. government gives little sign of trusting the "democratic" process that it claims to have initiated with elections in 1982, but it continues to maintain cordial relations with the Salvadoran military. It provided $12 million of military assistance to El Salvador in 1994; between August and December 1993 four hundred U.S. soldiers traveled to El Salvador to participate in "civic action" (mainly road-building) projects (Zielensky 1994); such projects were continued into mid-1995. Will these roads serve as military conduits in future counterinsurgency operations? Thanks to a 1992 constitutional amendment, the Salvadoran military is prohibited from intervening in domestic security issues, which are now the sole responsibility of the newly created National Civil Police, which is under civilian control and replaces the former security forces (National Guard, National Police, and Treasury Police). However, former president Cristiani twice used emergency powers to bring the army into the streets after that amendment took effect: once to protect the coffee harvest in 1992, and a second time to patrol major cities against a supposed wave of delinquency in 1993. And new president Armando Calderón Sol, who took office in May 1994 as Cristiani's replacement, lost little time in placing more than 7,000 soldiers on patrol throughout the country (including northern Morazán).

With the military formally relegated to a backseat in dealing with civil disturbances, death squads again function, now as an alternative shadow apparatus of repression. Not surprisingly, one of these death squads took the name of the commander (and probable intellectual author) of the El Mozote massacre, calling itself the Domingo Monterrosa Commando

Unit (Palumbo 1994). Many death-squad assassinations in the 1990s have been disguised as robberies or civil assaults in order to confuse human rights monitors. But the disproportionate representation of opposition activists and politicians among the victims leaves little doubt that these are political crimes aimed at punishing the regime's opponents, driving them underground, and destabilizing the peace process (CDHES-NG 1993). A 28 July 1994 report by the Joint Group for the Investigation of Illegal Armed Groups with Political Motivation in El Salvador described a panorama of violence more complex than that of the past, but also noted that "there are signs of active participation of active-duty members of the Armed Forces and National Police in many of the actions of political violence" (Joint Group 1994:56). It is clear that the purge of human rights violators in the military was far from complete.

The military's hysterical reaction to the Truth Commission report (see chapter 7), the urgency with which President Cristiani pushed through the Amnesty Law, and the shelter that the institution provides to human rights criminals bespeak the Salvadoran military's fundamental conservatism, its incapacity to develop a self-critique of its historic role, and the veiled threat that it continues to represent to civil society.

HISTORY AND MEMORY

Every image of the past that is not recognized by the present as one of its own concerns
threatens to disappear irretrievably.

—Walter Benjamin, *Illuminations*

In the debate that unfolded before, during, and after the public release of
the Ad Hoc Commission report on military officers and the subsequent
Truth Commission report, ideas about history and memory took center
stage. Many people on the Right argued that the past should be forgotten
because keeping it alive in present memory would impede the process
of national reconciliation. Thus a senior government official wondered
"whether it is better to bring to justice those believed responsible for
brutality or whether society is better served by trying to forget the past."
And he opted for the latter, arguing that "[a]t some point we just have to
say enough and move on. . . . Otherwise we will always be caught in the
past" (quoted in Farah 1993). For this official, the past was a time of un-
mitigated hatred between adversaries who have now resolved their differences at the negotiating table and must learn to live together; the
memory of such painful experiences will impede, perhaps even prevent,
completion of this task. Similar statements were made by President Alfredo Cristiani, his successor Armando Calderón Sol, and other officials
(Centro Universitario de Documentación e Información 1993a:5, 7; *Diario
de Hoy* 1993a).

But others have argued that the past cannot be erased just by force of
will. For those who were victims, who survived assassination attempts,
torture, rape, etc., or who were friends and relatives of those who did not
survive, the past intrudes upon, lives in, and must therefore be accom-

modated to the present (see Suárez-Orozco 1992; Salimovich et al. 1992). Rufina Amaya will never forget her internment in the home of Alfredo Márquez, the sight of her half-blind husband, Domingo Claros, running from the church, his execution at the hands of the soldiers, and, after her courageous escape, the cries of her children as they were brutally put to death. Rufina may or may not want to exact revenge. My sense is that revenge interests few people on the Left in El Salvador. But she and others do want some public accounting of the El Mozote massacre, beyond that which the Truth Commission, obstructed in its investigation by every barrier that the military and the Ministry of Justice could put up, has provided. Most important—and this is a sentiment very widely shared in northern Morazán—she wants guarantees that such horrible things will never occur again: *"El Mozote, nunca más"* ("El Mozote, never again").

This brings up another, more concrete, aspect in which the past lives on. Here I refer to the presence in the population of members of the Armed Forces (and others) who carried out or ordered the torture, rape, and murder of civilians. These are the people referred to in the Truth Commission and Ad Hoc Commission reports. Many of them are wealthy and powerful. To come to terms with them will require an enormous degree of political will. But to fail to do so by declaring a blanket amnesty, as did the Legislative Assembly in the bill passed on 20 March 1993, may encourage them to repeat the past, as Cynthia Arnson pointed out:

> The declaration of an amnesty for the ostensible purpose of national reconciliation may, in fact, only guarantee that new crimes are committed. Wiping the slate clean and pretending that human rights abuses did not take place is not the same as ensuring that they will not happen again. . . .
>
> It may be that at some point in the peace talks the different sides in the Salvadoran conflict agree to an amnesty except in several significant human rights cases agreed to by both sides. Such an agreement would represent a truly Pyrrhic victory. It would prevent the deep wounds of the past from healing, allow resentments to continue to burn, and ultimately endanger the hopes for true social reconciliation. (Arnson 1992:88)

To attempt to erase this history of trauma and suffering, of struggle, of defeat and victory would be to reject the lessons that might result from examination of the past; such lessons are hypostatized only when memory enters into a truly dialectical relationship with the present, as a creative element shaping it from within (see Taussig 1987; Benjamin 1968: 253–264). An effort is currently being made along these lines in northern Morazán, where the pastoral team led by the priests Rogelio Ponceele, Miguel Ventura, and, until June 1993, Esteban Velásquez works alongside grassroots organizations to place the El Mozote massacre within a historical narrative of popular resistance.[1]

Each year since 1991, the priests, assisted by catechists from the region, have conducted a memorial service in the open fields near the village. On 12 December 1992, the eleventh anniversary of the massacre and the first since the end of the civil war, the Christian Base Communities of El Salvador (CEBES), the Community Development Council of Morazán and San Miguel (PADECOMSM), the Communal Women's Movement (MCM), and Segundo Montes City organized an assembly in nearby Arambala. Carloads and several busloads of people arrived from the capital and other departments to accompany El Mozote survivors and regional peasants and workers in the commemoration. Photographs of the excavation carried out by the Argentine forensic team stood against the wall of Arambala's small chapel, located adjacent to the ruins of its destroyed church. After several brief speeches, songs by the Torogoces, and a poem read by a Chilean internationalist, about five hundred people marched to a field near El Mozote's Plain for more speeches and a mass. On that hot, still December afternoon Rufina Amaya told once again the story of her capture, escape, and all the horrible things that she had experienced. The people planted an *izote* tree, known for its stubborn capacity to grow back after being cut down (and adopted by some in the FMLN to symbolize the fortitude of the resistance struggle), and left wreaths of flowers commemorating the deceased at its foot.[2] The theme of the afternoon was "El Mozote, nunca más."

THE MUSEUM OF THE REVOLUTION

A similar process of historicization is under way in the FMLN Museum of the Salvadoran Revolution, Heroes and Martyrs, in Perquín, where professional curators from the capital have helped the *Frente* select items for exhibition from among its extensive collection of photographs, pamphlets, equipment, and war materiel. That the FMLN amassed and guarded such a large quantity of artifacts, including samples of the arms, munitions, radios, medical supplies, educational pamphlets, political statements, and photographs spanning the entire period of the civil war is

FIGURE 9 Jorge Meléndez (Comandante "Jonas"), one of the highest-ranking members of the FMLN (ERP faction), speaks at the 12 December 1992 commemoration of the El Mozote massacre, held in a field outside the center of the former hamlet three days before the final FMLN demobilization. Rogelio Ponceele, a priest who entered northern Morazán in 1980 and spent the entire war there, listens prayerfully at the extreme left of the stage. Between them stands Aparicio Orellana, a Catholic catechist and former FMLN combatant.

evidence of the organization's self-conscious approach toward the history it was making and its awareness of the importance of preserving traces of that history for future generations.

The Museum of the Revolution is intended as a "living museum" in which curators will periodically mount new exhibits drawing on different parts of the artifact collection. The viewer enters the Heroes and Martyrs Room and passes through four additional rooms to end the tour in a two-room concrete-block building that served as local headquarters for Radio Venceremos for several months in 1992. The museum also includes several outdoor exhibits: a mock guerrilla encampment replete with trenches and staff headquarters located in a coffee grove, and the crater from a 500-pound bomb in front of which is mounted an unexploded bomb of that size disarmed by FMLN demolition experts.

The master narrative of the museum is that of oppression and resistance, with the FMLN placed at the forefront of a process that began in

1932, if not before. A map in the second room delineates the boundaries of the four FMLN strategic "fronts"—the western, central, paracentral, and eastern—and attaches to each the name of a martyr of the 1898 Indian uprising or the 1932 rebellion: Feliciano Ama, Modesto Ramírez, Anastacio Aquino, and Francisco Sánchez, respectively. El Mozote figures at three points in the museum display. First, photographs of the forensic work at El Mozote are displayed on the south wall of the Heroes and Martyrs Room. This room is dedicated to the memory of the movement's precursors and supporters, and to those who fell along the way. Inclusion alongside Archbishop Romero, Rutilio Grande, and other "heroes and martyrs" associates the El Mozote dead with a purpose and an agency that only some of them consciously pursued, and allocates them an active, as opposed to a merely passive, role in what is ultimately portrayed as a victorious struggle. The message is implicit but unmistakable: the Salvadorans who died at El Mozote did so in order that survivors and future generations would be able to live in peace and with dignity.

The second and third references to El Mozote strengthen the place of the first reference in the narrative order and reinforce that order. Behind

FIGURE 10 The Museum of the Salvadoran Revolution, Heroes and Martyrs, a local FMLN project, opened on 12 December 1992 with a gala celebration. The sign reads: "Welcome to Perquín Morazán, Museum of the Salvadoran Revolution, Living Expression of the Collective Memory."

FIGURE 11 Samuel Vidal Guzmán worked as a museum guide in 1992. As a Catholic catechist and former health brigade worker with twelve years of experience in the FMLN, he was uniquely equipped to explain Morazanian history to museum visitors.

the main museum building is a concrete patio open on all four sides and roofed with aluminum sheeting. The principal artifact on the patio is a ten-foot piece of the tail section of Col. Domingo Monterrosa's helicopter, which was destroyed by a remote-controlled bomb in the skies over Joateca along with the colonel and high-ranking members of his entourage on 23 October 1984, shortly after the initiation of a major army push into northern Morazán known as Torola IV. Such was the symbolic importance (as well as the strategic significance) of this event that the

FMLN secured pieces of Monterrosa's helicopter and guarded them for over nine years. There is an artifact connected to the helicopter pieces in the Radio Venceremos Room, which houses receivers, radios, tape recorders, and mixers used during the war by the radio collective. There the visitor encounters the transmission unit adapted by FMLN technicians to send a remote signal to a small receiver that had been hidden, with dynamite attached, in a Venceremos broadcast transmitter "captured" by the army on a spur of Tizate Hill near Joateca following a confrontation staged by the FMLN (López Vigil 1991:316–338; Henríquez 1992: 253–262). A small typed sign explains that the helicopter was destroyed by eight *tacos* (sticks) of dynamite.

The symbolic importance of Monterrosa's destruction is played up by a second, smaller piece of his helicopter mounted on a stand in front of the Radio Venceremos building and near the bomb crater. As northern Morazanians were often the targets of Salvadoran Air Force pilots, the crater and the bomb are obvious symbols of state repression and its tie with U.S. imperialism, while the twisted pieces of Monterrosa's helicopter evidence what happens in a just world to people like Monterrosa who kill innocent civilians. Since it was the FMLN (the ERP specifically) that planned and carried out the operation, the exhibit presents the organization as the moral representative of an oppressed peasantry, following here the logic of liberation theology and its vision of a God of the poor who sanctions violence in defense of life when nonviolent channels have failed (Ellacuría 1991a:39–42; Lancaster 1988). The destruction of the helicopter some five hundred feet above Joateca had a cathartic effect (even if temporary) among civilians who remained in the zone, as noted by Father Rogelio Ponceele (López Vigil 1987:93):

In La Joya, quite close to the place where Monterrosa was killed, there was a celebration of the word with the community to give thanks to God. The theme of the liturgy was "God carries out justice through the medium of his people." And there were recreational games and a dance. We were so happy because of what had taken place. Some Europeans were scandalized when I told them that. It bothered them that we rejoiced at Monterrosa's death. They didn't realize what that signified for the advance of the people. They didn't realize that it wasn't only the death of one person, but the deaths that person had brought about and those that he could have brought about in the future. We didn't rejoice because of the tragic death of a person nor will we make a definitive judgment about it. That does not suit us. But we see in that death how God rejects the bad and never abandons his people. That is why we rejoice.

Some people would like to see El Mozote left as a memorial to the events that took place there. Adjacent to the plaza a small, black, sheet-metal statue in the form of a nuclear family (man, woman, two children) holding hands commemorates the victims. It was placed there by the Human Rights Institute of the University of Central America (IDHUCA) on 11 December 1991, the tenth anniversary of the massacre (Brown 1992:58). The memorial is propped up with stones, among which have been placed wooden crosses, bits and pieces of (human?) bone, and spent 5.56 mm cartridges from M-16s, the principal weapon of the Atlacatl Battalion.

IMAGINING EL MOZOTE

Since the war ended, El Mozote has been on the "must-see" list of solidarity tourists as well as internationalists working with the FMLN and with grassroots organizations in northern Morazán. Each day, when the weather permits, groups of foreigners and middle-class Salvadorans drive

FIGURE 12 The FMLN defused this 500-pound bomb, which currently resides in the Museum of the Salvadoran Revolution, Heroes and Martyrs. Museum curators located the bomb directly in front of an actual crater, the product of a bomb of similar size and configuration dropped on Perquín by a Salvadoran Air Force plane in April 1981.

FIGURE 13 The Human Rights Institute of the University of Central America placed this memorial in El Mozote in December 1991. The brass plaque at the base reads, "They have not died. They are with us, with you, and with all humanity."

through Arambala and, skirting the Arambala plaza and the remains of an adobe church destroyed by an air force bomb, they head up and over a low rocky pass. From the crest, the Arambala–Joateca road twists steeply downward toward the Sapo River. But long before one reaches the river, a narrow dirt road joins in from the right. This is the road to El Mozote. In good weather, which means dry, one can drive a four-wheel-drive vehicle with high clearance all the way to the former church; otherwise, people must park their vehicles a kilometer short of the plaza and make the remainder of the journey on foot. Either way the visitor traverses a gentle grade and then passes through a dark glade shaded by bamboo and mango trees. The road, low and soft, then breaks into the sunlight and passes between grassy pastures fenced in with barbed wire. The school, reconstructed in 1994–95, is up a dirt road to the left; one-story cement-block houses, a few still abandoned, intermittently front the road on the right. Another quarter mile and one enters a dusty plaza, formerly the nerve center of hamlet life, situated between El Chingo and La Cruz hills.

Many homes have been reconstructed and new ones are being built, but when I carried out most of the fieldwork for this project in 1992–93, the decaying walls of the roofless buildings, where nature had encroached into courtyards and even into the very structures, were among the few remaining signs of a vibrant, progressive community reduced to rubble, ashes, and torn flesh. It was a place where, for visitors like myself, wild imagination was kept in check by knowledge of the magnitude of the horror that took place there. A member of the Radio Venceremos team once recounted the following to Ignasio López Vigil (1991:162):

> Since then [the massacre], El Mozote has been converted into a sacred field. When years later we had to pass there with a guerrilla column, something very strange occurred that I have not related. It was an overcast night, and in approaching the place where the hamlet had been, thousands of glow-worms lit up at the same time. I mean thousands and thousands so that all the surrounding countryside was illuminated. And soon, as if due to a mysterious order, they all went out at the same time. And they lit up with that spectral light. And all turned off. I swear that I had never seen a thing like that in my life. And I believe that not one of those who that night was in our column has been able to forget the light of the glow-worms.

I, too, experienced El Mozote as a mysterious, if less transcendental, place during my first visit, having walked there from Arambala one scorching July day in 1991, six months before the cease-fire that ended the war. As I wound my way down into the flat and deserted green saddle between El Chingo and La Cruz hills, I heard the chirping of thousands of unseen grasshoppers and perceived the very faint drone of a spotter plane flying high overhead, out of missile range. That day the sound had an impact upon me the way that glow-worm light did upon the *compas*: the faint imprint of a thousand histories flickering on and off and on, each distinct and meaningful, and intertwined with others in a dense network of collective becoming. I walked up an overgrown path toward the school and toured the ruins. Regarding my experience there I wrote the following journal entry:

> I was looking for a spot of blood, a sign of struggle, anything that might give away what had occurred. The only thing I found was an empty tin of military issue food, and that could have been left there last year . . . or yesterday. . . . On the way out [of the hamlet] I was spooked by the sound of a bird whose rhythmic calls reminded me of

the sounds that commandos make in the movies. Though I had seen nothing, I felt as though I had been privy to a terrible secret. All that life, all those relationships, those plans, even if they only involved the repetition of a generations-old pattern, wiped out. Not by a hurricane or an earthquake, which some would attribute to the will of a sacred deity, but through a deliberate, carefully devised plan which interpreted every man, woman, and child in the north of Morazán as an intolerable threat to the social order of the rich.

What El Mozote may symbolize to others—how what happened there is played and replayed in their minds—I cannot say. The vast majority of the visitors, American and European tourists and solidarity workers or middle-class Salvadorans from the cities, arrive at the area unaccompanied. They leave no more the wiser, and often unimpressed. The few remaining collapsed roofs and fallen walls, which appear little different from those in scores of other battle-scarred Salvadoran communities, do not give up their histories without human assistance. The fortunate visitors obtain guides in Segundo Montes, or, better yet, Rufina Amaya traces for them the path of her internment and escape in order that the cruel and barbaric acts that took place at El Mozote might become part of the heritage of another generation.

Whereas northern Morazanians wish to see the story of El Mozote enter the annals of Latin American history as another atrocity perpetrated on innocent civilians by the state and the imperialist giant to the north, the Salvadoran and U.S. governments would like to see this story expire. But like the 1932 matanza, the El Mozote massacre has spread beyond the confines of northern Morazán. It should be obvious that I intend this book to add new details to the story of El Mozote and to disseminate that story to hitherto uninformed audiences. For me this work continues the tradition of Father Ponceele's memorial masses, the FMLN's Museum of the Revolution in Perquín, the historic ballads of the Torogoces musical group (one of its songs describes the death of Monterrosa), and other cultural and intellectual projects for which history serves as a political resource for the construction of a more equitable and just future.

THE REPOPULATION OF EL MOZOTE

Much of this book has dealt with El Mozote's past, or with efforts on the part of northern Morazanians to prevent the suppression of its past. In these accounts "El Mozote" acted upon the horizon of the present through the competing versions of the events that transpired there. Domingo Monterrosa, Rufina Amaya, Tutela Legal, Juan Mateu Llort, Todd Greentree, the Argentine forensic team, Mark Danner, the Truth Commission, and others produced chronicles, testimonies, hypotheses, assertions, and guesses to explain the why, what, and wherefore of the massacre.

It would be remiss of me to leave El Mozote hushed and abandoned under the harsh rays of the August sun at the same time that the community is being brought to life again.[3] To be complete, the story of El Mozote must also include the present, which is being fashioned by over 150 families who repopulated the area between January 1992 and September 1995.

Even as the brutal 1981 massacre marks El Mozote as a place of death, economic necessity has driven people to come to terms with that death in order to live. Hundreds of manzanas of cultivable land, made more fertile by twelve years of abandonment and rest, attract former residents currently living hand-to-mouth as petty merchants, construction workers, and service providers in cities, and as farm laborers in capitalist-dominated agro-export zones. Some former residents who repatriated to Segundo Montes City from exile in Colomoncagua, Honduras, between November 1989 and March 1990 are also working their land in El Mozote because they have none in Segundo Montes; some would move back to their native community but for the absence of basic services there.

Table 6 summarizes basic information about fourteen of the twenty households that had repopulated the El Mozote area as of August 1993. Twelve of these fourteen households were headed by former residents, and eleven of the twelve had lost family members in the massacre. Most of these people recall that they left the area because of a generalized "fear" or a more specific fear of an "army operation." About two-thirds abandoned the community in 1980, and the remainder left in 1981. They fled to familiar places to which they had traveled historically to make money, purchase needed goods, transact official business, and sell their products: Lourdes (department of La Libertad), a customary prewar destination for seasonal migrants; regional marketing and administrative centers such as San Miguel and San Francisco Gotera; La Montaña, where lumbering served as a reliable source of dry-season labor for many local peasants; and Joateca, a more "placid" peasant community eighteen kilometers east of El Mozote. No one attempted to repopulate El Mozote until the signing of the Peace Accords between the government and the FMLN, and the majority scheduled their returns after the FMLN's

National Army for Democracy (END) completed its demobilization and the mayors in exile reassumed their posts in the region's eight municipal centers.[4] The returnees indicated that land and the hope for a better life drew them back to northern Morazán and to El Mozote.

The repopulation of El Mozote is a response to the desire to return to places of origin, but it is also a product of the experience of displacement and the difficulty—impossibility for most people—of gaining a level of economic security comparable to that which they enjoyed before they fled the community. This is another side of El Mozote's history, and the histories of countless other rural communities in El Salvador whose inhabitants were similarly branded as guerrilla supporters and treated accordingly. Following are three brief accounts of the experiences of El Mozote survivors who, like other persons displaced from northern Morazán, were made objects of discrimination, surveillance, and repression by government officials, military units, and employers in the cities, towns, and displaced-persons camps where they sought refuge from the war (Lawyers Committee for International Human Rights and Americas Watch Committee 1984; Americas Watch Committee 1985:17; Cagan and Cagan 1991).

1. Rogelio and María

The experiences of Rogelio and María, whose story I have touched upon in chapters 5 and 6, illustrate the point. It will be recalled that Rogelio left his home in La Ranchería for Lourdes with several of his sons in April 1981 to earn cash with which to purchase fertilizer for the spring corn planting. María followed him in September, and they left the land in the care of their sons-in-law and their families, who were savagely murdered in or near their homes by the Atlacatl Battalion during the massacre. During his ten-year displacement, Rogelio worked mainly as a field hand picking coffee, cutting sugarcane, and clearing irrigation ditches. But the intense heat of La Libertad took a toll on his fifty-eight-year-old body, and he often took ill and was unable to work. To keep the family afloat, María learned to pick coffee when she was fifty years old.

The influx of displaced persons into Lourdes generated heavy competition for the limited number of laboring positions available, and many employers did not want to give work to people from far away because they claimed that they were from the guerrillas. María argued with them: "How can that be? If we were from the guerrillas, we would be there with

Table 6   Families Repopulating El Mozote as of August 1993

Initials	Current Family Size	Prewar Residence	Members Killed in Massacre	Date Left	Reason for Leaving
1. JSC	3	El Mozote	Yes	4/81	Fear
2. SH	4	El Mozote	Yes	1980	Fear
3. FRM	9	El Mozote	Yes	8/80	Guerrillas
4. OP	11	El Mozote	Yes	12/81	Army operation
5. AOL	6	Joateca	No	Before war	Army operation
6. MSM	9	Tierra Colorada	Yes	1981	Fear
7. MDP	8	El Mozote	?	8/81	Fear
8. SA	6	Perquín	No	?	?
9. MMM	9	El Mozote	Yes	12/9/81	Army operation
10. LM	6	El Mozote	Yes	10/81	Fear
11. CC	7	El Mozote	Yes	8/80	Fear
12. SC	9	El Mozote	Yes	3/81	Fear
13. MO	4	El Mozote	Yes	7/80	Fear
14. SB	2	Los Toriles	Yes	12/11/81	Army operation

Source: Direct investigation, June–July 1993.
Note: In most cases the destination column refers to town center (e.g., Joateca) or city (e.g., San Francisco Gotera) within the department of Morazán. Otherwise destination is recorded as the hamlet or town to which the refugees were displaced, followed by the municipality (if in Morazán), department (if in El Salvador), or country.

them. We came here for work." To earn additional money, María bought and sold mangoes, chickens, bread, chocolate—virtually anything that she could get her hands on—in the local market and produced embroidered tortilla cloths in her "spare" time. She and her husband rented an apartment for several years and then purchased a lot on time from an army colonel and constructed a small house. (Having stolen lives and property from peasants formerly residing in conflict zones, some members of the officers' corps victimized the survivors a second time by subdividing real estate into house lots for sale to the refugee population created by the military's depredations.)

Tragedy struck a few years later when paramilitary forces disappeared one of María and Rogelio's sons, who left behind a widow and several children. Shortly thereafter, a second son was similarly abducted and killed. For María and Rogelio, Lourdes proved a perilous refuge, only marginally better than El Mozote. Their last two sons left El Salvador for

Destination	Date Returned	Reason for Returning	Land Owned in El Mozote
Lourdes, La Libertad	8/92	Work	5.0 mz
SF Gotera	3/93	Better life	1.5 mz
Sabanetas, Arambala	3/28/93	Land	10.0 mz
Colomoncagua, Hon.	2/92	Peace	62.0 mz
Colomoncagua, Hon.	12/6/92	Land	0.4 mz
San Miguel, S.M.	4/92	Peace	Little
Sabanetas, Perquín	2/21/93	Better life	1.0 mz
El Carrizal, Arambala	2/4/93	Land	2.5 mz
Joateca	2/28/93	Land	3.0 mz
Lourdes, La Libertad	8/92	Land	?
SF Gotera	8/92	Land	Some
SF Gotera	8/92	Land	Some
?	2/20/93	Better life	6.0 mz
Joateca	8/92	Love of land	0.5 mz

the United States, where they currently reside, but the parents seldom hear from them.

Rogelio and María returned to El Mozote because Rogelio owned twenty-five manzanas of land there, and perhaps because they remembered that time before the war when they had been relatively self-sufficient (see chapter 5). Now Rogelio works the cornfield alone, a spry seventy-year-old who skips along trails with the speed and confidence of a man half his age, but whose diminutive frame, weakened with age, cannot withstand the rigors of what has become, for all practical purposes, a frontier life.

2. Andrés

Forty-seven-year-old Andrés survived the massacre because his home lay a few hundred meters outside the operation's area. But his young wife, who was visiting a sick relative in El Mozote, became trapped inside the circle of soldiers. Once Andrés realized what was taking place, he gathered their two young children and fled northern Morazán for Lourdes. In the competition for scarce work, he, like Rogelio and María, experienced discrimination due to his origin. He moved to San Salvador and for years earned his living loading trucks there and, later, in San Miguel. Bitter over the death of his wife and the difficulties that he had to overcome to raise two children without her, he returned to El Mozote to farm his sixty-two manzanas of land.

3. Miguel

Other survivors remained in northern Morazán and sought shelter in the cold, moisture-laden northern mountains, which the army seldom entered. Miguel left El Mozote for Honduras in August of 1980 and spent eighteen months in the border town of Marcala; then he crossed back into El Salvador and settled in the high pine forests of Sabanetas in La Montaña. In Sabanetas, Miguel established a small business buying and selling corn, and ran it until he was forced to leave in 1984 or 1985 (the exact year is uncertain) by the Arce Battalion, another of the army's five U.S.-trained immediate-reaction infantry battalions.[5] According to Miguel, the Arce Battalion soldiers told the people living in Sabanetas that they were going to do the same thing there as had been done in El Mozote. Miguel took the threat seriously and fled, leaving behind goods worth over five thousand colones. When he returned several months later to recover the merchandise, it had all been stolen. He spent the next six months in El Social near Perquín, where he says he ran afoul of a local FMLN commander who suspected him of collaborating with the government. Unable to work in peace, Miguel left the zone for San Miguel, where he spent the remaining seven years of the war. Like the peasants mentioned above, Miguel returned to El Mozote because he owned land there, in his case ten manzanas.

Others recount equally difficult experiences of flight and repression, poverty and struggle. They are drawn back to El Mozote by the prospect of returning to the land, working for themselves rather than for others, and raising their families in a moral community absent the *vicios* (vices) common in many of the cities and towns where they took refuge. Every one of the twelve former inhabitants who provided information about his/her flight from the community, life in exile, and return to El Mozote owned land in the area, even if only a small field; a few returnees (e.g., see table 6, JSC and OP) possessed substantial amounts. Even so, the earliest returnees seeking to resurrect El Mozote, or, perhaps better stated, to create it anew, endured terribly difficult conditions, perhaps as formidable as those faced by the settlers who first populated the hamlet fifty years ago. Because of an absence of wells, they drew water from open water courses made turbid by the spring rains. Children had to walk forty minutes to reach the nearest school in Arambala, which provides instruction only through grade four. And local commerce consisted of a single, small, poorly stocked store located in Tierra Colorada—a long walk for those who resided in Los González or La Ranchería.

Securing subsistence in a sparsely settled community that was abandoned to nature for more than ten years posed the greatest challenge. Trees and thick brush covered formerly cultivated fields and obliterated most secondary trails. Cutting the forest and clearing the land for planting was laborious and time consuming when the only available tools were axes and machetes. Most peasants were fortunate if they succeeded in planting small fields of corn with which to sustain their households. The perennial henequen plants, which might have survived prolonged periods of inattention, were burned by the army during the war to deny the guerrillas access to the products and to pressure civilian masas to leave the area.[6] No one was in the position to invest labor and very scarce capital into preparing and planting a field of henequen that had to be tended for three to four years until the first returns would be realized. And even if some farmers had planted henequen, the fiber extracted from the plant and the artisan goods produced from the fiber had been devalued by the importation from Honduras of bags and lassos woven from cheap, durable synthetic fibers. Soldiers also destroyed sugarcane fields and carted off the trapiches that processed sugarcane into panela.

Perhaps worst of all, the first returnees residing in El Mozote had no dependable source of cash to invest in production and to purchase the clothing, shoes, medicines, fertilizer, and other goods that they consumed but did not produce. The wealthier peasants and merchant agriculturists who had employed land-poor and landless peasants in their dry-season sugarcane- and henequen-processing operations had died in the massacre or made new lives for themselves in the cities.

The returnees to El Mozote might have looked forward to assistance from international foundations and humanitarian organizations that aided the repopulation of Tenancingo, Cabañas; Las Vueltas and San

Antonio Los Ranchos, Chalatenango; Segundo Montes, Morazán; and other communities abandoned during the early eighties (Edwards and Siebentritt 1991; Cagan and Cagan 1991; Americas Watch Committee 1987: 157–184). In northern Morazán peasants organized through Segundo Montes City, CEBES, MCM, and PADECOMSM acquired programs in education, health, and production with the financial and technical assistance of groups such as Doctors without Borders (France), Aid in Action (England), Voices on the Border (United States), and the European Union. However, El Mozote's repopulation was unsponsored and, until recently, gradual; and the protagonists were people who, for the most part, shunned publicity, lacked international contacts, and were reluctant (for obvious reasons) to make demands on the state.

On 20 March 1994 Salvadorans voted in the first postwar elections, the culmination of the two-year peace process. Concepción Márquez, who works in education in Segundo Montes, was one of 5 victorious FMLN mayoral candidates in northern Morazán (of 8 contenders). Nationwide, the FMLN gained 21 seats in the legislature and more than a dozen mayoralties. But overall, ARENA won a smashing victory and remained in control of the presidency, the legislature, and 212 of the 262 municipal councils (Vickers and Spence 1994:6). Thus, the ability of Meanguera's new mayor to respond to the needs of her constituents in El Mozote appeared to rest on the relationship that FMLN-controlled communities could establish with politically hostile departmental and federal authorities, as well as on El Mozote's success in winning programs in competition with larger and equally needy populations concentrated in Segundo Montes and in the town of Meanguera.[7] The prospects were not good.

But in October 1994, when I returned to El Mozote for the first time in seven months, the difference in the social landscape was surprisingly palpable. A steep section of the road in Tierra Colorada had been paved with stone, greatly facilitating the entrance to El Mozote of vehicles with low wheel clearance. Several dozen new homes were visible along the road; others clustered around the plaza, where, as before the war, people gathered for late afternoon chats in the shade of a large amate tree. I learned from the president of the local council that, according to a recent census, the population comprised 155 families, more than 750 people in all. About 85 percent of them had arrived since my last visit. When I asked people why they had moved back to El Mozote, I was given the same answers that Shelli McMillen obtained during the summer of 1993: almost all of the returnees owned or had inherited land in El Mozote and viewed peasant agriculture as an attractive alternative to low-wage employment in agro-export zones or the informal sector of the urban economies of San Miguel, San Salvador, and other cities. They returned with dreams of economic improvement, but with very little capital to make those dreams into realities.

The U.S.-based CARE, a relief and development agency, had donated materials for latrine construction, and CARE health promoters arrived daily from their office in San Miguel to instruct the peasants in latrine construction and utilization, and in the importance of water purification. CARE also had organized a credit committee, which was financing (at 14–16 percent interest) subsistence cultivation of corn, beans, and other agricultural products. Fifty yards east of the amate tree, a new *casa comunal,* constructed of bamboo and sheet metal, rested on the foundation of the former casa. Marcos Díaz's store, now run by a surviving sister and her husband, was open for business, although the offerings were few in comparison to those when Díaz himself tended the counter. The school was in the process of being rebuilt with money from USAID channeled through the National Reconstruction Secretariat.

The CARE- and USAID-funded school-construction projects might never have been undertaken but for a preelection visit to El Mozote by Rep. Joseph Moakley, who lobbied the State Department on behalf of the community. While the current residents appreciate the assistance, it is poor recompense for the damage wrought by the U.S.-trained and U.S.-armed Atlacatl Battalion.[8] It is ironic that the U.S. government waits for a Japanese apology for having instigated the war in the Pacific, but has never considered apologizing for its role in the all-out civil war on Salvadoran workers and peasants.

MEMORY AGAIN

I have often wondered what it must be like to reside in El Mozote, a place that I imagine to be saturated with painful memories, whether imagined or rooted in the real. Is it difficult, I wonder, to tread the same ground over which your siblings, grandparents, parents, nephews, cousins, lovers, friends, and neighbors were marched to their deaths? Do people pause each time they pass the ruins of the sacristy, the church, and the homes of Israel Márquez, Alfredo Márquez, and others where people were interned and cold-bloodedly murdered? Or do the practical necessities of life, the daily "inconveniences" of extracting a living from this overgrown landscape, take precedence in the residents' thoughts? Neither I nor Shelli McMillen ever conversed about El Mozote in quite these terms with those who live there now. However, the willingness of many people to discuss in detail the community's past and the numerous losses they suffered when the Atlacatl nearly eradicated the community, as well as the seeming incapacity of others to speak with us about that past at all, suggest that for many, images of the massacre are submerged just below the surface of the mind like a suppressed nightmare capable of breaking unpredictably into consciousness.

Things would have been simpler, I believe, had the FMLN won a clearcut military victory and embarked on the construction of a government committed to the poor. But the war remained stalemated for years, and its resolution was contradictory and ambiguous. In exchange for a series of concessions outlined in the Peace Accords, the FMLN acknowledged the legitimacy of the ARENA-dominated government, which then proceeded to use the power of incumbency to undermine the accords wherever possible. As a result, two and one-half years after the cease-fire the repressive National Police continue to patrol half the nation's territory, the army has been in the streets, death squads enjoy a mini-resurgence, and the intellectual authors of the most egregious human rights violations stride freely through the Zona Rosa after being "graciously" pardoned as a result of Cristiani's Amnesty Law (see CDHES-NG 1993). The government is attempting to roll back the gains won by the FMLN and its supporters as a result of twelve years of struggle. To the extent that it is successful, the FMLN and its sympathizers will have an increasingly difficult time fitting El Mozote into a narrative history of sacrifice, struggle, and victory. And those who died there will, more and more, appear to the survivors to have died in vain. Already malaise has visited northern Morazán, especially among elderly people condemned to loneliness by the deaths of children and grandchildren, and among many former FMLN combatants whose sole gain from the war consisted of a few pieces of cheap furniture, some kitchen utensils, agricultural work tools, and a month's supply of food.

If El Mozote cannot for long be assimilated into a narrative of oppression, struggle, and victory, it will at least remain a symbol of the first of those terms. Along with the murder of Archbishop Romero and the assassination of the Jesuit priests at the University of Central America, El Mozote is one of El Salvador's (and Latin America's) major symbols of state repression, if for no other reason than that the majority of the victims there were young children, the aged, and the infirm—those least interested in challenging the social order and least able to defend themselves from its guardians. As the government plan to base El Salvador's future development on selling the nation as an offshore manufacturing platform for transnational capital—a mini-Taiwan, as it were—reaches its limits, and as the reconstruction funds that have temporarily stabilized the economy dry up, it is inevitable that social mobilization and social protest will grow to levels that threaten the system's architects and its principal beneficiaries. When the president, whether Armando Calderón Sol (1994–2000) or some other front man for the oligarchy and bourgeoisie, calls out the military to quash peaceful marches, work stoppages, and demonstrations in city and countryside, we can only hope that one of the cries that rallies the popular classes to resist this new wave of repression will be "EL MOZOTE, NUNCA MÁS!"

AN ALTERNATIVE ANTHROPOLOGY

EXERCISING THE PREFERENTIAL

OPTION FOR THE POOR

To articulate the past historically does not mean to recognize it as "the way it really was" (Ranke). It means to seize hold of a memory as it flashes up at a moment of danger.
—Walter Benjamin, *Illuminations*

Visitors to northern Morazán and to El Mozote often enjoy the hospitality of the little concrete-block hotel at the visitors' center in Segundo Montes. There, one can get a bed in a small room for twenty-five colones (roughly three dollars) a night and take meals at the outdoor cafeteria or walk down the dirt road to eat at La Guacamaya Subversiva next to a community grocery and BANCOMO (Community Bank). In the mornings delegations of foreigners assemble for tours of Segundo Montes or day trips to El Mozote, Perquín (the former "guerrilla capital" of Morazán), or elsewhere. In the late afternoon and early evening, the visitors return and over soft drinks and beer in the cafeteria they replay the day's experiences.

One of the few persons they regularly seek out is Rufina Amaya, whose account of the El Mozote massacre was first broadcast by Radio Venceremos and appeared in abbreviated form several weeks later in the *New York Times* and the *Washington Post*. Since 1990, Rufina has shared her story dozens of times. On various occasions she has even guided visitors around El Mozote, pointing out the former site of the Alfredo Márquez house in which she was interned with the other women and children. Then she retraces the route down the main street, around a corner, and up the little footpath to the home of Israel Márquez, toward which the soldiers marched her along with other adult women to a certain death.

The tree behind which she crouched grows a little larger each year. It is rooted only a hundred meters from the slopes of Cerro Chingo, where Rufina hid in a patch of maguey before she finally made her escape from the smoldering ruins of El Mozote.

But most visitors are unaware that the wooden shacks located a few meters from their sleeping quarters are home to at least a half dozen other former residents of El Mozote, each with a story about the community and about flight and survival that is as affecting, if not quite as graphic or shocking, as the story told by Rufina Amaya. Nor do they know, or are many of them interested to know, that the pitted sheet-metal roofing and loosely boarded walls throughout the five settlements that compose Segundo Montes house thousands of other people who survived assassinations, massacres, captures, and bombings. These survivors—there is no better word to signify their situation—are working to construct a new community out of the ruins of numerous destroyed ones. Visitors to the region are much more interested in the social experiment in progress than they are in the tragedies that engendered it. Thus, few of the stories actually get told to foreigners, not because of a deficit of storytellers, but because listeners are so few and far between. And when Salvadorans do gain an audience, as has, at times, María Teresa Tula, exiled to the United States, they are often not believed, as Tula noted:

It's interesting. When there are macabre crimes and murders committed in this country then people demand justice. I've seen it on television here. When someone commits a bloody crime like a rape or a murder, they can be sentenced to die in the electric chair. And yet when these same kinds of savage crimes are committed in El Salvador, no one demands justice. They don't believe what goes on in my country. Even journalists who have interviewed me use language that delegitimates my experience. They write, María Teresa Tula "alleged" or "said" that she was tortured. The way they frame my responses makes it sound like there is some doubt about what happened or that I imagined what happened to me. This is very painful for me and anyone who gives testimony about their own torture.

Sometimes I say, "How come they don't believe me?" I'm not going to take off my clothes in public and say, "Look, here are the scars from my wounds where I was tortured." I'm not going to hold up a piece of x-ray film and say, "Here is the evidence of how my spinal cord was injured during my torture." I'm not telling my story because I want pity. I don't want people to say, "pobrecita, poor thing." We don't want people to feel sorry for us. (cited in Stephen 1994b:175–176)

According to a census carried out in December 1991 by the Initiative for Alternative Development (IDEA) with the assistance of community leaders, Segundo Montes's 1,774 families (representing a population of 7,900 on the eve of the Peace Accords) lost 5,056 members during the war, among whom 1,976 were victims of "repression" broadly defined and another 2,375 died in "combat," fighting, with few exceptions, on the side of the FMLN (IDEA 1992).[1] These banal figures illustrate two vivid truths: first, that Segundo Montes is replete with survivors of the civil war with stories to tell; and second, that the massive repression intended to intimidate into silence the northern Morazanian peasantry engendered instead an equally massive collective resistance that, prolonged for over twelve years (and replicated in other areas of the country), partly explains why the more numerous and better-armed government forces failed to win the civil war.

Wouldn't it be preferable if, instead of reading my narrative about El Mozote, we could listen directly to those who lived there recount the pride that they had in their community, the joy of the fiestas, the difficulty of making a living, the hard work involved in securing the cemetery and school and in organizing the agricultural cooperative? They would tell us of the bodies that showed up one day in the cemetery, the sounds of the shells that fell on La Guacamaya on the other side of the hill, and the rumors of an impending invasion of army troops who would exterminate the population. We would want to hear from those who fled to La Montaña and were threatened by the Civil Defense forces there, as well as those who, resting in their flight near Rancho Quemado, looked south and saw huge flocks of turkey vultures circling above the Plain and then followed with their eyes the black smoke curling upward from smoldering fires. At that moment they knew that El Mozote was finished and that there would be no return. Many would also recount weathering years of discrimination, persecution, and intimidation as refugees and displaced persons in Colomoncagua, La Montaña, Lourdes, San Miguel, San Francisco Gotera, and perhaps even the United States, where the government argued that all but a select few Salvadorans were economic refugees fleeing poverty rather than political refugees fleeing repression. Like a torrent of water in a stream swollen by summer rains, our narrators would rush onward, collapsing the past into the present with descriptions, accounts, stories of their return—impoverished but hopeful—to a devastated land where instead of salvation they found more tribulation: continuing military repression and harassment (until the war ended), barren soil, a lack of employment opportunities, and rudimentary shelter.

It would be best, I think, if we were shucking corn, sorting beans, or engaged in some other repetitive task that relaxes the mind. "Boredom," Walter Benjamin (1968:91) tells us, "is the dream bird that hatches the egg of experience. A rustling in the leaves drives him away."[2] Then, perhaps, we would drive the ticking hands of the clock back to zero and learn again how to let the words of the storyteller fill our heads. Therein lies the danger of this account of El Mozote's people and their history, and of analogous accounts of other peoples and events: the conversion of stories, vibrant and living, into information, dead and self-contained, through their inscription and analysis. But if in this book I have taken stories told to me and transformed them into information for reproduction, consumption, and disposal, I have at least sought to mitigate the worst of the effects by organizing that information in a way that owes more to the oral historian than to the archivist, more to the testimonial than to the ethnography. The work has been polemical, deliberately so; I have assumed (I think) a consistent political register marked by an identification with the plight of the poor and a cynicism regarding the claims of power; and I have tried to show how the El Mozote massacre, a short episode in a long civil war, draws people and relationships together over vast distances and decades of time. It is linked in a complex chain of causalities to Cortés and Pedro de Alvarado; it references the violent dispossession of peasants from the fertile volcanic uplands during the last quarter of the nineteenth century and the first quarter of the twentieth (it is likely that some of the refugees from those displacements settled in northern Morazán); El Mozote descends from the great matanza of 1932, when several thousand desperate peasants challenged the oligarchical system and tens of thousands were indiscriminately slaughtered by its defenders. And without doubt "El Mozote" is a call for reflection upon the human dimension of the U.S. counterinsurgency strategies launched at the beginning of the 1960s. El Mozote is one tragic chapter in the long, bloody history of capitalism. It is emblematic of the capitalist history being made at these present moments (the moment at which I am writing and the one in which you are reading), as well as a portent of those histories that are to come and the brutalities that will surely accompany them. On the other hand, I have also suggested an alternative future in which El

Mozote, to borrow a phrase from the epigraph to this chapter, becomes one of those memories that future generations "seize hold of . . . at a moment of danger."

THE "PREFERENTIAL OPTION" AND THE LIMITS
OF ANTHROPOLOGY

Benjamin states that "there is no story for which the question as to how it continued would not be legitimate" (1968:100).[3] The testimonial—which provides the architectural framework for my narrative—is a type of story distinguished from other categories of stories by the intimate relationship between the teller and the account. For nontestimonial stories, a storyteller's audience can become storytellers in their own right—simplifying, embellishing, or restructuring what they have heard as they see fit before sharing it with others. But the testimonial loses its moral force and much of its truth value when recounted by anyone other than the witness who lived the experiences that are at the heart of the narrative. It is at that point that my effort to model *this* story on the testimonial encounters its limits.

As a storyteller in the generic sense rather than a witness to a lived experience, I have been able to do no more than share the testimonies that northern Morazanians shared with me during interviews and conversations. Invariably, I have translated their accounts in ways that might not please every one of the people who contributed to the construction of this narrative, but such is the contradiction between the speaker and the scribe, the telling and its translation.[4] In anthropology this contradiction—between those who are at liberty to describe the cultures of others and those others less able to contest their objectification, whose beliefs and practices are described—lies at the heart of the ethnographic enterprise; it will exist as long as some people have the desire and, more significantly, the opportunity and the power to make objects of the lives of others. Because the contradiction has its roots in a concrete relationship, a form of being-in-the-world, it cannot be canceled out, bracketed off, elided, or absolved by elaborate word play or innovations in ethnographic writing, such as the ones discussed by George Marcus and Michael Fischer (1986). (Who, ultimately, determines the form and content of the text, and whose career is advanced or jeopardized according to the text's reception?) A distinguished Vietnamese filmmaker and critic writes,

On one plane, we, I and he [the anthropologist], may speak the same language and even act alike; yet, on the other, we stand miles apart, irreducibly foreign to each other. This is partly due to our distinct actualities and our definite history of involvement and power relationship. What I resent most, however, is not his inheritance of a power he so often disclaims, disengaging himself from a system he carries with him, but his ear, eye, and pen, which record in his language while pretending to speak through mine, on my behalf. (Minh-ha 1989:48)

Edward Said provides a similar, if more global, formulation: "Without significant exception, the universalizing discourses of modern Europe and the United States assume the silence, willing or otherwise, of the non-European world. There is incorporation; there is inclusion; there is direct rule; there is coercion. But there is only infrequently an acknowledgment that the colonized people should be heard from and their ideas known" (1993:50).

Imperialism enabled anthropology, as one of Said's "universalizing discourses," to speak for and about others. And the contemporary forms of imperialism, as virulent as the earlier ones even if less visible, enable its current practice, presiding over the unequal access to resources that makes it possible for a few, mostly European American, anthropologists to study a great many informant peoples of color.[5] There exists no contradiction between anthropology and imperialism per se; the majority of anthropologists only object when imperialist intervention threatens the physical existence of the subjects who are the bearers of the ideas and practices that they study. In El Salvador those prospective subjects— "exotic" Native Americans—were mostly killed off during the 1932 matanza, with the result that El Salvador never developed a reputation in the United States or Europe as a desirable field site for anthropological work.[6] With notable exceptions few U.S. anthropologists protested in print the slaughter perpetrated by their government and the Salvadoran military on tens of thousands of mestizo peasants, workers, and students.[7] On the other hand, more anthropologists responded to the Guatemalan military's scorched-earth policies that were wiping out thousands of highland Mayans who had for decades served up the ethnographic "raw material" for the molding of academic reputations. But even in Guatemala, the response was muted; only a handful of the dozens of anthropologists who had carried out research there got involved.[8]

Since at least the early 1970s the officers of the American Anthropological Association have struggled to prevent political and economic contradictions of the larger universe from threatening the discipline's tenuous internal "unity," which, in a period of shrinking resources for the social sciences and humanities, is a prerequisite for maintaining academic positions and funding levels vis-à-vis competing social sciences. In 1970 anthropologists participating in Department of Defense–sponsored counterinsurgency studies in Thailand were absolved of wrongdoing by the Ad Hoc Committee (chaired by Margaret Mead and known as the Mead Committee), while two members of the Committee on Ethics who had publicly criticized this embrace of imperialism were chastised. In one of the association's brighter moments, the Mead Committee report was overwhelmingly voted down (Wakin 1992), and a year later, in 1971, the AAA issued its Principles of Professional Responsibility, which assigned "anthropologists' paramount responsibility . . . to those they study" and forbade participation in clandestine and secret research (Fleuhr-Lobban 1991:248). The Committee on Potentially Harmful Effects of Anthropological Research (COPHEAR) existed during the next three years (1972–74), but it died "primarily for want of cooperation and success in collecting information sufficient to carry out its charge," and a proposal for a successor Committee on Ethnocide and Genocide was dropped by the Executive Board prior to the 1974 meetings (Berreman 1991:62–63).

In the following (post-Vietnam) period most anthropologists demonstrated little public concern over violations of their subjects' human rights. There are several reasons for this, but they don't appear among those listed by Theodore Downing and Gilbert Kushner (1988:3) in their introduction to *Human Rights and Anthropology*. There they attribute the "relative paucity of anthropological literature specifically focused on human rights" to "(1) the small number of anthropologists, (2) disciplinary tradition and (3) lack of funding for human rights research." These explanations strike me as less than satisfactory. First, their "small number" has not prevented anthropologists from devoting a great deal of attention to indigenous conceptions of time, Australian aboriginal kinship systems, Native American religion, or a host of other issues. Second, to attribute the lack of interest in human rights to anthropology's "disciplinary tradition" begs the question. Anthropology's historic subjects have, as defined by that "tradition," been among the oppressed, so why haven't the various dimensions of oppression (social, economic, political) assumed a more prominent role within anthropological discourse? And more importantly, why haven't more anthropologists committed themselves to political *engagement* on behalf of their subjects, rather than confining most of their energies to sharing materials with like-minded colleagues through specialist books and journals? Finally, one might ask how many funding proposals have anthropologists really introduced to carry out human rights research? Must all research wait on the largesse of a benevolent patron before being undertaken?

Some in the field argue that extreme cultural relativism or a rigid commitment to science and "objectivity" account for some anthropologists' political passivity before human rights violations. Radical cultural relativists cannot agree on a universal code of human rights (Schirmer 1988:92; Dundes Renteln 1990; cf. Messer 1993:224), while some science-oriented anthropologists hide behind a self-imposed "neutral observer status" and professional division between research and application to justify their lack of involvement.

Consider what has occurred in the last twenty-five years within the North American anthropological community. Shortly after its formation, the Committee on Ethics underwent a metamorphosis from a committee "concerned with ethical principles and practice to one devoted primarily to personnel matters: fairness in employment and promotions, issues of plagiarism, priority of publication, and conflict of interest" (Berreman 1991:59, cf. Hill 1987:15). Responding to the "needs" of the growing number of "practicing anthropologists" (i.e., those employed outside academia by business, government, and, to a lesser degree, private voluntary organizations) in the American Anthropological Association, the Executive Board recommended replacing the Principles of Professional Responsibility with a new Code of Ethics. Drafted in 1982 by the Committee on Ethics, the draft Code of Ethics would have watered down the "Principles" by lowering the priority of anthropologists' responsibility to their informants, eliminating restrictions on clandestine research, and removing the principle of anthropological accountability for ethical violations. Berreman believes that "these omissions have resulted not in a code at all, but a mild statement of intent, and one conspicuously devoid of ethical content . . . a license for unfettered free-enterprise research." He concluded, "It seems that the era of Reaganomics spawned the nightmare of Reaganethics" (1991:52, 66).[9]

The 1982 draft Code of Ethics was not adopted, but by 1990 the Principles of Professional Responsibility had been amended so as to eliminate six clauses in the 1971 Principles that prohibited clandestine and secret research (Wakin 1992:235). An even more radical overhaul to the ethics code was proposed at the November 1995 meeting of the American Anthropological Association in Washington, D.C., where the reigning ethics committee, buckling under to the growing presence of practicing anthropologists and their "practical" needs, proposed to abandon all standards of anthropological accountability and move from ajudication to education. Among the reasons offered to the twenty to twenty-five people in attendance at the lunchtime meeting to discuss the new ethics code—a measure of the general disinterest in this topic—were the lack of staff for investigation, lack of funds to carry insurance in case of lawsuits brought against the association, and the fact that even were the association to expel a member for violations of the ethics code, it lacks all power to prevent that person from continuing to practice anthropology.

Now, at last, anthropology has discovered human rights, which was selected as the theme of the 1994 annual meeting.[10] Overbey (1994:1) tells us, "By far the most popular topic of the meeting, human rights [with 29 sessions] surpasses sessions on culture (24), gender (24) and even identity (21)." But does the number of sessions reflect a profound anthropological commitment to human rights, or is it the cumulative result of individuals' strategies to pass paper and session proposals by the AAA screening committee? Will human rights issues remain a high priority in future meetings with different thematic foci? And will anthropologists become public advocates for *structural* change at the risk of being barred from further access to field sites and those subject peoples who reside in them (Ringberg 1995), or will they instead continue to write for specialized, academic audiences of peers while their subjects' health, livelihoods, and environments are destroyed before their eyes by the forces of global capitalism?[11]

I am not optimistic that many anthropologists will dedicate themselves to seeking structural change instead of merely working toward readjusting the brutal international system of domination and exploitation so as to make it a little less brutal. Anthropologists are "establishment" products, and those who have found jobs within the system have made their peace with it: most are locked into a comfort zone of middle-class rewards, reveling in their "liberalism" and parrying the stickier moral questions that occasionally confront them as they jet back and forth between materially understocked field settings in the South and materially overstocked homes in the North. A significant percentage are now employed outside academia. For most (not all, of course) of these "practicing anthropologists," anthropology has become a job for which the parameters and constraints (what can and cannot be investigated and said) are set by their employers. "[T]he educated and cultured of the world, the well-born and well-bred, and even the deeply pious and philanthropic" cannot escape the contradiction that they "receive their training and comfort and luxury, the ministrations of delicate beauty and sensibility, on condition that they neither inquire [too closely] into the real source of their income and the methods of distribution nor interfere with the legal props which rest on a pitiful human foundation of writhing white and yellow and brown and black bodies" (Du Bois 1986).

Is Du Bois's thesis so radical? *Should* we expect otherwise? *Should* we expect an entire category of mostly European American, "accommodated" intellectuals to develop a trenchant critique of the system that feeds them, and, more importantly, to work actively toward both a national and global redistribution of wealth, power, and privilege, *including their own?* Could anthropology survive in a worldwide system of social and economic equality in which the ethnographer toils without the support of either the imperial headquarters or a neocolonial subsidiary and in which the erstwhile "informants" have *the absolute right of refusal* to serve as subjects of anthropological projects?

In a utopian world of social, economic, and gender equality—which in my view should be the one that we are seeking to mold collectively— anthropology in its present form (perhaps in any form) would simply not exist because everyone would have the opportunity to speak on his/her own behalf, meaning that no one would be able to speak *unilaterally* on behalf of others. Should such a society be created (for it will certainly not "evolve"), where would lie the hierarchically structured "field" that serves as the historic (and current) ground for anthropological discoursing?

To say that anthropology might disappear does nothing to hurry along its demise, for anthropology will doubtlessly persist as long as do the inequalities that enable its practice. And those inequalities are growing both inside the capitalist "centers" and in the "peripheries" into which capital is expanding (Asia, Latin America) or from which it is retracting (e.g., large areas of West Africa).[12] My encounters with the survivors of El Mozote, and with many other people in northern Morazán and elsewhere, lead me to suggest, therefore, that anthropologists hesitant to abandon the discipline follow the lead of liberation theology and adopt a "preferential option for the poor."

Before his death on 16 November 1989 at the hands of elements of the

Atlacatl Battalion, the Jesuit priest and theologian Father Ignacio Ellacuría described the preferential option for the poor as

> . . . a movement towards a greater solidarity with the cause of the op-
> pressed, towards a growing incorporation into their world as the priv-
> ileged place of humanization and Christian divination. Such incor-
> poration is not done in order to take perverse pleasure in miserable
> poverty, but in order to accompany the poor in their desire for libera-
> tion. Liberation cannot consist of passing from poverty to wealth by
> making oneself rich by means of the poverty of others. It consists
> rather of surmounting poverty through solidarity. We are, of course,
> talking about the poor-with-spirit, the poor who accept their situa-
> tion as the foundation for constructing the new human being. Out of
> the materiality of poverty, this construction of the new human being
> arises actively from the poor-with-spirit, impelling them towards a
> process of liberation in solidarity that leaves out no human being.
> (1991b:70)[13]

In short, "this new human being is defined in part by active protest and
permanent struggle" (Ellacuría 1991b:70). It is not necessary to be a Christian to agree with Ellacuría's main point. And anyway, the concepts of the
preferential option and the construction of the "new human being" have
their secular revolutionary coordinates as well (Frank 1969), even if in
Latin America these have drawn considerable moral force from progressive Catholic theology and practice (Lancaster 1988:132–136). It is with
these ideas in mind that I offer a few suggestions by which anthropologists and other social scientists can begin to practice a preferential option.

Practicing the preferential option for the poor means struggling and
working closely with grassroots organizations in the investigation of human rights abuses;[14] it means scrutinizing the institutions and agencies
that are at the forefront of the "New World Order"; it means anthropologists working actively in their own communities to oppose the growing
assault on social programs such as welfare, public education, and public
housing; it means dedicating more time to translation and dissemination
of materials produced by people who have little or no access to a larger
public in the decision-making imperial centers and sponsoring, as well,
speaking tours in which witnesses testify directly to the chaos being
wreaked upon them as well as to their resistance to it;[15] and finally, it
means working within colleges, universities, and other institutions to in-

crease the representation on faculties and staffs of people of color *beyond the token level* so as to sharpen anthropology's internal critique, politicize the discipline, and hasten the arrival of a day when anthropology will die a dignified death rather than the unseemly one toward which it lurches at present.[16] Whether intercultural investigation and knowledge production would proceed on the basis of another set of relationships, methods, and procedures; whether people would assume all responsibility for explaining themselves to others; or whether, in the future, such explanation would even be warranted or desirable, I cannot say. I can only say that the practice of anthropology *as we now know it* would be inconceivable.[17]

HUMAN RIGHTS AND THE VIOLENCE OF EVERYDAY LIFE

In this work I have discussed the massacre, murder, torture, indiscriminate bombing, and forced relocation of noncombatants in the context of international agreements about human rights such as the Universal Declaration on Human Rights and the Geneva Convention (with special reference to Protocol II). These agreements, which embody civil and political rights, serve human rights advocates as international standards against which the behavior of particular governments and groups are compared. However, the Salvadoran government is also legally obligated to uphold a wide range of economic, social, and cultural rights inscribed in the Salvadoran Constitution as well as in international agreements to which the government is a signatory (Montes, Meléndez, and Palacios 1991:162–163). During the civil war international human rights monitors had little to say about the systematic violation of economic, social, and cultural rights. Either such violations are so common in the neocolonial world as to be taken for granted (and in that manner partially legitimized) or their significance pales beside the massive systematic violations of the right to life, freedom from persecution, and violations of other rights that mark open warfare. For instance, all eleven categories of rights assessed in the Americas Watch Committee and the American Civil Liberties Union's comprehensive 1982 *Report on Human Rights in El Salvador* involve civil or political rights (1982:37–174). But from the perspective of a preferential option for the poor, the right to health care, housing, decent work, protection against hunger, and other economic, social, and cultural necessities are as important as civil and political rights or more so. María Teresa Tula explains,

I guess I just have to keep talking because we realize that it is something that the U.S. public needs to know. They have to hear people who are from what is called the "Third World" talk about the kinds of human rights abuses we suffer. These abuses are not just about torture and killing. There are many other kinds of human rights abuses as well, like the lack of education. Right now, 70 percent of Salvadorans don't know how to read and write. We don't have access to basic medicine. We have insufficient nutrition and substandard or no housing. They never talk about these conditions. They just talk about establishing democracy in our country. (cited in Stephen 1994b:176)

These violations of basic human rights are regular and predictable products of capitalism, and they define what Nancy Scheper-Hughes (1992) calls "the violence of everyday life." The maintenance of such violence is only possible through the use of state-sponsored violence that "tries to hinder the struggle against injustice by taking preventive measures" (Ellacuría 1991a:40). As a result the human rights of the majority of Salvadorans are doubly violated: in their daily intercourse workers and peasants are deprived of the essentials to life; and when they protest and organize to seek redress, they are murdered, beaten, tortured, and disappeared. Pacifists eschew violence in favor of nonviolent routes to change, but the history of El Salvador and many other countries demonstrates that revolutionary violence is but the original violence of the ruling classes and their supporters turned back upon them—the violence that derives from exploitation, political repression, and ideological depreciation. "The rebel armed resistance," stated Edward Herman and Frank Brodhead, "was an *effect* not a *cause* of violence" (1984:10). Without the original sources of violence, revolutionary violence (of the FMLN and opposition groups in other countries) would not exist; it would have no rationale.

The Peace Accords, demobilization of the FMLN, and the general elections of March 1994 have not stemmed the violence of everyday life in El Salvador, which will continue to grow in magnitude unless there is a twofold redistribution of wealth: a redistribution from North (imperialist capitalist centers) to South (neocolonies) and an internal redistribution of wealth from that small minority of immensely wealthy Salvadoran capitalists to the large majority of struggling workers, peasants, and unemployed whose labor was the source of their fortunes. Drawing on material from a wide variety of sources, the Human Rights Committee of El

Salvador, Nongovernmental, summarized the dismal state of social and economic rights almost two years after the end of the civil war. El Salvador's literacy rate remained unchanged at 67 percent; infant mortality was 50 per 1,000 live births, one of the highest rates in Latin America; over half the children under the age of 5 showed signs of malnutrition; and 44 percent of the population lacked access to health services. Sixty percent of the population was classified as "impoverished," and 28 percent lived in "conditions of extreme poverty nationally" (CDHES-NG 1993: 21–22). The authors concluded, "All these 1993 statistics show the persistence of structural conditions that could, at some moment in El Salvador's future as they did in the past, become the immediate cause of widening internal social conflicts and even military conflicts" (23). In other words, a radical reconfiguration of Salvadoran society is the sine qua non for a reduction in the everyday violence from which most other forms of violence originate.

Since 1993 income distribution has worsened despite hundreds of millions of dollars in international assistance for reconstruction and $700–800 million in annual remittances from Salvadorans living outside the country. Social tensions are again on the increase, as the unique experiment that began when the Salvadoran government and the FMLN signed the Peace Accords in Mexico City on 16 January 1992 begins to unwind. The Peace Accords neither went far enough nor have been carried out in their entirety, principally because of opposition from the bourgeoisie, the government, and the military. The unjust social structures of capitalism (national and imperial) have hardly been touched, and they daily expose millions of Salvadorans to illness, hunger, and despair. All this goes to indicate that Mark Danner erred when he referred (in the subtitle of his book) to the massacre at El Mozote as "a parable of the cold war." The El Mozote massacre cannot be consigned to the dustbin of a completed epoch that revolved on an East–West axis; it is better conceived as a single, brutal episode in a continuing war between the haves and the have-nots of El Salvador, the United States, and elsewhere. Right now in Latin America the wealthy make war on the poor through free-trade agreements and structural adjustment programs (see NACLA 1993), while in the United States, welfare recipients, public schools, and affirmative-action policies are among the major targets of domestic structural adjustment. ("Structural adjustment," whether the International Monetary Fund–sponsored version or the domestic government–sponsored version, has the goal of "readjusting" income distribution to the benefit of the wealthiest 5 to 10 percent of the population.) In the long run in El Salvador the campaign now under way to reduce the state's role in the economy and to channel all exchanges of goods and services through the market will cause more pain and suffering than did the twelve-year civil war concluded in February 1992. Everyday life will become increasingly violent for the vast majority of the population. But impelled by the depredations of the present and drawing on the reservoirs of past struggles, Salvadorans will continue to organize and struggle to create an alternative future. There is no option to this. It behooves those of us who identify with the preferential option for the poor to listen, to learn, and to struggle at their sides, for in this very intertwined global economy that capital has configured to the benefit of the few, their future—the future of the masses there and here—is the future of us all.[18]

A MEMORIAL

After many requests, human rights advocates secured from the Calderón Sol administration release of the remains exhumed from the sacristy by the Argentine forensic team in 1992, and CEBES planned a full evening and night of activities for a memorial to the victims, culminating in a dawn reburial on 11 December 1994. On the afternoon of 10 December, I met up in El Mozote with Jacinto Márquez—friend, field assistant, peasant agriculturist, oral historian, catechist, and former FMLN combatant. Jacinto is from Paturla, Joateca, and had been a civilian in Joateca at the moment that Domingo Monterrosa ascended into the sky for what became his last helicopter ride. The brief account recorded here is based on our combined observations.

Seven hundred to a thousand people, between residents and visitors, arrived at the plaza for activities that would last from 3 P.M. on 10 December to 6 A.M. the following morning. María Julia Hernández, the Tutela Legal director, gave a brief speech in which she noted how Cristiani's Amnesty Law had made it impossible to deliver those responsible for the El Mozote massacre before the criminal authorities; she emphasized, "We have to recuperate the historical memory of our country," and said that the people themselves had an enormous role to play in this.

During an afternoon mass, carried out by Miguel Ventura, Rogelio Ponceele, and a visiting Irish priest, seven people, among them cate-

FIGURE 14 Seven closed caskets containing the remains of at least 143 persons disinterred in the sacristy at El Mozote in October–November 1992 await reburial following an all-night vigil on 10–11 December 1994. (Photograph courtesy of Mark Hoffman)

chists, the mayor of Perquín, representatives of grassroots organizations, and Rufina Amaya, climbed the stage erected near the ruins of the church to place symbolic offerings on the simple altar table. The objects represented past sufferings, present realities, and future hopes. A CEBES catechist brought a cardboard figure of a child to represent the children massacred in El Mozote; the president of the El Mozote local council contributed handfuls of earth from the land that had been abandoned for twelve years; Miriam Ramos, mayor of Perquín, set down a brick as a manifestation of "the force that the mayors are making to reconstruct the destroyed communities." Finally, Rufina Amaya placed on the altar a bunch of red flowers to symbolize both the massacred children and the blood that "provides the force to walk, eat, and live."

The evening and the long, cold night were taken up with cultural activities: singing, musical performances, and Canadian and Salvadoran videos about the massacre projected onto a large, white sheet. Meanwhile, candles illuminated a shelter of branches and leaves that covered the floor of the former church, where women and a few men prayed over seven, open wooden coffins that contained, all jumbled together like different varieties of dry cereals, the brown and white bones of the minimum 143 victims recovered by the Argentine forensic team from the adjacent sacristy. Rogelio Ponceele intoned into the microphone, "We are in a vigil. . . . we are for the first time in a vigil with the mortal remains before us. This night is a kind of wake that we are going to share together."

Finally, at four in the morning on 11 December 1994, the seven coffins were closed, blessed, and borne in a candlelight procession around the plaza to their final resting places in two deep graves flanking a new stone, mortar, and metal monument commemorating the El Mozote massacre that took place thirteen years earlier. Before the procession began, Ventura delivered a powerful speech in which he touched on the causes of the conflict and the protagonistic role of the people, who "in the armed conflict . . . were strong not only because of the armaments that they built and accumulated, but fundamentally due to their conviction and belief in the capacities of one another. They discovered that illiterate, poor, and malnourished humans harbored within them the hidden force of a love capable of giving the life for another and this made them even stronger than death." He criticized the current neoliberal project designed to "exclude the majority [and] cultivate conditions for new confrontations," and noted how a revolutionary process that began with such enthusiasm had weakened in the postwar period because of a tendency for the masses to give precedence to personal needs over collective ones:

> The risk today, esteemed brothers and sisters, is to fall into the trap designed by the powerful and carried out by all the communications media to make us forget the existence of that new force of the poor and above all the memory of the martyrs. This thirteenth anniversary of El Mozote has to be the appropriate occasion to assess the great achievements that sacrifice and martyrdom have wrought during the last twenty years of Salvadoran history, and like Mary the Virgin, to proclaim that God has carried out marvels among this people, has hurled down the powerful from their thrones and put the humble in their places.

He followed by noting that future generations would make pilgrimages to El Mozote "to feed their spirits [and] inspire their ideals for change and the construction of a new society."

The priests blessed the graves, and those bearing the coffins lowered them by ropes and covered them with dirt. Many people, myself included, pressed close to watch and to throw in handfuls of soil in a final parting. During the final moments the eastern sky lightened to a gray-blue, then blue, and finally gave way to a brilliant, rose-colored dawning. The ceremony ended with a collective *Padre Nuestra* (Lord's Prayer), and the weary crowd broke up and headed for home.

REFERENCE MATERIAL

CHRONOLOGY

1981

1 December	FMLN's clandestine Radio Venceremos broadcasts that the army is going to invade northern Morazán.
8 December	Atlacatl Battalion disembarks from helicopters in Perquín, part of an invasion force of 4,000 troops approaching from the north, south, and east. In the evening the FMLN begins to retreat from La Guacamaya.
9 December	Radio Venceremos loses its transmitter when "Toni" is shot and killed; surviving members of the broadcast team hastily retreat to Jucuarán on the coast of Usulután.
10 December	Atlacatl Battalion enters El Mozote.
11 December	Massacre at El Mozote; massacre at La Joya.
17 December	Atlacatl troops depart northern Morazán.
24 December	Radio Venceremos returns to northern Morazán and broadcasts the first news of the massacre.
25 December	About 200 persons displaced from northern Morazán arrive at a camp in San Francisco Gotera.
29 December	FMLN troops retake La Guacamaya.

1982

3 January	Raymond Bonner and Susan Meiselas cross the Honduran border into northern Morazán as guests of the FMLN. Alma Guillermoprieto follows them several days later.
27 January	Articles appear in the *New York Times* (Bonner 1982a) and the *Washington Post* (Guillermoprieto 1982) asserting that a massacre occurred at El Mozote.
28 January	President Ronald Reagan certifies before the U.S. Congress that the Salvadoran government has improved its human rights performance and is increasing its control over the military.
30 January	Todd Greentree and Maj. John McKay of the U.S. Embassy in San Salvador visit northern Morazán.
31 January	Ambassador Deane Hinton sends a cable to the State Department detailing the results of the Greentree/McKay investigation. The cable is written by Greentree but cleared by Hinton.

2 February   Assistant Secretary of State for Inter-American Affairs Thomas Enders defends Reagan's certification before the House Subcommittee on Western Hemisphere Affairs.

28 March   Elections are held for a Constituent Assembly.

1984

23 October   Col. Domingo Monterrosa, commander of the Atlacatl Battalion, is killed when the FMLN blows up his helicopter over Joateca, a few miles from El Mozote, during maneuvers of Torola IV operation.

1989

11 November   The first refugees from Colomoncagua, Honduras, return on foot to El Salvador and settle in the vicinity of Meanguera.

16 November   During an FMLN nationwide offensive some members of the Atlacatl Battalion murder six Jesuit priests, their housekeeper, and her daughter on the campus of the University of Central America.

1990

16 October   Tutela Legal files the first legal brief on the El Mozote case.

11 December   The first memorial mass takes place at El Mozote.

1991

14 August   Salvadoran military invades northern Morazán for the last time.

31 December   The FMLN and the Salvadoran government sign an agreement to end the war; the FMLN celebrates with a New Year's Eve party in Joateca.

1992

16 January   FMLN and Salvadoran government sign formal Peace Accords at Chapultepec Castle in Mexico City.

1 February   Cease-fire between the Salvadoran military and the FMLN begins; FMLN combatants congregate in camps supervised by ONUSAL.

February   The first families arrive to repopulate El Mozote.

27 April   United Nations creates the Truth Commission.

27 May	Inspection of El Mozote massacre sites begins.
13 October	Argentine forensic team begins excavation of the sacristy.
17 November	Excavation of the sacristy is completed; all remains are transferred to a laboratory in Santa Tecla for further examination and analysis.
8 December	Atlacatl Battalion is demobilized, precisely eleven years to the day after it landed at Perquín to take part in Operation Rescue.
12 December	The third memorial mass, presided over by Father Rogelio Ponceele and Father Miguel Ventura, is held in a field in El Mozote.
15 December	FMLN completes demobilization.

1993

25 January	Excavation is completed in remains of the house of José María Márquez.
28 January	Archaeological work at El Mozote ceases.
15 March	The Truth Commission releases its report, titled *From Madness to Hope.*
20 March	Salvadoran legislature passes the Amnesty Law.
24 March	Secretary of State Warren Christopher forms a commission to look into charges that the U.S. government withheld evidence about Salvadoran government complicity in human rights abuses during the war.
15 July	The Christopher Commission releases its report.
6 December	Mark Danner's article "The Truth of El Mozote" is published in the *New Yorker;* the article later becomes a book called *The Massacre at El Mozote: A Parable of the Cold War.*

1994

March	Rep. Joseph Moakley visits El Mozote and pressures the embassy and State Department to assist the returning population. CARE is dispatched to provide agricultural loans plus water and latrine projects. USAID finances reconstruction of the school during 1994–95.
20 March	El Salvador holds its first postwar elections. The FMLN wins 25 percent of the vote nationwide and is victorious in five of the eight northern Morazanian municipalities, including Meanguera; where Concepción Márquez, former refugee and schoolteacher in Colomoncagua, assumes office as mayor.

24 April   ARENA wins a landslide 68 to 32 percent victory over the FMLN in the presidential run-off, with ARENA's Armando Calderón Sol elected the nation's president.

June   A telephone caller claiming to represent the Domingo Monterrosa Commando Unit makes death threats against Jesuits at the University of Central America and against attorneys investigating the death squads.

28 July   The Joint Group for the Investigation of Illegal Armed Groups with Political Motivation in El Salvador releases its report; the group attributes continuing acts of political violence to, among others, members of the Armed Forces and the National Police. A list of names developed with the report is never publicized.

September   A census in El Mozote reveals that the hamlet comprises 155 households, a sevenfold increase from July 1993.

10–11 December   An all-night vigil takes place at El Mozote, sponsored by CEBES. At 4:30 A.M. 11 December, following an afternoon and night of speeches, a mass, music, and videos, the remains of the 143 massacre victims exhumed from the sacristy by the Argentine forensic team in 1993 are reburied in seven coffins in two graves flanking a new monument commemorating the massacre.

NOTES

CHAPTER 1

1. This discussion about the amount of press coverage El Mozote has received draws on materials accessed through Lexus-Nexus, an online database that contains texts from most major English-language newspapers and press services from the United States, Canada, and England.

2. And this is true not only as regards the traditionally denominated "Third World"—above all, the nations of Africa, Asia, and Latin America—but also in that mobile sector of the Third World that greases the wheels of First World capitalism and provides the cheap service labor (the domestic help, the gardeners, the cooks) that makes it possible for middle-income groups to acquire and enjoy their privileged lifestyles. These people, too, are invisible. Southern California may be the prototype in this regard:

> Without all the immigrants willing to do the menial work that native-born Americans . . . have forsworn, no cars would get parked at Westside restaurants, no lawns would be tended, and no infants looked after. Their employers, though, hardly acknowledge their existence, while for every Anglo child who grows attached to the maid another is confused by her presence. "I was alone all day," the five-year-old daughter of one of Allegra's friends told me boastfully. "The maid was there," her mother interjected, "but she only speaks Spanish and the child thinks she won't talk to her on purpose." (Rieff 1991:112)

The maid doesn't count. She doesn't exist as a tangible social being worthy of attention. She is, as Rieff notes, an "enabler" of middle-class comfort, a human appliance that can be turned on and off.

3. "The Truth of El Mozote" was published as a book in April 1994, with the title *The Massacre at El Mozote*. As best I can tell, the text of the book reproduces that of the article with but a few minor changes. However, for the book Danner added chapter notes and a lengthy (100-plus page) appendix of documents related to the case.

4. The principal utility of Danner's article is to provide a systematic narrative of the embassy "investigation" of the massacre and an analysis of how this investigation and its results were structured, constrained, and modified to conform to a preordained and unquestionable U.S. support for the Salvadoran government. Still, focusing on the cover-up and limiting the precipitating conditions to domestic conflicts without taking into consideration the influence of U.S. counterinsurgency doctrine and the military- and police-aid packages through which it

was materialized lets the U.S. government off pretty easy. I address U.S. counter-insurgency policy in chapter 3.

5. It should come as no surprise that three of the best-known testimonials from Latin America are by women: *I, Rigoberta Menchú* (Menchú 1984); *Let Me Speak!* (Barrios de Chungara 1979); and *Don't Be Afraid, Gringo* (Alvarado 1987) record the testimony of female peasants and workers.

6. Perhaps the best example is Francisco Metzi's *The People's Remedy* (1988). Metzi was born in Mozambique to Belgian expatriates. His testimony chronicles his experiences as a health-care worker during three years with the Popular Liberation Forces in Chalatenango. Metzi's identification with the guerrilla struggle is prominently displayed by his use of the first-person *we* when discussing collectively experienced problems and proposed solutions (e.g., "We had often debated how to solve this problem. . . . Unfortunately, we soon came to realize that we had serious limitations" [pp. 164–165]). Metzi eventually returned to El Salvador, despite the tremendous risk:

> Life was intense there. There were precious moments of intimacy with the *compas,* as we huddled together, the rocky soil digging into our flesh, and formed a human wall of resistance against the icy wind that fiercely lashed against us. Today I can clearly recall the stories of peasants or youths from San Salvador about the humiliations they had suffered in the garrisons and the police headquarters, or in the streets. Their hopes for a new dawn for their children are still vivid to me. Under the stars, we shared our loves and frustrations, and our dreams of life after the victory. Experiences of such quality are difficult to repeat. When life is on the line everyday, men and women show what human beings are really made of.
>
> Such living is not easily forgotten. Therefore, it should come as no surprise that, once again, I'm carrying my backpack full of medicine and walking the Salvadoran soil, this time with a greater sense of reality and a stronger dose of hope. (p. 194)

7. They are also affected by the hand of the enabler, since most testimonies are recorded and edited by academics and others with the interest, leisure, and capability of disseminating to a wide audience the voices of subaltern peoples.

8. This book's short examination of El Mozote is part of a broader project addressing thirty years of repression and resistance in northern Morazán. Prior to working in El Mozote, I carried out ethnographic and oral historical research in the municipalities of Jocoaitique, San Fernando, Perquín, Arambala, and Joateca. I was assisted in the task by Phyllis Robinson in Jocoaitique and Roxanna Duntley in Perquín. Following completion of the first draft of this book in August 1994, I continued my research in northern Morazán between September 1994 and July 1995.

CHAPTER 2

1. Dunkerley (1982:92–96) and Pearce (1986:130–132) discuss the early years of the ERP.

2. Members of revolutionary organizations and their supporters adopted pseudonyms during the war to protect friends and family from persecution as a result of their activities. Many of these names "stuck" and accompanied their bearers into the postwar period as the names by which they are commonly known.

3. Before 1992, social control in El Salvador resided in the hands of the security forces and the Armed Forces, both of which were commanded by the minister of defense and staffed by officers who had matriculated from the Captain General Gerardo Barrios Military School. The security forces were divided into the National Guard and the Treasury Police, which worked in rural areas like northern Morazán, and the National Police, which patrolled El Salvador's cities.

4. This very brief description simplifies a much more complex situation, which will be the subject of a future work treating northern Morazán before, during, and after the civil war. Needless to say, I will devote a significant amount of attention to the role of peasant catechists as progressive organic intellectuals in some ways similar to, in others different from the Shambaai rainmakers discussed by Feierman (1990).

5. Before 1980 many adult male army reservists served in cantonal patrols under the authority of an active-duty army sergeant who resided in the municipal center. When the war began in earnest in 1981, the army dissolved the patrols into a Civil Defense containing all adult males, armed the men, and ordered them to protect their communities against the guerrillas. Before they were routed by FMLN forces in 1982, Civil Defense forces in northern Morazán murdered many politically nonaligned people.

6. The other groups were the Popular Forces of Liberation (FPL), the Armed Forces of National Resistance (FARN), the Salvadoran Communist Party (PCS), and the Central American Workers Revolutionary Party (PRTC).

7. The same Salvadoran place-name frequently refers to several administrative divisions or locally named areas at different institutional levels. Thus, La Guacamaya is one of four cantones that compose the municipality of Meanguera. But "La Guacamaya" also refers to a dispersed hamlet within cantón La Guacamaya. To minimize confusion, I generally indicate the administrative status to which a place-name refers.

8. The First Company approached El Mozote via Arambala. However, at least one other company arrived at El Mozote by a more northerly route that led it through Tierra Colorada.

9. The excavation of the sacristy in October–November 1992 led to the discovery of the remains of at least 143 individuals, only 1 of whom proved to have

been an adult male. The witness (or witnesses) who testified to Tutela Legal—quite probably Rufina Amaya—thus erred on this point. It is important to keep in mind that testimony was collected almost ten years after the fact and that over the course of a decade memory, even of events as shocking as these, can falter.

10. Although I have talked to Rufina Amaya on numerous occasions, we have never discussed her experiences between 10 and 12 December 1981, which she has recounted in great detail during formal testimony before human rights commissions, judges, and the Truth Commission; in interviews with journalists such as Mark Danner; to delegations of foreigners; and in public forums in El Salvador and Europe. It made no sense to me to drag Rufina once again over events that cannot be related without pain. Rather, we discussed the formation of the community, the church, marriage and kinship, and family relations—in effect, issues that few if any visitors bother to ask her about.

11. I have not attempted a precise counting of the victims. But in the course of fieldwork, Shelli McMillen and I did learn of several living people erroneously listed among the victims in the Tutela Legal report. A precise accounting would require extensive genealogical interviews with as many survivors as possible. To carry out this task would probably require contact with people in various cities and towns in El Salvador, in other Central American nations, and perhaps in the United States as well. I do believe that most current estimates understate the actual death toll.

CHAPTER 3

1. In this chapter I employ the words *oligarchy, elites,* and *bourgeoisie* interchangeably. Technically, of course, this is not correct, since the oligarchy comprises merely one faction, albeit the dominant one, of the Salvadoran bourgeoisie, and some elites wielding considerable political influence (the Catholic archbishop, high state functionaries, and others) fall outside the bourgeoisie altogether.

2. Paige interviewed seventeen members of the coffee elite divided between the "agro-industrial elite" (processors) and the "agro-financial elite" (growers). The former tended to be members and officials of the Asociación Salvadoreña de Beneficiadores y Exportadores de Café (ABECAFE), the large processors association; the latter belonged to the Asociación Salvadoreña de Café (ASCAFE), the principal growers association.

3. For a contemporary U.S. example of social isolation, see David Rieff's (1991) seminal book *Los Angeles: Capital of the Third World.*

4. According to Paige (1993:38), "The poor as an organized social force demanding their fair share of the nation's wealth simply do not exist in the elite's view of a gradually improving standard of living for all. And the army too lies largely outside elite critical vision despite its continued centrality in Salvadoran

society. The silences in the conversations of the agro-industrial elite are at least as significant as the opinions they express."

5. In Brazil, Argentina, and Uruguay the military "made war against the left as a foreign enemy and claimed to be waging a third world war against subversion" (Fagen 1992:46). In Argentina the military regime perfected the technique of disappearing its accused opponents; thousands of them were tortured, drugged, and thrown alive from airplanes.

6. I interviewed one former member of the Atlacatl who admitted participating in Operation Rescue, but I do not believe that he spoke truthfully of what he had seen and done. He claimed to have spent the operation guarding the Torola River bridge rather than deep within the operations area itself. This was a patent falsehood. The blocking force consisted of regular army and security-force personnel, not members of the battalion, which was a special forces group. As I noted in chapter 2, the Atlacatl Battalion was helicoptered to Perquín and then traveled south on land, so none of its members would have been at the Torola River bridge, south of El Mozote, during the operation. Furthermore, the former soldier denied that any of his comrades had discussed what occurred at El Mozote when they returned to barracks. This young man, now in his early thirties, has renounced militarism and lives in a Christian community. The priest of that community was present during our interview, which took place in the church. The former soldier's elisions and inconsistencies indicate that he was too embarrassed and guilt-ridden to confront the horrific acts in which he directly and/or indirectly participated; perhaps his conversion (he is a member of a group of charismatic Catholics) entails an effort to atone for his sins. Finally, it is notable that not a single member of the Atlacatl has come forward to testify publicly about the El Mozote operation. I take this as a sign not only of enormous shame and guilt, but of a well-reasoned fear of the likely consequences of doing so.

7. Baloyra (1982:62) also notes that "the oligarchy maintained its class superiority by 'inviting' a select few [military officers] to join its ranks after they had retired from the military, and few in the military were welcomed with open arms into the more exclusive clubs of San Salvador."

8. One such case took place in June 1976. President and Colonel Arturo Molina proposed a modest but badly needed land reform that would have involved the expropriation of 120,000 acres from large ranchers and cotton growers and redistribution of the land to 12,000 landless families in San Miguel and Usulután. However, the affected landowners, who would have received full compensation for their land, organized the Eastern Region Farmers Federation to oppose the reform law. The National Association for Private Enterprise also opposed the law, which it said would set a dangerous precedent, and took out advertisements in San Salvador newspapers intimating that Molina was capitulating to communism (McClintock 1985:177; Armstrong and Shenk 1982:83–84; Baloyra 1982:55–62). The reform effort was abandoned despite support from USAID, political parties, pop-

ular organizations, and sectors within the army. Thenceforth "the military government turned its attention to brutally putting down the mobilization of the peasantry the reform had been intended to appease" (McClintock 1985:178)—the task for which, after all, the military had been retained.

9. In October 1960 senior and junior officers cooperated in the overthrow of President José María Lemus. In 1972 Capt. Benjamín Mejía led a revolt in support of Christian Democratic Party claims that the military's National Conciliation Party had stolen the elections (Baloyra 1982:40–43). And in 1979, Capt. Francisco Emilio Mena Sandoval, Capt. Bruno Navarrete, and Capt. Marcelo Cruz Cruz fled the Second Brigade base at Santa Ana and joined the FMLN. Most of the army soldiers who accompanied them were killed shortly thereafter at the battle of Cutumay Camones (Mena Sandoval 1991:95–102).

10. Dickey draws a stark contrast between "Anglo-Saxon legal and political institutions" and "the traditional Latin way of resolving the discrepancy between progressive ideals, which are accepted in principle, and the almost feudal social and economic realities of the region" (1984:35). Dickey believes that military officers who publicly manifest their respect for human rights while continuing to butcher unarmed men, women, and children embody this Latin American traditionalism.

11. The School of the Americas was forced out of Panama and moved to Fort Benning, Georgia, in 1984 as a consequence of the Panama Canal Treaty. According to Father Roy Bourgeois, who is working to get the school closed down, the Panamanian newspaper *La Prensa* called it "the School of Assassins, where soldiers are trained to kill their Salvadoran, Guatemalan and Nicaraguan brothers" (SOA Watch n.d.:1). Bourgeois states that "the SOA has trained more than 56,000 soldiers from 18 Latin American countries in low-intensity warfare, psychological operations (PSYOPS), counter-insurgency techniques, commando operations, interrogation methods and intelligence gathering" (Bourgeois 1994:14). In May 1994 the U.S. House of Representatives defeated by a vote of 217 to 175 a bill introduced by Rep. Joseph Kennedy to close the school (Ibid.:15).

12. I cannot leave this chapter without noting another consequence of U.S. counterinsurgency policy. In 1975 the arrival of the FALANGE (Anti-Communist Liberation Armed Forces) initiated the era of death-squad repression. According to McClintock (1985:175), the FALANGE was a creation of ANSESAL (the Salvadoran National Security Agency), a descendant of the earlier Security Services. When Roberto (alias "Blowtorch Bob") D'Aubuisson left ANSESAL in 1979, he removed all the intelligence files and worked to set up an informal paramilitary apparatus that would reactivate the discredited ORDEN. With the assistance of Guatemalan rightists such as Mario Sandoval Alarcón—*that* country's death-squad captain—D'Aubuisson established the Broad National Front as a political cover for the dirty war that the Salvadoran Right believed was necessary to save the nation from communism. Shortly thereafter the Broad National Front was incor-

porated into the nascent ARENA Party to contest the 1982 elections. This is the political party that rules El Salvador today, thanks in no small part to thirty years of U.S. counterinsurgency doctrine (cf. Pyes 1986a, 1986b; Nairn 1984).

CHAPTER 4

1. A "sanitized" copy of the cable was released to Raymond Bonner in 1983 after he filed an FOIA request; it is available from the National Security Archive microfiche set, El Salvador 1977–84, #02515. The complete version was made available in November 1983 and was later published in Danner 1994 (pp. 195–201).

2. In the following discussion and analysis I will treat Greentree as the cable's author, despite the fact that it was sent over Hinton's name. But I must caution that many people contributed to it. Greentree told Mark Danner that, despite alterations, "he 'did not feel that what went out distorted beyond acceptability' what he had written" (Danner 1994:114). For bibliographic purposes I cite the cable as Hinton 1982a.

3. In the early 1980s Argueta abandoned his parish seat in Jocoaitique for the safer climes of Joateca, located on the periphery of the FMLN-controlled zone. Around 1983 he was forced from the area by the FMLN. Following the cease-fire in January 1992, Argueta returned to Joateca, and following the FMLN's demobilization in December 1992, he sought to reoccupy the Jocoaitique church and convent.

4. In the version of the cable released to Bonner, all statements identifying the mayor of Jocoaitique had been excised.

5. Formed on 18 April 1980, the FDR (Frente Democrático Revolucionario [Democratic Revolutionary Front]) "brought together all the democratic and revolutionary organizations in El Salvador except the Christian Democratic Party" (Armstrong and Shenk 1982:154). The FDR allied with the FMLN as the civilian, political wing of the revolutionary movement. The alliance resulted in the FDR/FMLN.

6. Edward Herman (1992–93) compares the *Wall Street Journal*'s attack on Bonner with the credibility the *Journal* gave to the unwarranted Reagan administration claim in the mid-1980s that the Soviet Union and its allies in Laos and Cambodia were employing chemical weapons (which took the form of Yellow Rain) against local insurgents. Following the Truth Commission report on the El Mozote massacre, *Wall Street Journal* editor Robert Bartley rushed to claim that "the *Journal* never denied that a massacre took place, only that 'neither the press nor the State Department has the power to establish conclusively what happened at El Mozote.'" Even after the war Bartley continued to criticize Bonner for failing to mention that his visit to northern Morazán had been guided by the FMLN. Herman and Rothberg (1993:4) point out the editorial double standard at work

here: "Only evidence taken in enemy territory is a propaganda exercise, whereas evidence proffered by Enders or the Salvadoran army, no matter how manufactured, is credible. On *Journal* principles such as these, it does not matter if there was a massacre at El Mozote; since it was in rebel-held territory, verification would have been impossible."

7. Times Books published Bonner's *Weakness and Deceit: U.S. Policy in El Salvador* in 1984. No comparable work provided as honest and detailed an account of the grave contradictions of U.S. policy in El Salvador in the early 1980s. It is all the more surprising that the book was never issued in a paperback edition.

8. With the excavation and the imminent publication of the Truth Commission report in March 1993, a team of journalists from *Sixty Minutes* revisited the massacre site accompanied by Raymond Bonner and Susan Meiselas. They also contacted Todd Greentree, who was then working as a foreign service officer in Katmandu. Greentree stated in the interview that he was unable to conclude on the basis of the interviews he had conducted that a massacre had actually occurred at El Mozote, but that he came away with the distinct impression that "something had—had gone wrong. Something bad had happened." When asked to be more specific, he stated "that there had probably been non-combatant casualties of a large number . . . possibly a massacre." Greentree also stated that he had conveyed that impression to Ambassador Hinton, and that it had found a place in his written report (*Sixty Minutes* 1993).

9. Elliot Abrams, Reagan's assistant secretary of state for human rights, undoubtedly got it right when he argued that Congress had copped out when it imposed the certification requirement on President Reagan. Certifying that human rights were improving in El Salvador and that the government was making progress in bringing the military under control allowed Reagan to make the decision about continuing aid himself and also provided congresspeople opposed to the policy an opportunity to distance themselves from the president without actually having to vote for cutting off aid and thereby risk being blamed for losing El Salvador to the communists were the FMLN to win (Danner 1993:118–120, 1994:130–132). Ultimately, "nearly everyone [both Democrats and Republicans] tacitly agreed . . . that in the end the Salvadoran government, by whatever means, *had* to win the war, or the country's security would be unacceptably threatened" (Danner 1993:119, 1994:132).

10. I carried out a survey using the Lexus-Nexus online database. "El Mozote" was cited at least once by each of the following sources: *Los Angeles Times, New York Times, Newsday, Washington Post, Washington Times, San Francisco Chronicle, Chicago Tribune, Boston Globe, Foreign Affairs, U.S. News and World Report,* the U.S. Department of State, *Economist, Guardian* (England), Notimex Mexican News Service, *Latin America Regional Reports: Mexico and Central America,* Federal News Service, *BBC Summary of World Broadcasts,* United Press Interna-

tional, *CNN News*, Reuters, *Christian Science Monitor*, Inter Press Service, States News Service, French Press Agency, *Vancouver Sun*, *Toronto Star*, *Ottawa Citizen*, *Calgary Herald*, and the *Montreal Gazette*.

11. Jameson is more concerned with "strategies of containment" in the interpretation of narrative than he is with their role in narrative production. But more generally, following Marx, he links the term to the ways in which material interest and social position act to affect what can, or, perhaps better stated, what cannot, be thought (1981:52).

12. See Derrick Bell's masterful story "The Slave Traders" for an analogous statement of the differential value attached to white lives versus those of people of color (Bell 1992).

13. Following the release of the Truth Commission report, Rep. Joseph Moakley (Democrat, Massachusetts) suggested that "[w]hat we need now is a Truth Commission report on our own government. . . . We must determine what they knew and when they knew it" (cited in Ross 1993).

CHAPTER 5

1. This population estimate is based on an extrapolation from the 1971 population of 164 (El Salvador Ministerio de Economía 1974a:91–93).

2. One informant said that the land holdings of Israel Márquez around El Mozote, in La Montaña, and elsewhere totaled over 200 manzanas (140 hectares).

3. A landowner had plenty of ways to get around these legal technicalities, at least before his/her death. For instance he/she could sell the land, *de facto* or fictitiously, to anyone: an unrelated person, a legitimate child, an illegitimate child, etc. In this manner, it was possible to cut prodigal children out of the inheritance or to reward a child's loyalty with a larger than average share. Men could also recognize illegitimate children after the birth, in effect changing their status from "illegitimate" to "legitimate." In general the children of parents married by civil statute were legitimate, those of *acompañados* (accompanied couples)—whether the accompaniment was a man's only relationship or a relationship in addition to marriage—were illegitimate.

4. There were landowners with more than 200 manzanas in other municipalities. Filadelfo Gómez of Perquín had 557.5 manzanas, in Jocoaitique Pedro Cruz had 400 manzanas, and in Torola Aníbal Orellana and Abelino Aguilar owned 552 and 550 manzanas, respectively. The FMLN inventory of 4 June 1992 listed 9 landowners in northern Morazán with holdings exceeding 200 manzanas (140 hectares) (FMLN 1992b). However, none of them came from Meanguera.

5. This statement is based on a survey of 143 present and former house sites conducted over a 4-day period during June–July 1993.

6. The replacement of human labor power by machines had advanced farthest in the henequen industry when the civil war broke out in 1980. Mechani-

cal scrapers functioned in every henequen-growing municipality of the region, although the majority of the mescal probably continued to be extracted by hand with wooden or iron stakes. The sugarcane-processing industry had also experienced technical changes. In about 1970 trapiches with horizontally mounted metal rollers replaced cruder and less efficient trapiches that employed vertically mounted wooden rollers to express the cane juice. The movement from *trapiches de madera* (trapiches with wooden rollers) to *trapiches de hierro* (trapiches with iron rollers) was accompanied by an increase in the efficiency of cane-juice extraction and a reduction (from five to four) of the number of trapiche workers. The first experiments with motorized trapiches were just under way when the civil war began. Farther north in La Montaña mechanical sawmills operated alongside manual two-man saws in the production of planks and other lumber products.

CHAPTER 6

1. Christian Base Communities were formed of small groups of progressive Catholics who met for Bible study and materialized their commitment to the faith by carrying out social projects and assisting the aged, infirm, and destitute. Participants read the Bible—with the assistance of lay catechists trained in San Miguel and elsewhere (see chapter 5)—as a historical document with relevance to their own situation: God is a God of the poor who will help them overcome oppression by the rich like he helped Moses deliver the Jews out of Egypt.

2. Finding a cold soda in El Mozote before the war was highly unlikely as the community lacked electricity and none of the store owners possessed natural-gas refrigerators, such as I encountered in Joateca in late 1992.

3. Before the war, Argueta charged two to five colones per head for baptisms, within reach of poor peasant households. But even at these low rates, Argueta earned considerable sums since he baptized as many as eighty children per baptismal service in communities and hamlets outside the parish seat. In March 1995 I attended a saint's day mass in Jocoaitique during which Argueta baptized thirty-seven infants and children at ten colones apiece.

4. Rutilio Grande was assassinated in 1977. Armando López and Ignacio Ellacuría were among the six Jesuits (along with their housekeeper and her daughter) murdered by elements of the Atlacatl Battalion on 16 November 1989 on the campus of the University of Central America in San Salvador.

5. This discussion is based on interviews carried out in 1992–93 with Miguel Ventura, "Chele Cesar," "Roberto," "Benito," "Franco," and more than a dozen catechists who lived and worked in northern Morazanian communities.

6. Also, Jocoaitique had a history of resistance to state authority dating to the 1930s. In the 1956 elections it was the only rural municipality in the entire country that voted for the liberal PAR (Revolutionary Action Party) against the entrenched

PRUD, forerunner of the PCN (National Conciliation Party). In Jocoaitique a charismatic schoolteacher, a telegraph operator, and even the wife of the blood-thirsty National Guard commander all became ERP collaborators. The last two were found out and assassinated in 1980.

7. Atilio got in trouble with the ERP and was in danger of being executed when he changed sides. He died in combat against the FMLN in November 1982. It is possible that Daniel feared that his son would implicate other members of the family in guerrilla activity, or that, as was common, uninvolved family members would be held responsible and punished by the army for Atilio's "crime," even though he had joined the army.

8. Ventura took advantage of the situation and began to organize catechists in previously untouched areas while maintaining contact with progressive Christians north of the Torola (Ventura 1991:11). Following Ventura's reassignment, the rebel movement recruited several bright and enthusiastic catechists (among them "Serapio" and "Aparicio") who played important roles in northern Morazán during and after the war.

9. Favio Argueta was born in El Mozote in 1942. His family moved to Soledad, Meanguera, when he was nine years old following a series of quarrels with a close relative. By his own count, fifty-five of his near and distant relatives were massacred at El Mozote.

10. Human rights violations in the period following the El Mozote massacre are discussed in chapter 8.

11. *Massacre* is defined by *Webster's New Universal Unabridged Dictionary* (1983, p. 1106) as "the indiscriminate, merciless killing of a number of human beings, or, sometimes, animals; wholesale slaughter." I accept this definition for the sake of the analysis here and recognize the difficulties entailed in specifying to everyone's satisfaction just what that "number" might be. The number employed here is ten. Had a smaller number been used, say five or six, the list in table 1 would have been several times larger, since the eradication of entire families and groups of friends and workers was a common tactic of military and security forces during the period 1980 to 1983. The United Nations Truth Commission divided homicides into three categories: single victims, "small groups of victims of less than 20 persons," and large groups with twenty persons or more, "which we would call massacres" (United Nations 1993, app. 5:6).

12. Lt. Col. Domingo Monterrosa Barrios was appointed the battalion's first commander in February 1981, according to a biographic sketch produced in January 1984 by the Defense Intelligence Agency. On 25 November 1983 Monterrosa was promoted to commander of the Third Infantry Brigade in San Miguel. He died in 1984 when his helicopter was blown up in one of the FMLN's most ingenious military operations of the civil war (see chapter 9). For a list of massacres attributed to the Atlacatl Battalion, see Americas Watch Committee 1991 (182

n.37). Also see Centro Universitario de Documentación 1992b for other human rights violations attributed to the Atlacatl in the late 1980s.

13. But later, Danner (1993:62, 1994:42–43) contradicts this statement with the observation, "As the guerrillas were reduced to the status of delinquents, all civilians in certain zones were reduced to the status of masas, guerrilla supporters, and thus became legitimate targets. North of the Torola, for example, it was believed that the civilians and the guerrillas were all mixed together, and were indistinguishable."

14. CONADES compiled its figures based on reports obtained from a number of different organizations. In northern Morazán these were the International Red Cross and the General Direction of Communal Development (DIDECO). Different organizations reporting on displacement for the same municipality (which was not the case in northern Morazán) often provided quite discrepant figures. The numbers cited here are mere estimates.

15. The information on which table 3 was based included affinal kin, i.e., the husbands and wives of consanguines of the oldest members of the "lineage." The percentage of people who died at El Mozote rises only from 28.7 percent to 29.1 percent if affinal relations are excluded from the calculations.

16. The genealogical study probably errs on the low side in its estimation of the percentage of the prewar population that was killed by the Atlacatl Battalion. The smaller the number of extended family unit survivors, the less likely that survivors would be interviewed by researchers—and vice-versa. In any case, I would not expect the dead to have exceeded 40 percent of the total prewar population.

17. In no way should these figures be taken as representative of the loss felt by the survivors. The massacre eradicated an entire community, if by *community* (and here I am thinking of rural community predicated on face-to-face relationships rather than the "imagined community" of the nation discussed by Benedict Anderson [1983]) we mean the extrafamilial social and economic relationships through which individuals acquire a sense of place and belonging.

18. According to Danner (1993:54, 1994:17), the school was bombed and damaged a week to ten days before the massacre occurred.

19. In the late 1970s the ERP had a safe house in Azacualpa, which it employed as a base to open up clandestine supply routes between Honduras and El Salvador, and as a temporary storage depot for the smuggled merchandise. The accidental explosion of this house, which was full of contact bombs and other ordnance, drew the attention of the authorities and forced the shutdown of the operation. I cannot say for certain that similar calculations played a role in the "preservation" of El Mozote. Certainly, no ERP leader has ever admitted as much publicly. Another possibility is that the ERP encouraged sympathizers to remain in the area in order to gain some advantage from its failure to organize the inhabitants of the hamlet. As long as the army in San Francisco Gotera allowed

Marcos Diáz to travel to San Miguel to restock his store, the ERP had convenient access to products that were otherwise difficult and dangerous to obtain, as Heriberto noted. My information about the Azacualpa operation was obtained from two people who participated in it, one of whom was severely burned in the explosion. The information was later confirmed by area residents and several former guerrillas.

CHAPTER 7

1. According to Yúdice (1991:24–25), Didion's postmodern aesthetic vision "transform[s] her testimony into a self-reflection on her own alienated vision. She cannot 'see' the subjects of the counterhegemonic project because they are marginal and such marginalized elements appear in hegemonic postmodern texts only as the horror which excites the writer." I have criticized Didion in similar terms in an unpublished manuscript (Binford 1993b).

2. Limited time and resources restricted the number of cases on which the commission was able to gather direct testimony. The commission supplemented information from direct testimonies to the commission staff with indirect sources of information acquired from human rights institutions and other groups that received testimony during the war. For an analysis and comparison of the two sources of information see United Nations 1993, app. 5.

3. Witnesses were guaranteed anonymity. According to the weight of available evidence, cases were placed into categories according to whether there was "overwhelming evidence," "substantial evidence," or "sufficient evidence."

4. Tutela Legal may also have interviewed some of the ten "guides" forcefully recruited by the Atlacatl before it left Perquín. Also, Danner (1993:79, 1994:69) believes that the anonymous testimony of at least one soldier contributed to the report.

5. "Chepe Mozote" (José Guevara) was also captured and escaped, but he did not give testimony in the case (Danner 1993:84, 86, 1994:76–77). In La Joya, Jocote Amarillo, and elsewhere, some peasants evaded the army, hid nearby, and observed firsthand the soldiers as they coldly dispatched those whom they captured. Several such witnesses provided testimony to Tutela Legal that was incorporated into Tutela's 1991 brief.

6. The material in this section is based largely on interviews with Gloria Romero and Mercedes Castro, formerly members of the Human Rights Commission of Segundo Montes, with Antonio of Tutela Legal, and with Father Esteban Velásquez. I also consulted the 1991 Tutela Legal report and studied newspaper files from *Diario Latino, Diario de Hoy,* and *La Prensa Gráfica.*

7. The same informant said that Álvarez referred to himself in conversation as "an army colonel . . . to the death, and that the rank will only be lost at death." In the early 1970s Bishop Álvarez held up the ordination of Miguel Ventura for

more than a year (Ventura 1991:2) and in 1975, probably on the recommendation of a desperate and angry Andrés Argueta, reassigned Ventura from the Torola parish in northern Morazán to Osicala, located south of the Torola River (see chapter 6).

8. From its founding in 1982, Tutela Legal earned a reputation as the most credible source of information on human rights violations in El Salvador. It consistently reported much higher figures than the U.S. Embassy and attributed the vast majority of the violations to government agents and government-linked death squads, gaining it the enmity of both the Salvadoran press and the U.S. Embassy (e.g., United States Embassy 1984, 1985, 1986b). These attacks compelled Tutela officials to defer from engaging the organization in any activity or relationship that could be employed by its adversaries to undermine its claims to neutrality and objectivity.

9. This statement, based on observations made during three trips to the sacristy site during the exhumations, is not completely borne out by a reading of U.S. press reports, which did sometimes include a quote or two from civilian observers, in an effort to add a bit of "local color" to the stories (see Farah 1992; Johnson 1992). The Salvadoran press expressed a complete lack of interest in the opinions and/or experiences of onlookers.

10. As we walked down the calle negra one day in March 1994, Claudia Bernardi told me that nothing in the team's previous experience had prepared them for the number of children that they encountered. In order not to jeopardize their credibility they had had to maintain a cool, professional attitude during the excavation, but all had been affected by what they were uncovering and they had spoken privately among themselves about their feelings. Claudia said that something ended for her the moment the last bone was lifted from the sacristy floor and boxed for removal; and yet she finds herself drawn again and again to El Mozote: "It is not," she told me, "a completely sad thing."

11. Both women and children joined the FMLN as guerrilla fighters. Women accounted for 15 to 20 percent of ERP combatants. Many women served in the communications, health, and propaganda sectors, but all also fought when called upon to do so. Nor was youth a barrier to participation in combat. In 1991 I met a few rifle-bearing combatants who could not have exceeded twelve or thirteen years of age. But this was exceptional. Most males and females entered combat in their late teens. Guerrilla camps were often served by large groups of female civilian cooks, but the need for mobility ruled out the presence of large numbers of small children. Women in the camps who bore children either dropped out of the armed struggle for a time (if not permanently) or sent the children to Honduras or elsewhere to be cared for by friends or relatives.

12. In 1985 the Department of State claimed that "[t]he majority of the U.S.-made M-16 rifles captured from the guerrillas by the Salvadoran military have been traced, by individual serial numbers, to shipments made by the United

States to South Vietnam, and subsequently captured by communist forces after the 1975 fall of Saigon" (United States Department of State 1985:33). The Atlacatl was the first Salvadoran army unit to be uniformly equipped with the M-16. Among the weapons included in a March 1981 assistance grant provided by the U.S. government were nine thousand M-16s (McClintock 1985:333).

13. Rufina was in the group of women marched from the Alfredo Márquez house (fig. 2, no. 23) about ninety meters to the Israel Márquez house (fig. 2, no. 3), inside of which the women were killed. Some of the children remained at the home of Alfredo Márquez. From her hiding place next to the house of Israel Márquez, Rufina heard the children's cries.

14. The ERP was less enthusiastic about the report than other groups within the FMLN. The ERP was the only FMLN group whose top leaders—Joaquín Villalobos, Ana Guadalupe Martínez, and others—stood accused of human rights violations and were recommended for the same sanctions as the military. Villalobos entered the postwar epoch as one of two FMLN leaders with a high degree of name recognition and public visibility (Shafik Handel of the Salvadoran Communist Party being the other), and the prohibition on his holding public office was considered a blow to the organization's political future.

15. If the report itself was not enough, the Truth Commission also appended a lengthy "Análisis de Prensa" (Press analysis) that concluded that the Salvadoran press "presents as reality only the views of COPREFA [the Armed Forces Press Agency]. . . . The informative silence, disinformation, and impunity in the face of crime forms part of a reality that the written press helps to forge" (United Nations 1993, app. 3:54).

16. I rather expect that, as contemporary as anticommunism may seem, its more virulent forms depend heavily upon worked-over images from the period of European exploration, conquest, and colonization. In El Salvador capitalism eradicated Native American populations; most of the indigenous people who survived three hundred years of Spanish-mestizo domination were killed in the 1932 rebellion. But the communist arrived to assume the Indian's place and with one great advantage for representation: anyone, regardless of physiognomy, can be a communist and bearer of the diabolical characteristics that are thought to characterize them. The demise of the Soviet Union and international communism poses much greater problems for Salvadoran ruling classes than for those in the United States, where inner city Latinos and especially African Americans are portrayed as the sources of many of capitalism's ills. However, I predict that as a master code of bourgeois social control, anticommunism will remain alive and well in El Salvador for the foreseeable future. I can envision nothing on the horizon to replace it.

17. Charles Cecil works at the California Academy of Sciences; Roger Heglar is professor emeritus from San Francisco State University. Cecil was recruited to the project by acquaintances in El Salvador, where he had carried out archaeolog-

ical work many years earlier. Llort was unhappy with the Argentinean archaeologists, who he thought were biased toward the Left. I spoke by telephone with Cecil on 4 August 1994 about the excavation of sites II and III.

18. Villalobos agreed to support Cristiani's decision to allow several high-ranking officers recommended for dismissal by the Ad Hoc Commission to remain at their posts in exchange for a guarantee of additional land and other benefits for ex-FMLN combatants. Villalobos was publicly criticized by the FPL, and he defended his position in an ERP party congress held at the National University on 17 January 1993. A good friend provided me with a copy of notes taken at the meeting.

19. Unfortunately, in the absence of the Argentine forensic team or a comparable group of experienced professionals, the Sumpul River excavations have been carried out by Juan Mateu Llort and the Salvadoran Institute of Legal Medicine. On 18 May 1993 Llort told the French Press Agency (1993) that the work would "be completely scientific and impartial." This is the same Llort who continued to defend the military *after* the exhumation of the sacristy at El Mozote provided conclusive evidence that a massacre had occurred. As the evidence of a massacre at El Mozote mounted, Llort declared that there existed no legal concept of "massacre," only "massive violence," and that those who refer to El Mozote as a "massacre" do so for political ends (*Diario Latino* 1992). Whether by "subtly" splitting legal hairs or just by crass dissimulation, Llort's job as an official in the ARENA government was to cover up rather than to uncover the truth surrounding human rights violations.

CHAPTER 8

1. Schwarz notes that "[t]he leverage that the United States can exert over the conduct of a regime . . . decreases dramatically when those whom the United States is attempting to influence perceive America to be constrained by its own national interest." In the case of El Salvador he asked, "How could the Salvadoran military take seriously U.S. threats to cease aid if Washington repeatedly made clear its intention to prevent a rebel victory?" (1991:40).

2. The charts in the Truth Commission report (United Nations 1993, app. 3) were constructed on the basis of information that appeared at about the same time as the occurrence of the acts reported. Press reports were analyzed from the following countries: the United States, Honduras, Costa Rica, Mexico, Venezuela, Colombia, Argentina, Germany, and Spain.

3. On the other hand, Romero's death received only about one-fifth of the coverage of the death of Jenzy Popieluszko, a Polish priest murdered in October 1984 by the Polish police. More coverage was given to Popieluszko in the *New York Times*, CBS News, *Time*, and *Newsweek* than to more than one hundred Latin American religious victims put together (Herman and Chomsky 1988:38–42).

Edward Herman and Noam Chomsky conclude in *Manufacturing Consent* that
"[t]he worth of the victim Popieluszko is valued at somewhere between 137 and
179 times that of a victim in the U.S. client states; or, looking at the matter in
reverse, a priest murdered in Latin America is worth less than a hundredth of a
priest murdered in Poland" (39).

4. Likewise, Iraq was a testing ground for "smart bombs" and other weapons
that the Pentagon had not previously employed in a "live" warfare situation.

5. Schwarz (1991:2) breaks U.S. expenditures down as follows: $1 billion in
military aid; $3.5 billion in nonmilitary (e.g., economic support funds, USAID)
aid; over $850 million in unsubsidized credits; and an estimated CIA investment
of over $500 million. Lower estimates of U.S. assistance to El Salvador generally
leave off the unsubsidized credits and CIA expenditures (cf. Americas Watch
Committee 1991:141).

6. The FMLN reduced the size of combat assault teams, expanded the war to
all fourteen departments and to the cities, provided troops with practical political training so that they would be capable of doing activist work among local
populations, expanded the use of mines to counteract government incursions
into controlled areas, and stepped up its sabotage of coffee-processing plants,
electricity pylons, and other economic targets. Simultaneously, the FMLN continued to develop its logistical capabilities in order to carry out large-scale lightning
assaults on military bases and other important targets.

7. The following actions are prohibited by Protocol II, and deaths resulting
from them are to be considered murder:

(1) direct ground attacks against individual or groups of unarmed noncombatants where no legitimate military objective, such as insurgent forces or war
materiel, is present;

(2) search and destroy or mop-up ground operations carried out by Salvadoran troops under the circumstances described above;

(3) indiscriminate attacks and bombardment of encampments of such non-
combatants, known to be such by Salvadoran forces where no legitimate military
objective is present;

(4) ground attacks against or bombardment of such unarmed noncombatants, either immediately prior to, during, or after the receipt from relief societies
of supplies essential for their survival, i.e., food and medicines. (Americas Watch
Committee 1984b:43–44)

8. Following complaints from Americas Watch, "civil defense" was added as a
sixth category in April 1985 (Americas Watch Committee 1985:132–133). It was not
until a February 1986 summary of political deaths of civilians during 1985 that
the U.S. Embassy included a category for "security forces/army." In this summary
the embassy blamed the "security forces/army" for a mere 9 civilian political

deaths compared to 152 purportedly committed by the "guerrillas" and 33 "possibly by guerrillas" (United States Embassy 1986a). In sum, the embassy claimed that guerrillas were killing between 16 and 20 innocent civilians for every 1 killed by the "security forces/army."

9. According to Tutela Legal, though, it had not improved at all. Tutela Legal employed an empirical counting procedure that respected the definitions and rights represented in the Geneva Convention (Americas Watch Committee 1984b: 6–7).

10. LeMoyne left the *Times*'s Central America desk in 1989, but in 1992, following the signing of the Peace Accords, he published a front-page article in the *New York Times Magazine* titled "Out of the Jungle." The magazine cover contained two photographs set side by side that apparently represented LeMoyne's vision of the FMLN's transformation. The photograph to the left, tinted green, portrayed a motley crew of FMLN combatants in the forest in full combat gear; to its right appeared a photograph of the leaders of the five groups that made up the FMLN, now trimmed, primped, and dressed in conservative suits and ties. The point could not have been more explicitly, or more crudely, drawn: the guerrilla [gorilla] had been domesticated!

11. Decree 50 lapsed in October 1987, when the government declared an amnesty and released more than 400 political prisoners, but it was replaced by the virtually identical Decree 618 (Amnesty International 1988:12; Americas Watch Committee 1987:68).

12. The ministry also claimed that "physical torture and moral pressure as means of obtaining information or confessions have been largely eliminated at the detention centers" (El Salvador Ministerio de Cultura y Comunicaciones 1987:50).

13. The postwar Truth Commission restricted itself to "grave acts of violence." Denunciations of property destruction, denial of free transit, denial of personal liberty, or arbitrary capture were included only if accompanied by a grave act of violence. "Grave acts" fell into the following six categories: homicide, forced disappearance, tortures and bad treatment, serious wounds, kidnapping for extortion, and sexual violation (United Nations 1993, app. 5:1–2).

14. A common strategy employed by the U.S. State Department during the war was to deny human rights violations when they jeopardized military aid. Then, later, past abuses could be acknowledged as present ones were being denied in order to argue that, comparatively speaking, the situation had improved and that aid should be continued or increased because the military was being brought under control (Americas Watch Committee 1991:119–120). I expect this strategy to continue to be employed during the postwar period to justify military assistance. Thus the same Truth Commission report that criticized U.S. government complicity in denying abuses in the past may be appropriated by current and future administrations as a baseline against which to measure the "improvement" in military performance in the present.

CHAPTER 9

1. As noted in chapter 7, Father Velásquez was forced by his superiors to leave the country in July 1993.

2. "Santiago" (Carlos Henríquez Consalvi) titled his memoir of the war *La terquedad del izote* (The stubbornness of the izote).

3. I gratefully acknowledge the contribution here of Shelli McMillen, who carried out many of the interviews that contributed to this section.

4. The guerrilla army was named the *Ejército Nacional de Democracia* (National Army for Democracy) in 1990 following the nationwide offensive of November 1989. The END demobilized between 1 February and 15 December 1992. During this period the troops congregated in six camps in northern Morazán under the supervision of the United Nations Observers Mission (ONUSAL).

5. Aside from the Atlacatl and Arce, the other immediate-reaction infantry battalions (BIRIS) were the Bracamonte, the Belloso, and the Atonal. Each BIRI had its own base but conducted operations in any part of the national territory.

6. North of the Torola River, one has to look long and hard to find a henequen plant. A few hundred meters south of the river, henequen is grown prolifically in carefully plotted, evenly spaced rows on the steep hillsides.

7. In March 1993 I served as Morazán departmental coordinator with the U.S. Citizens Election Observers Mission (MOECEN) and observed the elections in Perquín, Jocoaitique, and Meanguera. In Meanguera the FMLN polled 856 votes, more than four times the 209 received by the second-place ARENA Party.

8. The United States provided the Salvadoran government $6 billion in economic and military assistance to defeat the FMLN yet committed to provide a paltry $300 million for reconstruction following the end of the war. However, according to USAID officials, due to a reduction in allocation actual expenditures will fall $10 to $15 million short. Of course, no amount of assistance can resurrect the dead or compensate families for such losses, but one might hope for a more generous response to the survivors of a "low-intensity" war for which the U.S. government bears such heavy responsibility. A particular irony marks road sign placement in the El Mozote case. During the first year following the war, a sheet-metal sign nailed to a couple of vertical two-by-fours, placed by the PADECOMSM Social Communications Commission next to the roadside at the junction where the dirt and gravel road for Joateca intersects the paved road to Perquín, directed visitors to the hamlet. The sign read

El Mozote 4 km.
A Thousand People Massacred by the Atlacatl Battalion
11 December 1981

By October 1993, that black-and-white sign had been removed and casually tossed on the roadside; in a crude effort to eradicate historical memory, a second sign advertising USAID-financed water and latrine projects in El Mozote had been erected on the same site.

CHAPTER 10

1. An additional 667 people died from "illness" and 38 from "accidents." Segundo Montes drew its refugee population from more than a dozen municipalities in Morazán. Meanguera contributed 1,289 inhabitants, 16.3 percent of the total and the largest number of any single municipality.

2. The complete citation is as follows: "If sleep is the apogee of physical relaxation, boredom is the apogee of mental relaxation. Boredom is the dream bird that hatches the egg of experience. A rustling in the leaves drives him away. His nesting places—the activities that are intimately associated with boredom—are already extinct in the cities and are declining in the country as well. With this the gift for listening is lost and the community of listeners disappears" (Benjamin 1968:91).

3. It is almost certain that the ideas and arguments in this section will raise the hackles of many in the anthropological establishment, and yet they are, I believe, little more than a logical extension of human rights analysis to the field of anthropological discourse and practice. I intend no malice. This is a critical reflection on anthropological practice, including my own. However, I do wish to question the self-satisfied back-patting of those who believe, as does James Peacock, president of the American Anthropological Association, that "[t]he 21st century should be anthropology's century" (Peacock 1994). Better had he said that the twenty-first century *should be* the century of the "wretched of the earth" (Fanon 1963). By contrast, Anna Grimshaw and Keith Hart (1994:259) suggest that "[i]t is entirely conceivable that the next century will have no place for a class of specialist intellectuals, called *anthropologists,* with a mission to tell people what is going on in their world."

4. Ricardo Falla (1994:2) explains that he writes about massacres in the Ixcán region of Guatemala to set down the "good news" of the testimony of those who survived: "The more terrible the account of what he witnessed, the more awesome the reality that he announces: I am alive." Falla goes on to note, "I am only the conveyor of this proclamation, not a firsthand witness. But I have been entrusted by chance or by history, whatever you wish to call it, to transmit what those firsthand witnesses have seen, smelled, touched, heard, felt, surmised, thought, struggled with. They have told their astounding story, and I cannot keep silent."

5. It could also be argued that contemporary imperialism has merely achieved new modalities, that it would be no less visible than the classical forms, if only we would learn what to look for. To take but one example, contract farming—in which the means of production and the production process are nomi-

nally under control of direct producers who are obliged to sell their product to multinational merchants and food processors—*appears* more benign than the classic plantation or hacienda, with its "big house," its workers' quarters, and its heavily armed foremen overseeing the labor of indigenous work gangs. However, the direct producers in contract farming assume virtually all of the risks of crop failure and enjoy few of the benefits of a bountiful harvest because of agribusiness corporations' control over standards and prices for agricultural commodities and, in many cases, over financing, inputs, and even the specifics of the production process itself. For a good example see Barry 1995.

6. El Salvador contains only a handful of anthropologists, most of whom obtained their university training in Mexico. Although courses in anthropology exist at several Salvadoran universities, none of the universities, including the public University of El Salvador (UES) and the prestigious, private Jesuit-run University of Central America (UCA), offer degrees in social anthropology (Ramírez and Rodríguez 1988). Ana Ramírez and América Rodríguez conclude that "[t]he [anthropological] work realized in El Salvador is still incipient, and the responses of 'salvage' ethnography do not permit seeing beyond the apparent, with a strong component of 'picturesqueness,' which contributes nothing toward a fruitful analysis of the relationship between cultural phenomena and social problems" (1988:13).

7. Martin Diskin (1983) and Philippe Bourgois (1991, 1982) were the major exceptions. Bourgois's case is particularly interesting. As a Stanford graduate student investigating the possibility of carrying out a doctoral dissertation on "ideology and material reality among revolutionary peasants" (1991:119) in Salvadoran refugee camps in southern Honduras, Bourgois crossed for a brief visit into El Salvador and inadvertently got caught, along with peasants and FMLN guerrillas, in a Salvadoran military search-and-destroy operation that lasted several weeks and involved the murder of numerous innocent men, women, and children. Bourgois barely escaped and, on his return to the United States, shared his experiences with Congress, the news media, human rights groups, and academics (Bourgois 1982). For his trouble, Bourgois was threatened with expulsion from graduate school. Faculty members accused him of, among other things, having violated the rights to privacy of his research subjects by contacting human rights organizations and having "potentially jeopardized the future opportunities of colleagues to research in Honduras and El Salvador by breaking immigration laws and calling attention to government repression in public forums" (1991:119).

8. Ricardo Falla (1994), Beatrice Manz (1988), Robert Carmack (1988), Victor Montejo (Montejo and Akab' 1992), Shelton Davis (Davis and Hodson 1982), and others contributed to this literature, and several anthropologists (e.g., Falla, Manz, Montejo) have been enduring advocates for Mayan peoples and critics of the Guatemalan military and government. Representing the neoliberal tradition in anthropology, David Stoll (also a contributor to the Carmack volume)

proposed a revisionist interpretation of the war in which he blamed rebels of the Guerrilla Army of the Poor for having organized peasants, "provoking" the ire of the Guatemalan army, which "naturally" responded by eradicating the entire populations of dozens of rural hamlets in the Ixil Triangle. In Stoll's view, a neutral civilian population was caught "between two armies" (Stoll 1993).

9. Fortunately, the draft code was never voted upon. However, the fact that the changes discussed by Berreman were proposed and then seriously entertained is evidence of a major shift in the ethical perspective of many practitioners.

10. Messer (1993:221) argues that the generally held belief that "anthropologists have been largely uninvolved in human rights formulations" is wrong. Through an extensive review of the literature she attempts to show that anthropologists have made two critical contributions to furthering human rights: "first, by providing cross-cultural research on the questions of 'What are rights?' and 'Who is counted as a full "person" or "human being" eligible to enjoy them?'; and second, by monitoring compliance with human rights standards and by criticizing human rights violations or abuses." Undeniably there exists a group of anthropologists committed to human rights who are working to broaden the concept of rights and to improve protection of those rights recognized internationally. However, the vast majority of anthropologists carry out research among peoples whose human rights (civil and political; economic, social, and cultural; rights to development; indigenous rights) are habitually violated (see Messer 1993, 1995; Doughty 1988; Corradi, Fagen, and Garretón 1992; Nagangast 1994). Only a small percentage are moved to action.

11. Ringberg (1995:48) asks whether academic anthropology is unethical. He points to a contradiction within the AAA's existing Code of Ethics (not the draft code) between one section, which focuses on anthropologists' responsibility to safeguard the welfare of their subjects, and another, which emphasizes anthropologists' responsibility not to behave in ways that jeopardize further research. True, there is a contradiction there, but the fact that it is seriously entertained, i.e., that anyone might really find themselves in an ethical dilemma as a consequence, is evidence of a deeper moral problem. Furthermore, I fear that Ringberg is correct in his statement that "[i]t appears to be the preserving of potential research opportunities that is the preferred choice" (48).

12. According to the U.N. Report on Development for 1992, the per capita income of the South was 6 percent of that of the North. Between 1960 and 1980 the per capita income of the "less developed countries" declined from 9 percent to 5 percent of that of the industrialized countries; comparable figures for sub-Saharan Africa went from 14 percent to 8 percent, and for Latin America from 38 percent to 30 percent (cited in Gayarre 1995:37). Economic inequality was also on the rise in the United States, which had become the most economically stratified of all industrial nations. In 1989 the top 20 percent of income earners received 55 percent of after-tax income; the lowest 20 percent of income earners received

only 5.7 percent (Bradsher 1995). According to New York University economist Edward N. Wolff, "We are the most unequal industrialized country in terms of income and wealth, and we're growing more unequal faster than the other industrialized countries" (cited in Bradsher 1995:D4).

13. The poor-with-spirit are the "active poor," those among the poor who have come to an understanding of their position, the injustice of it, and of the need to struggle in order to overturn it (Ellacuría 1991b:60). The poor-with-spirit are the subjects of history, analogous perhaps to the Lukacian class-for-itself.

14. See, for instance, Ricardo Falla's *Massacres in the Jungle* (1994).

15. EPICA, Voices on the Border, CISPES, and other groups have played important roles in bringing subaltern voices into print and before live audiences. Also, small presses such as Curbstone (Willimantic, Conn.) have published testimonies that larger commercial and university presses reject. On this theme, I also believe that, unless a strong case can be made otherwise, anthropologists have the responsibility to return any profits from books, lectures, and the sale of photographs to the host communities whose collaboration made possible these scholarly and artistic works. A recommendation to that effect should be made part of the AAA Code of Ethics; those accused of making a profit from their research of oppressed peoples should be investigated, and violators should be sanctioned.

16. The amount of resistance to permitting Them access to Our secrets should not be underestimated. At the University of Connecticut, where I teach, a majority decision (5–4) of the faculty of the Department of Anthropology to hire Dr. Soheir Morsy to fill a senior-level position as a medical anthropologist was overturned in the spring of 1993 by the dean of the College of Liberal Arts and Sciences following complaints by one faculty member and a spate of letters from graduate students worried that the presence of a critical Third World scholar (the candidate was Egyptian) might jeopardize their potential future careers with USAID, the Center for Disease Control, the National Institutes of Mental Health, and other institutions that these students mistakenly believe have the best interest of the world's poor at heart (see Shanahan 1994). In defending the dean's decision, Jeffrey Backstrand (1994), a graduate of the medical anthropology program, stated that "Morsy is a critical medical anthropologist, a researcher who focuses on inequalities of power and economics as they relate to the health status of individuals and communities. . . . In contrast, applied medical anthropologists are concerned with investigating the social, cultural, economic and behavioral causes of poor health, but with a focus on developing practical solutions." The possibility that "inequalities of power and economics" might be the major causes of poor health or that practical solutions are likely to have little positive impact unless they address those inequalities seems to have completely escaped the writer, so fully is he immersed in liberal ideology.

17. Stanley Diamond claimed that "[a]nthropology, abstractly conceived as the study of man, is actually the study of men in crisis by men in crisis" (1974:93).

Diamond thought that as an alienated person in an alienating society, "the anthropologist is himself a victim." The ultimate object of the study of others must therefore be self-knowledge (a point first made by Paul Ricoeur, who defined hermeneutics as "the comprehension of self by the detour of the comprehension of the other" [cited in Rabinow 1977:5]). In other words, the objectification of the other is ultimately to benefit Us: "We study men, that is, we reflect on ourselves studying others, because we must, because man in civilization is the problem. Primitive peoples do not study man. It is unnecessary; the subject is given" (Diamond 1974:100). Diamond portrays the beneficiaries of imperialism as its principal victims, and the real victims as the mirrors in which the beneficiaries will find reflected their own images, the *sine qua non* of their salvation. A more egoistic conception of anthropology is difficult to conceive.

18. Miguel D'Escoto, Catholic priest and head of the Nicaraguan Foreign Ministry, had just completed a fifteen-day march for peace in February 1986 and was addressing a group of foreign visitors. As the interview wound down, a delegation member asked him what message he would like them to take back to citizens of the United States: "Tell them," D'Escoto said, "that *we* are deeply concerned about *them*." The visitors were taken aback, as they were expecting that D'Escoto would indict the U.S. government for sponsoring a brutal counterrevolutionary war against the Nicaraguan people. Then D'Escoto continued:

> Tell them . . . that we are deeply concerned about them because a country that exports repression will one day unleash that repression against its own people. A nation that wages war against the poor in Nicaragua will ignore the needs of its own poor. A country which in the name of "democracy" fights wars against the self-determination of other peoples cannot remain a democracy. I have felt for a long time . . . that the U.S. people will one day be the most repressed people in the world. (cited in Nelson-Pallmeyer 1989:51)

REFERENCES

Alder, Daniel, and Thomas Long. 1992. "El Salvador: Tales of the Struggle." *NACLA* 26, no. 3:25–30.

Allende, Isabel. 1989. "Writing as an Act of Hope." In *The Art and Craft of the Political Novel*, ed. William Zinsser, pp. 39–63. Boston: Houghton Mifflin.

Althusser, Louis. 1971. "Ideology and Ideological State Apparatus." In *Lenin and Philosophy*, pp. 127–186. New York: Monthly Review.

Alvarado, Elvia. 1987. *Don't Be Afraid, Gringo*. San Francisco, Calif.: Institute for Food and Development Policy.

Americas Watch Committee. 1991. *El Salvador's Decade of Terror: Human Rights Since the Assassination of Archbishop Romero*. New Haven: Yale University Press.

———. 1987. *The Civilian Toll 1986–1987: Ninth Supplement to the Report on Human Rights in El Salvador*. New York: Americas Watch Committee.

———. 1986. *Settling into Routine: Human Rights Abuses in Duarte's Second Year: Eighth Supplement to the Report on Human Rights in El Salvador*. New York: Americas Watch Committee.

———. 1985. *The Continuing Terror: Seventh Supplement to the Report on Human Rights in El Salvador*. New York: Americas Watch Committee.

———. 1984a. *As Bad as Ever: A Report on Human Rights in El Salvador*. New York: Americas Watch Committee.

———. 1984b. *Protection of the Weak and Unarmed: The Dispute over Counting Human Rights Violations in El Salvador*. New York: Americas Watch Committee.

Americas Watch Committee, and American Civil Liberties Union. 1982. *Report on Human Rights in El Salvador*. New York: Vintage.

Americas Watch Committee, and Lawyers Committee for International Human Rights. 1984. *Free Fire: A Report on Human Rights in El Salvador*. New York: Americas Watch Committee.

Amnesty International. 1988. *El Salvador "Death Squads"—A Government Strategy*. London: Amnesty International Publications.

Anderson, Benedict. 1983. *Imagined Communities: Reflections on the Origin and Spread of Nationalism*. London: Verso.

Anderson, Thomas. 1971. *Matanza: El Salvador's Communist Revolt of 1932*. Lincoln: University of Nebraska Press.

Annis, Sheldon. 1987. *God and Production in a Guatemalan Town*. Austin: University of Texas Press.

ARENA (Alianza Republicana Nacionalista). 1988. "Cartilla de Formación Política." San Salvador: ARENA.

Argueta, Manlio. 1983. *One Day of Life.* New York: Aventura.

Armstrong, Robert, and Janet Shenk. 1982. *El Salvador: The Face of Revolution.* Boston: South End Press.

Arnson, Cynthia. 1992. "Human Rights: Has There Been Progress?" In *Is There a Transition to Democracy in El Salvador?* ed. Joseph S. Tulchin, pp. 85–93. Boulder, Colo.: Lynne Rienner.

Backstrand, Jeffrey. 1994. "Hiring Not Influenced by Gender, Ethnicity." *Hartford Courant,* 11 August, p. D10.

Baloyra, Enrique. 1982. *El Salvador in Transition.* Chapel Hill: University of North Carolina Press.

Barrios de Chungara, Domitila. 1979. *Let Me Speak! Testimony of Domitila, a Woman of the Bolivian Mines.* New York: Monthly Review.

Barry, Tom. 1995. *Free Trade and the Farm Crisis in Mexico.* Boston: South End.

———. 1986. *Low Intensity Conflict: The New Battleground in Central America.* Albuquerque, N.Mex.: Inter-Hemispheric Education Resource Center.

Barry, Tom, and Deb Preusch. 1988. *The Soft War: The Uses and Abuses of U.S. Economic Aid in Central America.* New York: Grove Press.

Bell, Derrick. 1992. "The Slave Traders." In *Faces at the Bottom of the Well,* pp. 158–194. New York: Basic Books.

Benjamin, Walter. 1968. *Illuminations.* Ed. Hannah Arendt. New York: Schocken.

Berreman, Gerald D. 1991. "Ethics versus 'Realism' in Anthropology." In Fleuhr-Lobban, ed., *Ethics and the Profession of Anthropology,* pp. 38–71.

———. 1968. "Is Anthropology Alive? Social Anthropology in Anthropology." *Current Anthropology* 9, no. 5:391–396.

Binford, Leigh. In press. "Community Development in Conflict Zones of Northeastern El Salvador." *Latin American Perspectives.*

———. 1993a. "The Conflict over Land in Postwar El Salvador." *Culture and Agriculture Bulletin,* no. 47:13–16.

———. 1993b. "Joan Dideon's *Salvador.*" Unpublished manuscript.

———. 1992. "El desarrollo comunitario en las zonas conflictivas orientales." *Estudios Centroamericanos* 47 (July–August):583–603.

———. 1991. "Peasants and Petty Capitalists in Southern Oaxacan Sugar Cane Production and Processing, 1930–1980." *Journal of Latin American Studies* 24: 33–55.

Bonner, Raymond. 1984. *Weakness and Deceit: U.S. Policy in El Salvador.* New York: Times Books.

———. 1982a. "Massacre of Hundreds Reported in Salvadoran Village." *New York Times,* 27 January, p. A2.

———. 1982b. "On the Attack with Salvador Rebels: Battle Starts Early and Lasts All Day." *New York Times,* 2 February, p. A8.

Bourgeois, Roy. 1994. "School of Assassins." *Z Magazine* 7, no. 9:14–16.

Bourgois, Philippe. 1991. "Confronting the Ethics of Ethnography: Lessons from Fieldwork in Central America." In *Decolonizing Anthropology: Moving Further*

Toward an Anthropology for Liberation, ed. Faye V. Harrison, pp. 111–126. Washington, D.C.: Association of Black Anthropologists and the American Anthropological Association.

———. 1982. "What U.S. Foreign Policy Faces in Rural El Salvador: An Eyewitness Account." *Monthly Review* (May):14–30.

Bradsher, Keith. 1995. "Gap in Wealth in U.S. Called Widest in West." *New York Times,* 17 April, p. A1.

Brown, Michael O. 1992. "The Pastoral and Theological Significance of the Investigation of the Massacre of El Mozote for National Reconciliation in El Salvador." Master's thesis, Washington Theological Union, Silver Springs, Md.

Browning, Christopher. 1992. *Ordinary Men: Reserve Police Battalion 101 and the Final Solution in Poland.* New York: Harper Collins.

Browning, David. 1971. *El Salvador: Landscape and Society.* Oxford: Clarendon.

Burkhalter, Holly, and Aryeh Neier. 1985. *Managing the Facts: How the Administration Deals with Reports of Human Rights Abuses in El Salvador.* New York: Americas Watch Committee.

Burns, Arthur. 1982. Confidential Cable from United States Embassy, Bonn, West Germany, to United States Department of State #02045, p. 5. National Security Archive #02488.

Cagan, Beth. 1994. "Salvadoran City of Hope: Segundo Montes on the Brink." *Dollars and Sense,* no. 19 (January–February):10–12, 36.

Cagan, Beth, and Steve Cagan. 1991. *This Promised Land, El Salvador.* New Brunswick, N.J.: Rutgers University Press.

Carmack, Robert M., ed. 1988. *Harvest of Violence: The Maya Indians and the Guatemala Crisis.* Norman: University of Oklahoma Press.

CDHES-NG (Comité de Derechos Humanos de El Salvador, No Gobernamental). 1993. "Report on the Human Rights Situation in El Salvador." *La Voz.* Special edition. San Salvador.

———. 1992. "Fuerza armada debe purificarse para que haya democracia." *La Voz* 1, no. 7.

———. 1991. "Situación de los derechos humanos y libertades fundamentales en El Salvador a dos años de gobierno del Lic. Felix Cristiani Presidente de la República." San Salvador: CDHES-NG.

———. 1986. *Torture in El Salvador.* San Salvador: CDHES-NG.

———. n.d. "Masacre en Morazán." San Salvador: CDHES-NG (probably published in early 1982). Mimeo, 16 pp.

Centro Universitario de Documentación e Información. 1993a. "Amnestía: instrumento de la impunidad." *Proceso,* no. 556 (24 March):4–8.

———. 1993b. "La depuración plantea una nueva crisis." *Proceso,* no. 545 (6 January):2–3.

———. 1993c. "Existe una multitud de testigos." *Proceso,* no. 554 (10 March):2–3.

———. 1992a. "La fuerza armada se resiste a la depuración." *Proceso,* no. 532 (30 September):2–3.

————. 1992b. "El injustificable accionar del Batallón Atlacatl." *Proceso,* no. 532 (30 September):12–15.

Christian, Shirley. 1986 [orig. 1983]. "El Salvador's Divided Military." In Gettleman et al., eds., *El Salvador: Central America in the New Cold War,* pp. 90–103.

Clements, Charles. 1984. *Witness to War.* New York: Bantam.

Cody, Edward. 1983. " 'Bombing' Charged in El Salvador; Archbishop Blames Salvadoran Army for Civilian Deaths." *Washington Post,* 7 February.

Colindres, Eduardo. 1977. *Fundamentos económicos de la burguesa salvadoreña.* San Salvador: University of Central America.

"Comandante Gonzalo, con tu ejemplo hacía nuevas victorias." 1982. *Señal de Libertad,* no. 19. Mexico.

CONADES (Comisión Nacional de Asistencia a la Población Desplazada). 1983. "Cuadro resumen de la población desplazada a nivel nacional por departamento." San Salvador: CONADES. Mimeo.

————. 1982. "El desplazado y su entorno: definiciones y orientaciones." San Salvador: CONADES. Mimeo.

Corradi, Juan E., Patricia Weiss Fagen, and Manuel Antonio Garretón, eds. 1992. *Fear at the Edge: State Terror and Resistance in Latin America.* Berkeley: University of California Press.

Dalton, Roque. 1987. *Miguel Marmol.* Willimantic, Conn.: Curbstone Press.

Danner, Mark. 1994. *The Massacre at El Mozote.* New York: Vintage.

————. 1993. "The Truth of El Mozote." *New Yorker* (6 December):50–133.

Davis, Shelton H., and Julie Hodson. 1982. *Witnesses to Political Violence in Guatemala: The Supression of a Rural Development Movement.* Boston: Oxfam America.

Defense Intelligence Agency. 1984. "Biographic Sketch" of Lieutenant Colonel Domingo Monterrosa Barrios. January. 2 pp. National Security Archive #04442.

Diamond, Stanley. 1974. "Anthropology in Question." In *In Search of the Primitive: A Critique of Civilization,* pp. 93–115. New Brunswick, N.J.: Transaction Books.

Diario de Hoy. 1993a. "Asamblea Legislativa aprueba amnestía general y absoluta." 22 March, pp. 11, 94.

————. 1993b. "Gral. Bustillo responsibiliza al gobierno por daños de comisión." 18 March, pp. 3, 17.

————. 1993c. "Informe comision verdad pretende devidir al pais." 16 March, pp. 3, 67.

————. 1993d. "Militares respalden al Presidente de la Corte." 22 March, p. 35.

————. 1993e. "Posición de la Fuerza Armada de E.S. Ante el Informe de la Comisión de la Verdad." 24 March, p. 11.

————. 1993f. "Vicios de la Comisión de la Verdad." 16 March, p. 3.

————. 1992a. "Corte pide no emitir juicios aventurados en caso El Mozote." 23 October, pp. 1, 3.

————. 1992b. "Desmovilizan al Batallon 'Atlacatl.'" 9 December, pp. 1, 3.

————. 1992c. "Hallen más creneos en zona de El Mozote." 22 October, p. 31.

————. 1992d. "Hasta fin de año preven diagnostico de El Mozote." 10 November, pp. 2, 27.

Diario Latino. 1993. "Asamblea estudia amnestía para señalados por comisión." 16 March, pp. 3, 73.

————. 1992. "Acto inhumano del Atlacatl, caso 'Mozote.'" 23 December, p. 16.

Díaz, Nidia. 1992. *I Was Never Alone: A Prison Diary from El Salvador.* Melbourne, Victoria: Ocean Press.

Dickey, Christopher. 1984. "Obdezco pero no cumplo" (I obey but I do not comply). In *Central America: Anatomy of Conflict,* ed. Robert Leiken, pp. 33–48. New York: Pergamon.

————. 1983. "El Salvador's Battle of Berlin Leaves Ruined City and Deep Despair." *Washington Post,* 5 February, p. A12.

Didion, Joan. 1983. *Salvador.* New York: Simon and Schuster.

Diskin, Martin, ed. 1983. *Trouble in Our Backyard: Central America and the United States in the Eighties.* New York: Pantheon.

Doggett, Marta. 1994. *Una muerte anunciada.* San Salvador: University of Central America Editores.

Dore, Elizabeth, and John Weeks. 1992. "Up from Feudalism." *NACLA* 26, no. 3:38–44.

Doughty, Paul L. 1988. "Crossroads for Anthropology: Human Rights in Latin America." In *Human Rights and Anthropology,* ed. Theodore Downing and Gilbert Kushner, pp. 43–71.

Downing, Theodore, and Gilbert Kushner. 1988. Introduction to *Human Rights and Anthropology,* ed. Theodore Downing and Gilbert Kushner, pp. 1–8. Cambridge, Mass.: Cultural Survival.

Du Bois, W.E.B. 1986. "'To the World' (Manifesto of the Second Pan-African Congress)." In W.E.B. Du Bois, *Pamphlets and Leaflets,* comp. and ed. Herbert Aptheker, pp. 194–199. White Plains, N.Y.: Kraus-Thompson.

Dundes Renteln, Alison. 1990. *International Human Rights: Universalism versus Relativism.* Newbury Park, Calif.: Sage.

Dunkerley, James. 1982. *The Long Road: Dictatorship and Revolution in El Salvador.* London: Verso.

Durham, William. 1979. *Scarcity and Survival in Central America.* Stanford, Calif.: Stanford University Press.

Durran, Mary. 1992. "Slowly Growing Pile of Bones Tells of a Terrible Day When the Army Came." *Guardian,* 17 November, Foreign Page, p. 14.

Edwards, Beatrice, and Gretta Tovar Siebentritt. 1991. *Places of Origin: The Repopulation of Rural El Salvador.* Boulder, Colo.: Lynne Rienner.

Eisner, Peter. 1993. "Ghosts of War: El Salvador Exhuming Bodies at Killing Ground." *Newsday* (16 February):29, city edition.

Ellacuría, Ignacio. 1991a. "Liberation Theology and Socio-historical Change in Latin America." In Hassett and Lacey, eds., *Towards a Society That Serves Its People*, pp. 19–43.

———. 1991b. "Utopia and Prophecy in Latin America." In Hassett and Lacey, eds., *Towards a Society That Serves Its People*, pp. 44–88.

El Salvador Ministerio de Cultura y Comunicaciones. 1987. *Human Rights and Fundamental Freedoms in El Salvador.* San Salvador: Dirección de Publicaciones e Impresos.

El Salvador Ministerio de Economía. 1974a. *Cuarto censo nacional de población, 1971.* San Salvador: Dirección General de Estadistica y Censos.

———. 1974b. *Tercero censo nacional agropecuario 1971.* San Salvador: Dirección General de Estadistica y Censos.

English, Adrian J. 1984. "El Salvador." In *Armed Forces of Latin America: Their Histories, Development, Present Strength and Military Potential*, pp. 402–415. London: Jane's Publishing.

Equipo Argentino de Antropología Forense. 1993. "Informe arqueológico." In United Nations, *De la locura a la esperanza*, app. 1.

Fabian, Johann. 1983. *Time and the Other.* New York: Columbia University Press.

Fagen, Patricia Weiss. 1992. "Repression and State Security." In Corradi, Fagen, and Garretón, eds., *Fear at the Edge*, pp. 39–71.

Falla, Ricardo. 1994. *Massacres in the Jungle.* Boulder, Colo.: Westview.

Fanon, Frantz. 1963. *The Wretched of the Earth.* New York: Ballantine.

Farah, Douglas. 1993. "Peace Begins to Become a Habit in El Salvador." *Washington Post*, 10 February, p. 23A.

———. 1992. "Skeletons Verify Killing of Salvadoran Children; Army Battalion Accused in 1981 Massacre." *Washington Post*, 22 October, p. A18.

FDR/FMLN (Frente Farabundo Martí para la Liberación Nacional). 1982. *A Massacre in El Salvador's Morazan Province, December 7–17, 1981.* San Francisco, Calif.: Solidarity Publications.

Feierman, Steven. 1990. *Peasant Intellectuals.* Madison: University of Wisconsin Press.

Fleuhr-Lobban, Carolyn, ed. 1991. *Ethics and the Profession of Anthropology.* Philadelphia: University of Pennsylvania Press.

Flores Díaz, Z. M. 1980. *Población, desarrollo rural y migraciones internas en El Salvador: Dept. de Morazán.* Departamento de Economía, Tesis de Licenciado. San Salvador: University of Central America.

FMLN (Frente Farabundo Martí para la Liberación Nacional). 1992a. *Acuerdos hacía una nueva nación: Recompilación de los acuerdos de paz sucritos con el gobierno de El Salvador.* San Salvador: FMLN.

———. 1992b. "Inventario de tierras, Departamento de Morazán." 4 June. San Salvador: FMLN. Mimeo.

Fondebrider, Luís, Patricia Bernardi, and Mercedes Doretti. 1993. Equipo Argentino de antropología forense informe arqueológico. In United Nations, *De la locura a la esperanza,* app. 3.

Foucault, Michel. 1979. *Discipline and Punish.* New York: Vintage.

Frank, Andre Gunder. 1969. "Liberal Anthropology vs. Liberation Anthropology." In *Latin America: Underdevelopment or Revolution,* pp. 137–145. New York: Monthly Review.

French Press Agency. 1993. "Forensics Experts Sift Earth for Remains of Massacre Victims." 18 May.

Gaspar Tapia, Gabriel. 1989. *El Salvador: El ascenso de la nueva derecha.* San Salvador: Centro de Investigaciones Social.

Gayarre, José Larrea. 1995. "The Challenges of Liberation Theology to Neoliberal Economic Policies." *Social Justice* 24, no. 4:34–45.

Gettleman, Marvin, et al., eds. 1986. *El Salvador: Central America in the New Cold War.* New York: Grove.

Golden, Tim. 1993. "U.N. Report Urges Sweeping Changes in Salvadoran Army." *New York Times,* 16 March, pp. A1, A12.

Grimshaw, Anna, and Keith Hart. 1994. "Anthropology and the Crisis of the Intellectuals." *Critique of Anthropology* 14, no. 3:227–261.

Gugelberger, Georg, and Michael Kearney. 1991. "Voices for the Voiceless: Testimonial Literature in Latin America." *Latin American Perspectives* 18, no. 3:3–14.

Guillermoprieto, Alma. 1982. "Salvadoran Peasants Describe Mass Killings." *Washington Post,* 27 January, p. A1.

Harnecker, Marta. 1993. *Con la mirada en el alto: Historía de las FPL Farabundo Martí a través de sus dirigentes.* San Salvador: University of Central America.

Hassett, John, and Hugh Lacey, eds. 1991. *Towards a Society That Serves Its People: The Intellectual Contribution of El Salvador's Murdered Jesuits.* Washington, D.C.: Georgetown University Press.

Hatfield, Mark O., Jim Leach, and George Miller. 1987. *Bankrolling Failure: United States Policy in El Salvador and the Urgent Need for Reform.* A Report to the Arms Control and Foreign Policy Caucus. Washington, D.C.: Government Printing Office.

Henríquez Consalvi, Carlos ("Santiago"). 1992. *La terquedad del izote.* Mexico: Diana.

Herman, Edward S. 1992–93. "The Wall Street Journal as Propaganda Agency: Yellow Rain and the El Mozote Massacre." *Covert Action Information Bulletin,* no. 43:36–40 ff.

———. 1982. *The Real Terror Network.* Boston: South End.

Herman, Edward S., and Frank Brodhead. 1984. *Demonstration Elections: U.S.-Staged Elections in the Dominican Republic, Vietnam, and El Salvador.* Boston: South End.

Herman, Edward S., and Noam Chomsky. 1988. *Manufacturing Consent: The Political Economy and the New Media*. New York: Pantheon.

Herman, Edward S., and Peter Rothberg. 1993. "Media Thugs Slug It Out." *Lies of Our Times* (June):3–4.

Hill, James M. 1987. "The Committee on Ethics: Past, Present, and Future." In *Handbook on Ethical Issues in Anthropology*, ed. Joan Cassell and Sue-Ellen Jacobs, pp. 11–19. Washington, D.C.: American Anthropological Association.

Hinton, Deane R. 1982a. Confidential Cable #00773 from United States Embassy, San Salvador, to United States Department of State, Washington, 31 January; lines with excisions: 8. National Security Archive #02515. The complete version of the cable was published in Danner, *The Massacre at El Mozote*, pp. 195–201.

———. 1982b. Limited Use Cable San Salvador #03844 from United States Embassy, San Salvador, to United States Department of State, Washington, 6 May. National Security Archive #03004.

———. 1982c. Unclassified Cable from United States Embassy, San Salvador, to United States Department of State, Washington, 8 January; 4 pp. National Security Archive #02387.

Hobsbawm, Eric. 1994. "Barbarism: A User's Guide." *New Left Review*, no. 206 (July–August):44–54.

IDEA (Iniciativa para el Desarrollo Alternativo). 1992. "Evaluación socio-económica de la Comunidad Segundo Montes." San Salvador: IDEA.

IDESES (Instituto para el Desarrollo Económico y Social de El Salvador). 1993. "Se reduce la FASS y se amplia la delincuencia mientras nace la PNC." *Boletín de Conyuntura*, no. 40 (February):11–15.

IDHUCA (Instituto de Derechos Humanos de la Universidad Centroamericana). 1993. "El significado del informe de la verdad." *Proceso*, no. 556 (24 March): 12–14.

———. 1992a. "El informe de la Comisión Ad Hoc y la reconciliación nacional." *Proceso*, no. 531 (23 September):14–16.

———. 1992b. "El injustificable accionar del Batallón Atlacatl." *Proceso*, no. 532 (30 September):12–15.

———. 1986. *Documentos sobre los derechos humanos*. San Salvador: University of Central America.

Inter Press Service. 1993. "U.N. Commission Blames Army for Most of War Atrocities." 18 March.

Jameson, Fredric. 1981. *The Political Unconscious: Narrative as a Socially Symbolic Act*. Ithaca, N.Y.: Cornell University Press.

Johnson, Tim. 1992. "Grisly Evidence of Killings Unearthed." *Calgary Herald*, 30 October, p. A5.

Joint Group. 1994. "Report of the Joint Group for the Investigation of Illegal Armed Groups with Political Motivation in El Salvador." 28 July. San Salvador.

Kaplan, Robert D. 1994. "The Coming Anarchy." *Atlantic Monthly* (May):44ff.

Kirschner, Robert H., Clyde Snow, Douglas Scott, and John J. Fitzpatrick. 1993. "Informe de la investigación forense." In United Nations, *De la locura a la esperanza*, app. 1.

Kovel, Joel. 1984 [orig. 1970]. *White Racism: A Psychohistory*. New York: Columbia University Press.

Krauss, Clifford. 1993a. "Christopher Picks El Salvador Panel." *New York Times*, 25 March, p. A9.

———. 1993b. "Testimony in '82 on Salvador Criticized." *New York Times*, 16 July, p. A3.

———. 1993c. "U.S. Lauds Salvador Report; Ex-Aides Are Critical." *New York Times*, 16 March, p. A13.

Lancaster, Roger. 1988. *Thanks to God and the Revolution*. New York: Columbia University Press.

Langguth, A. J. 1978. *Hidden Terrors: Truth about U.S. Police in Latin America*. Toronto: Pantheon.

Lawyers Committee for Human Rights. 1989. *Underwriting Injustice: AID and El Salvador's Judicial Reform Program*. New York: Lawyers Committee for Human Rights.

Lawyers Committee for International Human Rights and Americas Watch Committee. 1984. *El Salvador's Other Victims: The War on the Displaced*. New York: Lawyers Committee for International Human Rights and Americas Watch Committee.

Lehmann-Haupt, Christopher. 1994. "The Nature of One Particular War." *New York Times*, 9 May, p. C15.

LeMoyne, James. 1992. "Out of the Jungle." *New York Times Magazine*, 9 February, pp. 24–29.

———. 1985a. "Bombings in Salvador Appear to 'Bend the Rules.'" *New York Times*, 20 December, p. A14.

———. 1985b. "Salvador Air Role in War Increases." *New York Times*, 18 July, p. A1.

———. 1984. "Salvadoran Villagers Report Army Massacre." *New York Times*, 9 September, sec. i, pt. 1, p. 1.

Lernoux, Penny. 1980. *Cry of the People: United States Involvement in the Rise of Fascism, Torture, and Murder and the Persecution of the Catholic Church in Latin America*. New York: Doubleday.

Lewis, Anthony. 1993. "Comment: Belated Proof of an Atrocity." *Guardian*, 10 December, p. 14.

Lindo-Fuentes, Hector. 1990. *Weak Foundations: The Economy of El Salvador in the Nineteenth Century, 1821–1898*. Berkeley: University of California Press.

López Vigil, José Ignasio. 1991. *Las mil y una historia de radio venceremos*. San Salvador: University of Central America.

López Vigil, María. 1987. *Muerte y vida en Morazán: Testimonio de un sacerdote.* San Salvador: University of Central America.

Lungo Uclés, Mario. 1990. *El Salvador en los 80: contrainsurgencia y revolución.* San José, Costa Rica: EDUCA-FLACSO.

MacLean, John. 1987. *Prolonging the Agony: The Human Cost of Low Intensity Warfare in El Salvador.* London: El Salvador Committee for Human Rights.

Manwaring, Max G., and Court Prisk. 1988. *El Salvador at War: An Oral History.* Washington, D.C.: National Defense University Press.

Manz, Beatrice. 1988. *Refugees of a Hidden War.* Albany, N.Y.: State University of New York Press.

Marcus, George, and Michael Fischer. 1986. *Anthropology as Cultural Critique: An Experimental Moment in the Human Sciences.* Chicago: University of Chicago Press.

Martín-Baró, Ignasio. 1991a. "The Appeal of the Far Right." In Hassett and Lacey, eds., *Towards a Society That Serves Its People,* pp. 293–305.

———. 1991b. "From Dirty War to Psychological War." In Hassett and Lacey, eds., *Towards a Society That Serves Its People,* pp. 306–316.

———. 1991c. "Violence in Central America: A Social Psychological Perspective." In Hassett and Lacey, eds., *Towards a Society That Serves Its People,* pp. 333–346.

Martínez, Ana Guadalupe. 1992. *Las cárceles clandestinas de El Salvador: Libertad por el secuestro de un oligarca.* San Salvador: University of Central America.

Massing, Michael. 1983. "About-face on El Salvador." *Columbia Journalism Review* 22, no. 4:42–49.

McClintock, Michael. 1985. *The American Connection.* Vol. 1, *State Terror and Popular Resistance in El Salvador.* London: Zed.

McManus, Doyle. 1993. "State Dept. Panel Defends Reports on Salvador Abuses." *Los Angeles Times,* 16 July, p. A1.

Medrano, Juan Ramón, and Walter Raudales. 1994. *Ni militar ni sacerdote (de seudónimo Balta).* San Salvador: Arcoiris.

Meiselas, Susan. 1993. "Declaración de Susan Meiselas ante la Comisión de la Verdad." In United Nations, *De la locura a la esperanza,* app. 2. San Salvador: United Nations.

Mena Sandoval, Francisco Emilio. 1991. *Del ejército nacional al ejército guerrillero.* San Salvador: Ediciones Arcoiris.

Menchú, Rigoberta. 1984. *I, Rigoberta Menchú: An Indian Woman of Guatemala.* Ed. and trans. Elizabeth Burgos-Debray. London: Verso.

Messer, Ellen. 1995. "Anthropology and Human Rights in Latin America." *Journal of Latin American Anthropology* 1, no. 1:48–97.

———. 1993. "Anthropology and Human Rights." *Annual Review of Anthropology* 22:221–249.

Metzi, Francisco. 1988. *The People's Remedy: Health Care in the New El Salvador Today.* New York: Monthly Review.

Millett, Kate. 1994. *The Politics of Cruelty: An Essay on the Literature of Political Imprisonment.* New York: W. W. Norton.

Millett, Richard. 1984. "Praetorians or Patriots? The Central American Military." In *Central America: Anatomy of Conflict,* ed. Robert Leiken, pp. 69–91.

Millman, Joel. 1989. "El Salvador's Army: A Force unto Itself." *New York Times Magazine,* 10 December, p. 95.

Minh-ha, Trin T. 1989. *Woman, Native, Other.* Bloomington: University of Indiana Press.

Montejo, Victor, and Q'anil Akab'. 1992. *Brevisima relación testimonial de la continua destrucción del Mayab' (Guatemala).* Providence, R.I.: Guatemala Scholars Network.

Montes, Segundo, Florenín Meléndez, and Edgar Palacios. 1991. "Economic, Social, and Cultural Rights in El Salvador." In Hassett and Lacey, eds., *Towards a Society That Serves Its People,* pp. 158–168.

Montgomery, Tommie Sue. 1982. *Revolution in El Salvador: Origin and Evolution.* Boulder, Colo.: Westview Press.

Moore, Powell A. 1982a. United States Department of State to David Pryor, 23 February; 2 pp. National Defense Archive #02650.

———. 1982b. United States Department of State to David Pryor, 26 February; 2 pp. National Defense Archive #02668.

NACLA. 1993. "A Market Solution for the Americas?" NACLA 26, no. 4:16–46.

———. 1986. "Duarte: Prisoner of War." NACLA 20, no. 1:13–39.

Nagangast, Carole. 1994. "Violence, Terror, and the Crisis of the State." *Annual Review of Anthropology* 23:109–136.

Nairn, Allen. 1984. "Behind the Death Squads." *Progressive* 48, no. 5:20–25, 28–29.

Nelson-Pallmeyer, Jack. 1989. *War against the Poor: Low-Intensity Warfare and Christian Faith.* Maryknoll, N.Y.: Orbis Books.

Nordstrom, Carolyn, and JoAnn Martin. 1992. *The Paths to Domination, Resistance and Terror.* Berkeley: University of California Press.

Norton, Chris. 1991. "The Hard Right: ARENA Comes to Power." In Sundaram and Gelber, eds., *A Decade of War,* pp. 196–215.

Overbey, Mary Margaret. 1994. "Human Rights 1994: Annual Meeting Highlights." *Anthropology Newsletter* 35, no. 7:1, 4.

Paige, Jeffrey. 1993. "Coffee and Power in El Salvador." *Latin American Research Review* 28, no. 3:7–40.

Palumbo, Gene. 1994. "Threats, Attack in El Salvador Arouse Fears That the Death Squads Are Back." *National Catholic Reporter,* 1 July, p. 14.

Peacock, James. 1994. "Challenges Facing the Discipline." *Anthropology Newsletter* 35, no. 9:1, 5.

Pearce, Jenny. 1986. *Promised Land: Peasant Rebellion in Chalatenango El Salvador*. London: Latin American Bureau.

Petras, James. 1988. "The Anatomy of State Terror: Chile, El Salvador, and Brazil." *Science and Society* 51:4–38.

Popkin, Margaret. 1991. "Human Rights in the Duarte Years." In Sundaram and Gelber, eds., *A Decade of War*, pp. 58–82.

Price, Richard. 1981. *First Time*. Baltimore: Johns Hopkins University Press.

Pyes, Craig. 1986a. "ARENA's Bid for Power." In Gettleman et al., eds., *El Salvador: Central America in the New Cold War*, pp. 165–174.

———. 1986b. "Roots of the Salvadoran Right: Origins of the Death Squads." In Gettleman et al., eds., *El Salvador: Central America in the New Cold War*, pp. 86–89.

Rabinow, Paul. 1977. *Reflections on Fieldwork in Morocco*. Berkeley: University of California Press.

Ramírez, Ana Lilian, and América Rodríguez H. 1988. "Algunas reflexiones sobre el desarrollo de la antropología en El Salvador." *Cuadernos de Investigación*, no. 29.

Rieff, David. 1991. *Los Angeles: Capital of the Third World*. New York: Touchstone.

Ringberg, Torsten. 1995. "Is Academic Anthropology Unethical?" *Anthropology Newsletter* 36, no. 1:48.

Rohter, Larry. 1996. "Where Countless Died in '81, Horror Lives On in El Salvador." *New York Times*, 12 February, p. A1.

Rosenberg, Tina. 1993. "Talking Peace in El Salvador." *Nation* (22 February):235–237.

———. 1991. *Children of Cain: Violence and the Violent in Latin America*. New York: Penguin.

Ross, Michael. 1993. "Democrats Seek Probe of U.S.-Salvador Ties; Congress: The U.N.'s Report Has Reignited Lawmakers' Debate about Washington's Support of Salvadoran Government." *Los Angeles Times*, 19 March, p. A16.

Said, Edward. 1993. *Culture and Imperialism*. New York: Knopf.

Salimovich, Sofia, Elizabeth Lara, and Eugenia Weinstein. 1992. "Victims of Fear: The Social Psychology of Repression." In Corradi, Fagen, and Garretón, eds., *Fear at the Edge*, pp. 72–89.

Schaull, Wendy. 1990. *Tortillas, Beans, and M-16s: A Year with the Guerrillas in El Salvador*. London: Pluto.

Schell, Orville E. 1984. "Salvador Slaughter." *New York Times*, 14 March, p. A27.

Scheper-Hughes, Nancy. 1992. *Death without Weeping: The Violence of Everyday Life in Brazil*. Berkeley: University of California Press.

Schirmer, Jennifer. 1988. "The Dilemma of Cultural Diversity and Equivalency in Universal Human Rights Standards." In *Human Rights and Anthropology*, ed. Theodore Downing and Gilbert Kushner, pp. 91–113. Cambridge, Mass.: Cultural Survival.

Schöultz, Lars. 1981. *Human Rights and United States Policy toward Latin America.* Princeton: Princeton University Press.

Schwarz, Benjamin. 1991. *American Counterinsurgency Doctrine and El Salvador: The Frustrations of Reform and the Illusions of Nation Building.* Rand Corporation.

Scott, Douglas D. 1993. "Identificación de armas de fuego en el sitio de ejucación de El Mozote." In United Nations, *De la locura a la esperanza,* app. 1.

Scott, James. 1990. *Domination and the Arts of Resistance.* New Haven: Yale University Press.

———. 1985. *Weapons of the Weak: Everday Forms of Resistance.* New Haven: Yale University Press.

Shanahan, Marie K. 1994. "Scholar Fights UConn after Job Offer Fizzles." *Hartford Courant,* 2 August, pp. A1, A11.

Simons, Marlise. 1986. "Protestant Challenge in El Salvador." In Gettleman et al., eds., *El Salvador: Central America in the New Cold War,* pp. 141–143.

Sixty Minutes. 1993. "Mozote." Transcript of a twenty-minute segment aired on 14 March. New York.

Snow, Clyde. 1993. "Análisis antropológico." In United Nations, *De la locura a la esperanza,* app. 1.

SOA Watch (School of the Americas Watch). n.d. "The U.S. Army School of the Americas." Photocopy, 3 pp.

Special Task Force on El Salvador. 1990. "Interim Report on the Speaker's Task Force on El Salvador" [The Moakley Report]. Congress of the United States, Washington, D.C., 30 April.

Stephen, Lynn. 1994a. "The Politics and Practice of Testimonial Literature." In Stephen, ed., *Hear My Testimony,* pp. 223–233.

———, ed. 1994b. *Hear My Testimony: María Teresa Tula, Human Rights Activist of El Salvador.* Boston: South End.

Stoessel, Walter J. 1982a. Confidential Cable #035529 from United States Department of State to United States Embassy, Italy, and United States Embassy, El Salvador. 10 February; 2 pp. National Defense Archive #02587.

———. 1982b. Limited Official Use Cable #024611 from United States Department of State to United States Embassy, El Salvador, 29 January. National Defense Archive #02503.

Stoll, David. 1993. *Between Two Armies in the Ixil Towns of Guatemala.* Berkeley: University of California.

———. 1988. "Evangelicals, Guerrillas, and the Army: The Ixil Triangle under Ríos Montt." In Carmack, ed., *Harvest of Violence,* pp. 90–116.

Suárez-Orozco, Marcelo. 1992. "A Grammar of Terror: Psychocultural Responses to State Terrorism in Dirty War and Post–Dirty War Argentina." In Nordstrom and Martin, eds., *The Paths to Domination, Resistance and Terror,* pp. 219–259.

Sundaram, Anjali, and George Gelber, eds. 1991. *A Decade of War: El Salvador Confronts the Future.* New York: Monthly Review.

Taussig, Michael. 1992. "Terror as Usual: Walter Benjamin's Theory of History as State of Seige." In *The Nervous System,* pp. 11–35. London: Routledge.

———. 1987. *Shamanism, Colonialism and the Wild Man.* Chicago: University of Chicago Press.

Tutela Legal. 1991. "Investigación sobre la masacre de centenares de campesinos en los caseríos El Mozote, Ranchería y Jocote Amarillo del cantón Guacamaya, en los cantones La Joya y Cerro Pando, de la jurisdicción de Meanguera y en el caserío Los Toriles de la jurisdicción de Arambala, todos del departamento de Morazán, por tropas del BIRI Atlacatl durante operativo militar los días 11, 12 y 13 de Diciembre de 1981: Hechos conocidos como 'Masacre de El Mozote.'" San Salvador: Tutela Legal.

United Nations. 1993. *De la locura a la esperanza: Informe de la Comisión de la Verdad para El Salvador.* San Salvador: United Nations.

United States Department of State. 1982. Press briefing, "El Salvador: Alleged Atrocities at Mozote." 1 February, 3 pp. National Defense Archive #02527.

United States Department of State, and Department of Defense. 1985. *The Soviet-Cuban Connection in Central America and the Caribbean.* Washington, D.C.

United States Embassy. San Salvador. 1986a. "Civilian Deaths from January 1 through December 31, 1985, Attributable to Political Violence according to the Press as Reported by the Embassy, by Category." Doc. 0043L, 9 February, San Salvador.

———. 1986b. "Political Violence 1985: A Comparison of Embassy/Tutela Legal Figures." Unclassified Cable, 13 March.

———. 1985. "Tutela Legal's April 1985 Violence Report Gets It Wrong." Unclassified Cable.

———. 1984. "Guerrillas Dupe Tutela Legal." Embassy Press Release.

Ventura, Miguel. 1991. Interview with Notimex. 2 October. Mimeo.

Vickers, George, and Jack Spence. 1994. "Elections: The Right Consolidates Power." NACLA 28, no. 1:6–11.

Villalobos, Joaquín. 1986. "El estado actual de la guerra y sus perspectivas." *Estudios Centroamericanos,* no. 449 (March):169–204.

———. 1982. "Análisis sobre la situación actual." *Señal de Libertad,* no. 19:5–10. Mexico.

Wakin, Eric. 1992. *Anthropology Goes to War.* Madison, Wis.: Southeast Asia Center.

Whitfield, Teresa. 1995. *Paying the Price: Ignacio Ellacuría and the Murdered Jesuits of El Salvador.* Philadelphia: Temple University Press.

Williams, Dan. 1985. "El Salvador Intensifies Its Air War against the Guerrillas." *Los Angeles Times,* 17 July, pt. 1, p. 1.

Williams, Robert G. 1986. *Export Agriculture and the Crisis in Central America.* Chapel Hill: University of North Carolina Press.

Willis, Paul. 1979. *Learning to Labour.* New York: Columbia University Press.

Wolf, Eric. 1982. *Europe and the People without History.* Berkeley: University of California.

Yúdice, George. 1991. "*Testimonio* and Postmodernism." *Latin American Perspectives* 18, no. 3:15–31.

Zielensky, Mike. 1994. "Opening the Files II: El Salvador." *Lies of Our Times* 5, no. 3:6–9.

INDEX

Leigh Binford is Associate Professor of Anthropology at the University of Connecticut, where he has taught since 1985. He is coauthor of *Obliging Need: Rural Petty Industry in Modern Mexican Capitalism*, with Scott Cook, and coeditor of *Zapotec Struggles: Histories, Politics, and Representations from Juchitán, Oaxaca*, with Howard Campbell. This book is part of the author's long-term study of the rise of peasant resistance and participation in the Salvadoran civil war. His previous work has been on topics ranging from artisan brickmakers to both peasant and capitalist agriculture in Oaxaca, Mexico. He lives in Storrs, Connecticut.

DATE DUE